Fake News Madness

A SAPIENT Being's Guide to Spotting Fake News Media and How to Help Fight and Eliminate It

By

Corey Lee Wilson

Fake News Madness

Fake News Madness

Fratire Publishing books can be purchased in bulk with special discounts for educational purposes, association gifts, sales promotions, and special editions can be created to specifications. All inquiries for such can be made below.

FRATIRE PUBLISHING LLC
4533 Temescal Canyon Rd. # 308
Corona, CA 92883
www.FratirePublishing.com
FratirePublishing@att.net
(951) 638-5502

FratirePublishing
Relevant Books for **SAPIENT** Beings

Fratire Publishing is all about common sense and relevant books for sapient beings. If this sounds like you and you can never have enough common sense, wisdom, and relevancy, then visit us and learn more about the 50 *MADNESS* series of book titles at www.FratirePublishing.com.

Printed paperback and eBook ePUB by Ingram Spark in La Vergne, Tennessee, USA
Copyright © 2020: First Edition December 2020
ISBN 978-0-9847490-5-8 (Paperback)
ISBN 978-1-953319-34-0 (eBook)
LCCN 2020919739

Fake News Madness

Contents

Acknowledgements

I owe a debt of gratitude to the following for "heavily" borrowing at times pieces of their and/or outright sections. I do this unashamedly to use the sapient phrase, "if it ain't broke—don't try to fix it." Most of the borrowed works and research cannot be improved upon—so why try? It's better to assemble these meaningful parts, profound messages, and eloquent arguments into a cohesive whole, told with high school and college students in mind, and that's what I've done and where my talent lies.

Below in alphabetical order are the major contributors to *The SAPIENT Being* that I borrowed verbatim, quoted, and conceptualized much of their content from a little to a lot. Wherever this happened, I did my best to acknowledge my source. If I didn't at times within the 15 chapters, I did so intentionally because doing so would have distracted from their message. Nonetheless, they are more than covered in the References section.

Bozell III, L. Brent: As the founder and president of the Media Research Center (MRC), Bozell runs the largest media watchdog organization in America and MRC and its news, research and reporting bureaus critique the bias in the national media and how they undermine American democracy. Bozell and Tim Graham are co-authors of *Unmasked: Big Media's War Against Trump* and a significant portion of the content from their 2019 book was used for *Fake News Madness* particularly Chapter 1 and more contributions to Chapters 2, 8, 14 and 15. Bozell's MRC organization contributed as well to Chapters 1, 4 , 9, 10, 11, 13, 14 and 15.

Dice, Mark: Is the author of *The True Story of Fake News: How Mainstream Media Manipulates Millions* and he contributed heavily to Chapters 6, 7 and 14.

Noyes, Rich: As the Research Director at the Media Research Center (MRC) and senior editor of the MRC's blog, NewsBusters.org., Noyes has authored or co-authored a significant portion of MRC's authoritative Special Reports and articles and many of them were very relevant to *Fake News Madness* and used in Chapters 4, 10 and 14.

Pew Research Center: Pew surveys and reports provide the backbone of various media statistics and they were used throughout *Fake News Madness* in Chapters 2, 5, 6, 9, 10, 11 and 15.

Prager U: Prager University is an American nonprofit organization that creates videos on various political, economic, and philosophical topics from a conservative perspective. The university was created by conservative Dennis Prager, an American syndicated talk show host, to teach fundamental concepts. Its content is sapient and relevant, and they educate millions of Americans and young people about the values that make America great. Prager U's contribution to Chapter 7 was significant and they also contributed to Chapter 14.

As the author of *Fake News Madness*, I also have a confession to make concerning my war against fake news journalism going all the way back to my college days. I say up front, "most likely," because I cannot prove that my campus newspaper *The Poly Post* didn't intentionally post an article in the Cal Poly Pomona campus newspaper titled: "Thefts, Vandalism, and High-Speed Pursuit Keep Campus Cops Busy!" that featured my arrest for reckless driving on campus thirty-five years ago to get back at me for correcting their newspaper articles time and again on fake news about current events.

The Poly Post continued their fake news choosing "high speed pursuit" when there were no speed limits broken—the only laws broken, which I readily admit to breaking, were failure to pull-over for a smog ticket which I choose to avoid until off campus knowing I had an expired driver license and I didn't want to get in trouble again on campus, and earn a third strike against me considering I was already on double-secret probation and there would likely be an expulsion from college for a third offense!

And yet, through some miracle, I was not expelled from college and instead placed on triple secret probation. Yes! Triple secret probation! I'm not making this up and if you're a fan of the comedy classic "Animal House," you know what double secret probation is. Triple secret? Never heard of it you're saying.

Neither did I, until I was first placed on disciplinary probation for a fraternity kidnap gone wrong, then placed on disciplinary probation a second time two months later for being the unlucky fraternity officer whose signature was on an unsanctioned toga party event form, and my third offense was failure to pull over (but not in excess of speeding limit) on campus after I borrowed a friend's un-smogged truck to tow our fraternity chariot to campus where I dropped it off and headed back to the frat house reasoning that campus cops can't pursue you off campus. Wrong!

Regardless, I became the only college student in the USA to graduate in 1985 on triple-secret probation and did so with a 3.26 GPA in Economics, recognized for my outstanding academics, leadership, and extra-curricular activities by *Who's Who of American College Students*, became President of my Delta Tau Chapter of The Phi Kappa Tau Fraternity winning Cal Poly Pomona's first ever Poly Gold Award, and topped it off by being selected as my fraternity's Shideler Award winner for being the most outstanding graduating senior in the USA.

Nonetheless, my first bitter experience with fake news journalism didn't stop me from fighting and helping to eliminate it as the subtitle of this book states: *A SAPIENT Being's Guide to Spotting Fake News Media and How to Help Fight and Eliminate It*. This is a primary reason why I choose the fake news topic as the first one to be published in the 50 *MADNESS* series of books—and the one I most highly recommend reading first before reading any of the others—because until you first learn to spot fake news and its media—you won't be able to help fight and eliminate it as well as identify the hundreds of other issues in the *MADNESS* series of books.

A SAPIENT Being's Preface

Millions of today's youth, college students, and young adults have been brainwashed over the decades by fake news coming from mainstream media (MSM), social media, and leftist academia to the point where they lack the open mindedness, objectivity, and critical thinking skills to recognize it and its harmful effects.

Fake News Madness offers an opportunity to be part of the solution to this problem. By spotting fake news media using ethical journalistic standards we can take action to fight and eliminate fake news with practical logic, facts, truth, and sapience—and together counter the biased and unethical journalism, mainstream news, and social media on and off campus.

For some of you this *MADNESS* book will be a revelation, an epiphany, a sapient being moment. For others, it will be a triggering event, denial of truth, and a painful intervention.

As the time-tested saying goes, "Everyone is entitled to their own opinions—but they're not entitled to their own facts." Facts are facts, the truth is the truth, but they can be skewed and manipulated for disingenuous methods and false narratives. Mainstream news, social media, and academia have perfected and promoted their liberal and leftist agenda without recourse. They are in many ways the media arm of the Democratic Party and many are infected with Trump Derangement Syndrome (TDS).

Only seven percent of American journalists identify as Republican and the rest claim that despite the fact they're all Democrats, they can be objective. It just ain't so! Psychologists and the Heterodox Academy have shown that when people associate almost exclusively with those who agree with them, they suffer from groupthink, viewpoint orthodoxy, and confirmation bias—and lose their ability to see events clearly and objectively.

In 2016 the fake news media narrative was more an unequivocal declaration: Donald Trump must not win. As well all know, he did, and the overwhelming pro-Clinton MSM predicted he would lose. And lose big! How could they get it so wrong? And how could one man be the number one obsession and enemy of fake news?

The primary focus of this book is an analysis of the depth and breadth of fake and false news in mainstream and social media, journalism academic institutions, data/fact checking resources, about Trump derangement syndrome, election predictions, application of journalistic code of ethics, practical logic, and more.

By using sapience as the foundation for addressing these issues facing America and the world today, together—left, right, and center—we can achieve common sense solutions that support the public trust, promote good will, and serve the common good. Sapience, also known as wisdom, trumps all other ideologies.

Sapience is the ability to think and act using knowledge, experience, understanding, common sense and insight. Sapience is associated with attributes such as intelligence, enlightenment, and unbiased judgement and also recognizes the humanistic concepts of Western European culture, American exceptionalism, and conservative values.

Are you interested in spotting fake news media and helping to fight and eliminate it? If yes, please read on and if you also believe in the message of this book and willing to fight for it— please considering joining one of these two programs below sponsored by the SAPIENT Being.

Make Free Speech Again On Campus (MFSAOC) Program

Provide high school and college students the opportunity to start SAPIENT Being campus clubs, chapters, and alliances where independent, liberal, and conservative minded students can meet safely and freely as sapient beings to learn the facts and truth concerning the important issues facing us today. Learn more about the process of practicing, protecting, and promoting viewpoint diversity, freedom of speech and intellectual humility as part of the Make Free Speech Again On Campus program for on or off and/or virtual campus groups at https://www.sapientbeing.org/programs.

This is a new membership drive with independent students in mind who want to hear both sides of an issue, from any topic, without intimidation. It's also a perfect opportunity for liberal and conservative minded students to pop each other's ideological bubbles, and together, openly, and honestly, discuss and debate the hottest and most contentious issues facing America and the world today. We accomplish this by following the highest standards of civil discourse and debating each other's ideas, premises, and principles without attacking their character with malice and prejudice. This is sapience at its best!

World of Writing Warriors (WOWW) Program

Return free speech, open dialogue and civil discourse to high school and college campuses without intimidation and threat of violence to those with differences in opinion, ideologies, and practices. Encourage open debate, dialogue, and the free expression of alternative and non-orthodox viewpoints with the goal of creating a World Of Writing Warriors (WOWW) program that upholds journalistic standards and promotes viewpoint diversity throughout all types of campus journalism and media at https://www.sapientbeing.org/programs.

The WOWW Program is a partnership between the SAPIENT Being and Fratire Publishing that provides a unique opportunity for promising and unpublished writers, student and graduate journalists, debate programs and sponsors, white paper researchers and authors of every discipline and background to contribute to any of the *MADNESS* titles or provide their own and be recognized for it. Because Fratire Publishing is a small but determined independent publisher, it makes the perfect home for the WOWW Program with its 50 MADNESS series of titles.

Are You a Sapient Being or Want to Be One?

Sapience, also known as wisdom, is the ability to think and act using knowledge, experience, understanding, common sense and insight. Sapience is associated with attributes such as intelligence, enlightenment, unbiased judgment, compassion, experiential self-knowledge, self-actualization, and virtues such as ethics and benevolence.

Being a sapient being is not about identity politics, it's about doing what is right and borrows many of the essential qualities of Centrism that supports strength, tradition, open mindedness, and policy based on evidence not ideology.

Sapient beings are independent minded thinkers that achieve common sense solutions that appropriately address America's and the world's most pressing issues. They gauge situations based on context and reason, consideration, and probability. They are open minded and exercise conviction and willing to fight for it on the intellectual battlefield. Sapient beings don't blindly and recklessly follow their feelings or emotions.

Their unifying ideology is based on the truth, reason, logic, scientific method, and pragmatism—and not necessarily defined by compromise, moderation, or any particular faith—but is considerate of them.

Most importantly, per a letter written by Princeton professor Robert George in 2017 and endorsed by 28 professors from three Ivy League universities for incoming freshmen being sapient means, "Think for yourself!"

George's letter continues:

Thinking for yourself means questioning dominant ideas even when others insist on their being treated as unquestionable. It means deciding what one believes not by conforming to fashionable opinions, but by taking the trouble to learn and honestly consider the strongest arguments to be advanced on both or all sides of questions— including arguments for positions that others revile and want to stigmatize and against positions others seek to immunize from critical scrutiny.

The love of truth and the desire to attain it should motivate you to think for yourself. The central point of a college education is to seek truth and to learn the skills and acquire the virtues necessary to be a lifelong truth-seeker. Open-mindedness, critical thinking, and debate are essential to discovering the truth. Moreover, they are our best antidotes to bigotry.

Merriam-Webster's first definition of the word "bigot" is a person "who is obstinately or intolerantly devoted to his or her own opinions and prejudices." The only people who need fear open-minded inquiry and robust debate are the actual bigots, including those on campuses or in the broader society who seek to protect the hegemony of their opinions by claiming that to question those opinions is itself bigotry.

So, don't be tyrannized by public opinion. Don't get trapped in an echo chamber. Whether you in the end reject or embrace a view, make sure you decide where you stand by critically assessing the arguments for the competing positions. Think for yourself. Good luck to you in college!

Now, that might sound easy. But you will find—as you may have discovered already in high school—that thinking for yourself can be a challenge. It always demands self-discipline, and these days can require courage.

In today's climate, it's all-too easy to allow your views and outlook to be shaped by dominant opinion on your campus or in the broader academic culture. The danger any student—or faculty member—faces today is falling into the vice of conformism, yielding to groupthink, the orthodoxy.

At many colleges and universities, they instill what John Stuart Mill called "the tyranny of public opinion" does more than merely discourage students from dissenting from prevailing views on moral, political, and other types of questions. It leads them to suppose that dominant views are so obviously correct that only a bigot or a crank could question them.

Since no one wants to be, or be thought of as, a bigot or a crank, the easy, lazy way to proceed is simply by falling into line with campus orthodoxies. Don't do it!

To be sure, our overly politicized culture has a hard time viewing any "verbal cacophony" as a sign of strength and vibrancy. And perhaps nowhere is this truer than on many college campuses where political correctness is rampant, groupthink is common, and social media "mobs" arise in a flash to intimidate anyone who openly strays from the prevailing orthodoxy.

At the SAPIENT Being we're not intimidated—and our primary purpose is to seek the truth by enhancing viewpoint diversity, promoting intellectual humility, protecting freedom of speech and expression while developing sapience in the process—no matter what the cost on the intellectual battlefield, campus classroom, and marketplace of ideas. This is our ethos! Is it yours?

Best regards and sapiently yours,

Corey Lee Wilson

Corey Lee Wilson

 S.A.P.I.E.N.T. Being

1 – The Fake News Orgy of the 2016 Presidential Election

Credit: NBC

The reason *Fake News Madness* was selected as the first book of the 50 MADNESS book titles to be published is because it sets the precedence for spotting fake news which affects every other book topic. If we cannot call attention to, analyze, and eliminate the presence of fake news and its negative impact, we cannot fully understand the topics and meanings of the 50 book titles in a sapient manner.

Many in America are unaware of the fake news phenomena and the liberal and leftist bias within it. Many are the victims of it—trapped in a viewpoint orthodox echo chamber or so tyrannized by public opinion, they're afraid to think for themselves. When truth and non-fake news once again assert their rightful place throughout America in mainstream media (MSM), journalism, and academia—freedom of speech, viewpoint diversity, and intellectual humility will prevail.

The search for truth and investigating and verifying what a bona fide fact is, and what makes it different from a belief or an opinion has been an age-old philosophical quest known as Epistemology. What is knowledge? What is truth? How do we "know" something? "While Socrates and Plato were searching for answers to these important questions over two thousand years ago, it's a strange situation we find ourselves in when the 'information age' has helped to cause millions of people to drown in misinformation.

Media Liberal Bias Confirmed

As well documented by the Media Research Center (MRC), only the liberal media denies that there is a liberal bias problem in the media, but decades of studies and polls (not to mention common sense) have proven an overwhelming bias in their coverage of just about everything. A Harvard study analyzing the media coverage of President Trump's first 100 days in office found that 80% of it was negative. Of course, that was obvious to anyone old enough to pay attention during the election, but it was surprising that Harvard, a very liberal university, would actually investigate the matter.

The study analyzed reports from *The New York Times, The Washington Post,* and *The Wall Street Journal;* as well as CNN, CBS, NBC, ABC, Fox News, and even the BBC, and found the average coverage was 80% negative. Also, not surprising was that CNN's coverage was 93% negative. Fox News, on the other hand, was shown to be 52% negative and 48 % positive, which fits in almost perfectly with their trademarked slogan "Fair & Balanced."

This kind of slanted coverage is certainly nothing new. A famous study of liberal bias in the American media was conducted in 1986 and found that most journalists working for the major national news outlets were Democrats with liberal views on issues like gay rights, abortion, affirmative action, and welfare programs. The study, later published in a book called *The Media Elite*, gathered its data by conducting surveys of journalists at the Big Three broadcast news networks (ABC, CBS, NBC), along with print outlets including *The New York Times, The Washington Post, The Wall Street Journal, Time,* and *Newsweek.*

It concluded that because liberals dominated most news organizations, their coverage reflected their political attitudes both consciously and unconsciously; even if they didn't think they were being biased because they unconsciously believed that their views were 'correct,' so in their minds they didn't see their coverage as biased at all.

A decade later in 1997, another major study of journalists was conducted by the American Society of Newspaper Editors and that found that 61% of reporters leaned Democrat, but only 15% leaned Republican with 24% of those surveyed appeared to be independent.

In 2002 a professor at Dartmouth College published his research on media bias in his book *Press Bias and Politics: How the Media Frame Controversial Issues*, which also showed that most mainstream media in America present liberal views in a more favorable light.

Another study in 2005 by researchers at UCLA found a "strong liberal bias" at most mainstream media outlets with the exception of Fox News and *The Washington Times*. A 2007 study at Harvard University also confirmed a liberal bias in television news.

Documenting TV's Twelve Weeks of Trump Bashing in 2016

In the twelve weeks since the party conventions concluded in late July 2016, Republican presidential nominee Donald Trump received significantly more broadcast network news coverage than his Democratic rival, Hillary Clinton, but nearly all of that coverage (91%) was hostile, according to a study by the Media Research Center (MRC).

In addition, the networks spent far more airtime focusing on the personal controversies involving Trump (440 minutes) than about similar controversies involving Clinton (185 minutes). Donald Trump's treatment of women was given 102 minutes of evening news airtime, more than that allocated to discussing Clinton's e-mail scandal (53 minutes) and the Clinton Foundation pay-for-play scandals (40 minutes) combined.

For this study, the MRC analyzed all 588 evening news stories that either discussed or mentioned the presidential campaign on the ABC, CBS and NBC evening newscasts from July 29 through October 20, 2016 (including weekends). The networks devoted 1,191 minutes to the presidential campaign during this period, or nearly 29 percent of all news coverage.

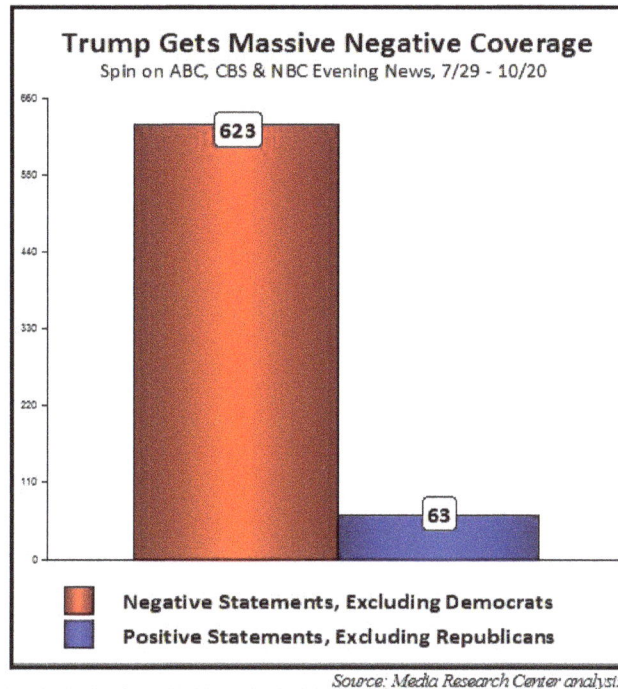

Trump Gets Massive Negative Coverage
Spin on ABC, CBS & NBC Evening News, 7/29 - 10/20

623

63

Negative Statements, Excluding Democrats
Positive Statements, Excluding Republicans

Source: Media Research Center analysis

MRC's measure of campaign spin was designed to isolate the networks' own slant, not the back-and-forth of the campaign trail. Thus, their analysts ignored soundbites which merely showcased the traditional party line (Republicans supporting Trump and bashing Clinton, and vice versa), and instead tallied evaluative statements which imparted a clear *positive* or *negative* tone to the story. Such statements may have been presented as quotes from non-partisan talking heads such as experts or voters, quotes from partisans who broke ranks (Republicans attacking Trump or Democrats criticizing Clinton), or opinionated statements from the reporter themselves.

Additionally, MRC separated personal evaluations of each candidate from statements about their prospects in the campaign horse race (i.e., standings in the polls, chances to win, etc.). While such comments can have an effect on voters (creating a bandwagon effect for those seen as winning or demoralizing the supports of those portrayed as losing), they are not "good press" or "bad press" as understood by media scholars as far back as Michael Robinson's groundbreaking research on the 1980 presidential campaign.

The results show neither candidate was celebrated by the media (as Obama was in 2008), but network reporters went out of their way to hammer Trump day after day, while Clinton was largely out of their line of fire. MRC's analysts found 184 opinionated statements about Hillary Clinton, split between 39 positive statements (21%) vs. 145 negatives (79%). Those same broadcasts included more than three times as many opinionated statements about Trump, 91 percent of which (623) were negative vs. just nine percent positive (63).

Even when they were critical of Hillary Clinton—for concealing her pneumonia, for example, or mischaracterizing the FBI investigation of her e-mail server—network reporters always maintained a respectful tone in their coverage.

Media Zeroed In On Trump's Controversies, Not Clinton's
(Minutes of airtime on ABC, CBS & NBC evening news, 7/29 - 10/20)

Trump: Sexist rhetoric/Mistreating women	102 minutes
Clinton: Questions about age/health	53 minutes
Clinton: Personal e-mail server	40 minutes
Trump: Won't release tax returns/Didn't pay?	33 minutes
Trump: Flip-flop on immigration?	32 minutes
Trump: Claiming Nov. election is "rigged"	27 minutes
Clinton: Clinton Foundation scandals	24 minutes
Trump: Feud w/Khan family	23 minutes
Trump: Too close to Putin/Russia	22 minutes
Trump: Flirting w/racism/Insensitive rhetoric	20 minutes
Trump: Questions about age/health	19 minutes
Trump: Promoting Obama birther theories	19 minutes
Trump: Lacks temperament/qualifications	18 minutes
Trump: Questions about Trump Foundation	14 minutes
Trump: Voicing 2nd Amendment threat to Hillary?	14 minutes

Source: Media Research Center.

This was not the case with Trump, who was slammed as embodying "the politics of fear," or a "dangerous" and "vulgar" "misogynistic bully" who had insulted vast swaths of the American electorate. Reporters also bluntly called out Trump for lying in his public remarks in a way they never did with Clinton, despite her own robust record of false statements.

As for those "horse race" assessments that were excluded from the Media Research Center's "good press/bad press" measure, those were decidedly anti-Trump as well. Out of 569 such statements about the health or prospects of Trump's campaign, 85% (486) were negative, vs.

15% (83) that were positive. For Clinton, the spin was reversed: out of 432 assessments of her status in the race, 62% (268) were positive, vs. just 38% (164) that were negative.

By far, the top topic since the 2016 party conventions had been the issue of Donald Trump's treatment of women, especially the 2005 *Access Hollywood* tape (which received nearly 50 minutes of evening news coverage) and the unproven allegations from several women that he engaged in inappropriate conduct in the past (26 minutes).

Add it all up, and Trump's alleged sexist behavior or rhetoric totaled 102 minutes of news coverage since the conventions. In contrast, references to Bill Clinton's past treatment of women, and Hillary Clinton's role in covering up her husband's wrongdoing, amounted to less than seven minutes of coverage during this same period, a roughly 15-to-1 disparity.

Other Trump controversies were given robust coverage: the issue of his tax returns (33 minutes), his concern that the November election could be "rigged" (27 minutes), and suggestions that Trump and his aides are too close to Putin's Russia (22 minutes).

In contrast, controversies involving Hillary Clinton received far less attention. Her "basket of deplorables" comment received just seven minutes of total coverage, while barely two minutes (134 seconds) was spent talking about her handling of the 2012 attack in Benghazi when she was Secretary of State.

Bill Clinton's crack that Obamacare was a "crazy system" was limited to just 140 seconds of evening news coverage, even though it signaled the kind of intra-party split that would surely have received far more coverage if it had been a Republican vs. a Republican.

A Quinnipiac poll found that more than half of all voters (55%) thought the media's coverage had been biased against Trump. With coverage like this, the question is, what are the other 45 percent thinking?

Mainstream Media (MSM) Missed the Revolution

Pundits looked at the gravitas and experience, the fund-raising process and endless endorsements, and the brand names of candidates such as Jeb Bush and Hillary Clinton and expected them to land the two nominations for those reasons. Indeed, these were foregone conclusions for most reporters. The "experts" were about to be exposed as dinosaurs, thoroughly out of touch with the American electorate as Bozell and Graham demonstrate.

The smartest people in the room believe their thumbs are pressed firmly on the pulse of the American public, but in reality their world extends only across a tract of land along the Manhattan—Washington, D.C., corridor, along with some prime coastal real estate in California. They were clueless as to the mood of an electorate in the real America that has lost its patience with the elites both in and out of government. This necessarily included them.

To understand the electorate in 2016 it is essential that one read Angelo Codevilla's article "America's Ruling Class—And the Perils of Revolution," published by *The American Spectator* six years before in 2010. The 12,000-word essay was a masterpiece that presented an existential struggle for the future of America between what he dubbed the "ruling class" and the "country class." It was prescient. Codevilla had perfectly described the opposing forces in the 2016 presidential campaign.

The ruling class is a fraternity/sorority whose membership includes those in a position of power over a population it views as less able—if not wholly unable—to handle its own affairs. "For our ruling class, America is a work in progress, just like the rest of the world, and they are the engineers."

The ruling class has no party affiliation.

"Differences between Bushes, Clintons, and Obamas are of degrees, not kind," the author wrote. "No prominent Republican challenges the ruling class's claim of superior insight, nor its denigration of the American people as irritable children who must learn their place. The Republican Party does not disparage the ruling class, because most of its officials are or would like to be part of it."

On the other side of the coin is the country class, with its "desire to get rid of rulers it regards inept and haughty.... The country class is convinced that big business, big government, and big finance are linked as never before, and that ordinary people are more unequal than ever.... The country class actually believes that America's ways are superior to the rest of the world's, and regards most of mankind as less free, less prosperous, and less virtuous."

As dumb was Trump was made to look by MSM, he got it—and fundamentally understood the divide—and the billionaire chose to champion the country class. That choice would necessarily pit him against virtually all levels of power in America today: against the establishment elite of both political parties, against the Chamber of Commerce oligarchy, against the unions, against academia, against Hollywood, and of course against the national news and social media.

Interestingly enough as Bozell and Graham point out, the country class uprising Codevilla had identified wasn't limited to the United States. The same phenomenon was emerging in other nations like Israel, France, Britain, Italy, Poland, Brazil, Netherlands and the Philippines. Many of the same issues, including unfair trade practices, uncontrolled illegal immigration, and Islamic terrorism, were triggering populist uprisings, and just as with the Trump phenomenon, the American and world news media chose sides.

Trump, the Race-Baiting, Clinically Insane, Neo-Fascist Sociopath

All of these predicators as Bozell and Graham point out was an early indicator of how badly the elites were going to misjudge Trump:

They dismissed him as an unsavory character. They missed the uprising he was leading. In the infamous Republican debate on CNBC in the fall of 2015, lead moderator John Harwood began by asking Trump: "Let's be honest. Is this a comic book version of a presidential campaign?"

But Harwood wasn't alone. The other CNBC "moderators" got into the act and proceeded to ridicule one GOP candidate after the next, until Senator Ted Cruz reached the end of his tether over their nonstop insults: "The questions asked so far in this debate illustrate why the American people don't trust the media.... You look at the questions. Donald Trump, are you a comic book villain? Ben Carson, can you do math? John Kasich, can you insult those two people over here? Marco Rubio, will you resign? Jeb Bush, why have your numbers fallen? How about talking about the substantive issues people care about?"

The audience roared its approval. The CNBC crew returned to Washington, D.C., and New York thoroughly humiliated, a case study on how to completely screw up a national debate.

CBS's Face the Nation brought on Slate writer Jamelle Bouie to smear Trump voters as racist: "Trump's supporters show all the hallmarks of people with high levels of racial resentment. They are—you know, they seem—a good number believe that President Obama is un-American or maybe even a Muslim and connected to terrorists. A good number referred to him as arrogant and elitist which, for myself, reads very much like 'uppity' as an old insult towards African Americans who have achieved some sort of stature in mainstream society."

PBS host Tavis Smiley threw the race card with more velocity on ABC's This Week: "Trump is still, to my mind at least, an unrepentant, irascible, religious, and racial arsonist," he screamed. "And so, when we talk about how Trump is rising in the polls, you can't do that absent the kind of campaign he's running, the issues he's raising."

As Trump's chances of winning the nomination grew, the historical analogies grew more ridiculous—and offensive. On February 26, 2016, the *Washington Post* editorial board decided to compare Trump's proposed crackdown on illegal immigration to murderers of millions: "He would round up and deport 11 million people, a forced movement on a scale not attempted since Stalin or perhaps Pol Pot. ... He routinely trades in wild falsehoods and doubles down when his lies are exposed."

The Angry Aftermath of Trump's Win: A 'Moral 9/11'

The New York Times had a headline asking, "Can The Media Recover from This Election?" *Fortune* magazine asked, "How much will Cable News' Record Ratings Drop Post-Election?" Then a survey conducted by CBS and *Vanity Fair* magazine found that Americans now saw mainstream media as the most unethical business, more so than the pharmaceutical companies, and the banking industry. Another survey from Monmouth University in New Jersey found that 6 out of 10 Americans believe that the mainstream media regularly reports fake news.

As Bozell and Graham summarize the fake news frenzy prior to the 2016 election: Trump was now a racist, a xenophobe, a misogynist, an ignoramus, a neo-fascist, and a sociopath, all rolled into one, clearly a menace and a threat to the future of the United States, if not humankind itself. But one thing was also for certain. It wasn't going to happen in 2016. The media, like virtually everyone else on the left, were still utterly convinced Hillary had this one in the bag.

As the campaign entered the final days, the media's overconfidence in a Clinton victory was everywhere. On MSNBC, Chris Matthews was gleefully reading from one of those anonymously sourced fake news *Washington Post* reports: "A wave of apprehension and anguish swept the Republican Party on Thursday, with many GOP leaders concluding it is probably too late to salvage his flailing presidential campaign. Republicans privately acknowledge it could be a landslide victory for Democratic nominee Hillary Clinton."

A few days later, CBS Evening News anchor Scott Pelley proclaimed, "Time is running out for Donald Trump.... No candidate down this far, this late has ever recovered (more fake news because Truman did in 1948 to beat Dewey)." Two days later, ABC's Jon Karl warned, "Donald Trump is down 17 points among women. You do not get elected president of the United States if you are down 17 points among women." On MSNBC's The Last Word with Lawrence O'Donnell, *Washington Post* columnist Eugene Robinson gushed over a Florida poll that claimed that 28 percent of Republicans were voting for Clinton and declared that "if it's anywhere near that then this election, not only that Florida fall to Hillary Clinton, but this election overall could, you know—we could be talking landslide." (Trump won Florida.)

With six days to go, former Bush and McCain staffer Nicolle Wallace insisted she was bringing the "cold hard truth" to the table on NBC: "The best-case scenario, if Trump and Co. do everything right? They lose with 266 electoral votes."

On the Sunday before the election, ABC political analyst Matthew Dowd (another former Bushie) called it for Hillary. "She's got about a 95 percent chance in this election, and I think she's going to have a higher margin than Barack Obama in 2012."

The Huffington Post proclaimed that Hillary Clinton was 98 percent likely to defeat Trump.

Ryan Grim of HuffPost argued, "It's not easy to sit here and tell you that Clinton has a 98 percent chance of winning. Everything inside us screams out that life is too full of uncertainty, that being so sure is just a fantasy. But that's what the numbers say." Grim later repeated, "If you want to put your faith in the numbers, you can relax. She's got this."

On the morning of Election Day, Eleanor Clift was measuring the drapes for a woman president in the Daily Beast: "There are likely to be more than 20 women in the Senate after Tuesday, and together with Clinton in the White House, they will send a strong signal to women and girls that nothing is holding them back, that the future is there for them."

As Bozell and Graham so correctly note: This arrogant, elitist overconfidence is precisely what made election night so enjoyable for Trump voters. On the CBS Evening News shortly before the polls began to close, reporter Nancy Cordes claimed that after being "dogged by her e-mail troubles, a restless electorate, and an unorthodox opponent," Clinton aides insisted Hillary's "perseverance through all of it, Scott, shows she's prepared for the nation's toughest job."

As ABC's prime-time election night coverage began, they turned to former evening-news anchor Charles Gibson, who promptly whacked Trump for not being as classy as his opponent, referring to Hillary Clinton's 2014 memoir *Hard Choices*: 'The chapter about when you should apologize, I think Donald Trump missed that chapter somewhere along the line."

Every single major news outlet picked Hillary Clinton to win a month before the election. Ironically, one of the worst prognosticators was Fox News. On the October 21 edition of Special Report, Bret Baier proclaimed that Hillary was going to trounce The Donald. The FNC electoral map had her winning the Electoral College 307- 181, with 50 toss-up votes.

But on Election Night—Things Were Not Going According to the Script

As Bozell and Graham noted: Hillary was supposed to pick up some red states while sweeping the battleground states. She was supposed to win Florida early, which would seal the deal—but she lost. She was supposed to capture North Carolina—but she lost. "As Ohio goes, so goes the nation," and she was going to pick up that state—but she lost that one too. A shell-shocked national media saw impossible developing! And then the roof caved in when blue states considered impregnable by the pundits started to fall. First Pennsylvania, then Wisconsin, and then, sealing the deal, Michigan.

Donald J. Trump had been elected the forty-fifth President of the United States.

Liberals found themselves talking to themselves. They tried being temporarily apologetic on NBC, with Chuck Todd admitting that "we have overlooked rural America a bit too much." Former anchor Tom Brokaw backhanded Trump 's voters as miscreants who "have to pull a pin on a grenade and roll it across the country, whatever it takes. 'We want change, and we want big change!'"

Leftist journalism professor Jeff Jarvis at New York University hyperventilated, choosing to blame the media for not being harsh enough: "I fear that journalism is irredeemably broken, a failure. My profession failed to inform the public about the fascist they are electing." Just as New York University fails to teach journalism when it employs the likes of Jeff Jarvis.

It was the same thing with comedians on election night. What was supposed to be a knee-slapping funfest became no laughing matter. Expecting a Hillary Clinton victory, CBS late-night host Stephen Colbert was given an hour on CBS-owned Showtime for a we-won trash-talk special. They titled it Stephen Colbert's Live Election Night Democracy's Series Finale: Who's Going to Clean Up This Shit?

As the real possibility of a Trump upset began to unfold, panic hit the set. Comedy Central Daily Show host Trevor Noah was in full hysteria, telling Colbert: "I don't know if you've come to the right place for jokes tonight. Because this is the first time throughout this entire race where I'm officially shitting my pants! I genuinely do not understand how America can be this disorganized or this hateful!"

MSNBC hosts Mark Halperin and John Heilemann (who also had a Showtime election series called The Circus) were on scene to add expert analysis to the comedy. Halperin clearly lost control as he wildly proclaimed, "Outside of the Civil War and World War II, and including 9/11, this may be the most cataclysmic event the country's ever seen!" Colbert cooed his appreciation, "I'm so glad you guys are here. I wouldn't want to be alone right now."

This Was a 'White-Lash' Against a Changing Country

In the midnight hour, CNN analyst (and former Obama White House aide) Van Jones took to crying racism in defeat: "It's hard to be a parent, tonight, for a lot of us. You tell your kids, 'Don't be a bully.' You tell your kids, 'Don't be a bigot. ...' And then, you have this outcome...

How do I explain this to my children? This was a 'white-lash.' This was a 'white-lash' against a changing country. It was a 'white-lash' against a black president."

National Public Radio (NPR) was still in anger mode after the election on Wednesday's Morning Edition news program, bringing on black author Attica Locke (who also writes for the Fox drama Empire), who rudely implied that each and every Trump supporter is a racist. NPR anchor David Greene politely suggested that it was not every one of them, but Locke refused to concede that there was a single nonracist: "I'm out with that. There's a part of me that honestly feels like that level of politeness, where we're not calling things what they are, is how we will never get forward."

Locke then went on Twitter to promote her taxpayer-funded radio rant: "Me on the election on NPR. The 'R' word is the new 'N' word, I guess. Why are folks afraid to say racist?" NBC Nightly News correspondent Richard Engel chronicled a global panic on the Wednesday night after Trump won: "There were gasps around the world. Headlines, 'Trumpocalypse' and 'Disunited States.' And echoes of the Brexit vote too, against the European Union establishment. But there are deeper concerns tonight that the world's shining light of democracy has gone dark."

New York Times columnist Thomas Friedman echoed Halperin's 9/11 metaphor on Friday night on HBO's Real Time with Bill Maher: "This is a moral 9/11! Only 9/11 was done to us from the outside and we did this to ourselves." Hillary losing was now the moral equivalent of losing 3,000 Americans in a terrorist attack.

That verdict came after Maher's own angry rant against Trump voters, who he believed had sealed their own doom: "Enjoy your victory, Trump voters. Because when you're dying because you don't have health insurance to treat the infection you got for a back-alley abortion you had to get because of fetal lead poisoning, you can say to yourself, at least I didn't vote for someone with a private e-mail server."

When Democrats win, it's a victory for hope and change and national unity. When Republicans win, it is a sad day, a victory for dark forces, their vicious lies, and flagrant fouls, manipulating the unruly throng. As Peter Jennings infamously said after the 1994 Republican wave election, it was "a nation full of uncontrolled two-year-old rage," a stomping, screaming temper tantrum, not a serious verdict on the future of America. These voters would need to see the error of their ways and know the damage they had committed.

They saw Trump's voters just as the Clinton campaign saw them: a basket of deplorables. All season long the pro-Hillary press treated Trump's followers with utter contempt. This was the country class showing its utter temerity in challenging the ruling class. These were extra-chromosomed rednecks in Make America Great Again (MAGA) hats. As Hillary put it, they were "irredeemable, but thankfully they are not America."

But those deplorables carried the day and they are America.

The pundits got it all wrong. They had accepted the comforting prophecies of the national media, not just regarding the coronation of Hillary Clinton, but on America's repudiation of Donald Trump. It was a resounding rejection of the ruling class—themselves (and this is the true reason Hillary lost not the idiotic conspiracy theories that followed Trump's historic win).

But these elites were not going silently into the night. The media would only double down, and triple down, and quadruple down as Trump made his way to the White House. All the rules learned at journalism school were tossed aside. If the news was harmful to this man, it was to be magnified; if it was favorable to him, it was to be ignored; and if needed, the "news" was faked.

The ruling class was not about to concede an inch of turf to the peasants.

2 – Pretty Much All of Journalism Now Leans Left

For the news media to serve citizens as an effective source for information, it is essential that the public respect their professionalism, independence, and fairness. Yet over the past twenty-five years, the news media's credibility has badly eroded.

A wide variety of public opinion polls have documented the fact that most Americans now see the media as politically biased, inaccurate, intrusive, and a tool of powerful interests. By a nearly three-to-one margin, those who see political bias believe the media bend their stories to favor liberals.

These polls document a crisis for the news media. Years of skewed reporting has squandered the public's trust. Recent surveys also show a widening partisan divide, as Democrats and liberals choose to believe the *New York Times*, CNN and MSNBC, and Republicans and conservatives put their trust in Fox News and the *Wall Street Journal*. The data presented here by the Media Research Center (MRC) tells the story of how journalists have devolved from respected professionals to resented partisans and have lost the esteem of their audience in the process.

Throughout most of the 20th century, journalists on the left and the right have long shared a reverence for the First Amendment. Today, though, journalists are becoming zealous to silence their ideological rivals—and the fervor is mainly on the left.

Ask journalists, and they'll likely tell you they play things right down the middle. They strive to be "fair." They're "centrists." Sorry, not true. The profound leftward ideological bias of the Big Media is the main reason why America now seems saturated with "fake news." Many Journalists, besotted with their own ideology, are no longer able to recognize their own bias.

Media today now means more than just television, newspapers, and radio. It includes social media. Facebook, Twitter, Instagram, YouTube and Snapchat, which have become major media companies that host and distribute content in quantities previously unimagined.

Because media has changed so dramatically with the creation of the Internet, smartphones, and social media; people don't just get their news from TV, radio, and newspapers anymore as you know. There are now countless blogs, YouTube channels, Twitter accounts, and Facebook pages dedicated to posting news and analysis—many of which rival or eclipse the reach of traditional media outlets.

The distribution of content posted on these platforms has complex implications regarding how it spreads online, what role these companies have in distributing (and suppressing) user generated content, and how information flowing through these platforms influences their audience.

Can We Trust the Media and Are They Fair?

After a century of journalism based on the ethos of fairness, objectivity, and balance, the news media, generally speaking, have abandoned their venerable values. According to Dr. Tobe Berkovitz and his November 2016 *Newsmax* piece titled "The Biggest Loser: Mainstream Media" mainstream media has become obsessed with an internal debate over the concept of "false equivalency," also called "false balance."

The false equivalency theory holds that once a candidate 's rhetoric ventures beyond the accepted mainstream paradigm and proves offensive to the sensibilities of elite gatekeepers (i.e., the media), that balance, objectivity, and fairness become moot.

Stories that rely on these classic journalistic principles become "false" because they do not treat a candidate who espouses potentially offensive ideas—building a wall and "extreme vetting" of Muslims—the same way they treat a candidate who does not hold those views.

In the current election cycle, the sacrificial lamb to false equivalency was NBC's Matt Lauer. He was vilified by his media brethren for daring to pose follow-up questions to the former secretary of state over her homebrew email server, and for not jumping on Trump every time he made a dubious statement. *New York Times* columnist Nicholas Kristof branded Lauer's performance "an embarrassment to journalism." Lauer's offense? He treated Trump and Clinton equally.

The 24-hour news cycle, the rise of social media, and the turn to overtly partisan journalism from both ends of the political spectrum are aggravating the social disruption and undermining the business of journalism in the 21st century. Today, "balance" has come to mean competing, uber-partisan talking heads who provide grist for the cable programming mill.

Is the Media Fair?

The profession of news sharing involves the presentation of facts. Opinion related topics should present multiple views. Unfortunately, editorial bias has become increasingly prevalent, with news often leaning to one side as noted in D.J. Wilson's Association of Mature American Citizens

(AMAC) article "Is the Media Fair?" When media bias prevails, whether left or right, or somewhere in between, journalistic objectivity is lost and the ability for audiences to decide issues for themselves falls to the wayside.

An examination of Trump's first 100 days in office reflects forward progress for his administration. Trump, at a historic pace, enacted more legislation and signed more executive orders than any other president in half a century. Trump's assertive stance on immigration has worked to decrease the flow of illegal entry into the United States through Mexico. The President's swift response to Syria's dictator Bashar al-Assad's use of chemical weapons on innocent civilians was a step to prevent and deter the end of chemical weapons.

Trump promotes America's energy independence, restoration of economic optimism, create jobs, rebuild the military, and to repeal and replace failing Obamacare.

Meanwhile, the media remained adversarial. Using Twitter as a forum, Trump singled out *The New York Times*, CNN, NBC, "and many more" in a February 2017 tweet which read, "The FAKE NEWS media is not my enemy, it is the enemy of the American people. SICK!"

A revised version deleted the word "sick" and added ABC and CBS to the list. Preceding the tweet, Trump openly criticized press coverage during a 77-minute news conference. One of the biggest things Trump says he learned in his first 100 days in office is the extent of dishonesty in the news media.

It's widely accepted that politicians, such as Trump, who do not subscribe to mainstream media's left leaning ideologies, become targets of the press.

A study, conducted by the Harvard Kennedy School's Shorenstein Center on Media, Politics, and Public Policy, analyzed Trump's first 100 days in office. The study found that "Trump received unsparing coverage for most weeks of his presidency, without a single major topic where Trump's coverage, on balance, was more positive than negative, setting a new standard for unfavorable press coverage of a President."

It was concluded that Fox was the only news outlet in the study that came close to giving Trump positive coverage overall. The study noted a variation in the tone of Fox's coverage, depending upon the topic. Media Research Center (MRC), conducted a study in April that showed that Trump received "by far the most hostile press treatment of any incoming American President." The study also concluded that TV news pushed a relentlessly negative agenda (see chart on next page).

The 'Mediacrats' Are Everywhere!

Congressman Lamar Smith, U.S. Representative for Texas' 21st congressional district and founder of the House Media Fairness Caucus, called for the media to adhere to the highest standards of reporting to provide the American people with facts, balanced stories, and fair coverage of the news. Smith stated, "The media and Democrats are so close in association and so close in their philosophical views that we might as well use one word to describe both, and that's Mediacrats."

Due to extreme negative coverage, Trump labeled the media as the "opposition party" to his administration, and he encouraged his supporters to "...do your part to fight back against the media's attacks and deceptions."

In an unusual break of protocol, Trump barred some reporters from attending his daily off-camera briefing. When speaking at the Coast Guard commencement in May 2017, Trump directly addressed his negative treatment by the media. "No politician in history, and I say this with great surety, has been treated worse or more unfairly."

Controversial Civil Rights Activist Malcolm X once said, "The media's the most powerful entity on earth. They have the power to make the innocent guilty and to make the guilty innocent, and that's power.

Because they control the masses." The press has slammed Trump for many things; the controversy surrounding former National Security Advisor Mike Flynn, allegations of a Russian-Trump interference in the 2016 election, the timing of the firing of FBI Director James Comey, Trump's relationship with German Chancellor Angela Merkel, legality of the travel ban, and withdrawal from the Paris Climate Accord.

Trump is sometimes criticized for the contents of his tweets, but the 45th President has an advantage: he can bypass the press and bring his voice directly to the people. According to Twitter, Trump has 80.3 million followers and counting as of May 28, 2020.

Pew Study: Media Bias Against Trump is Real and Extreme

The President and his supporters have often lamented unfair coverage from sources they dub 'fake news,' and this study below reported by Rusty Weiss in the October 2017 Liberty Unyielding, titled "Pew Study: Media Bias Against Trump is Real and Extreme," confirms their suspicions.

While the fact that the media has been unfair to Trump should come as no surprise to anyone paying attention, the rate of negative coverage might raise an eyebrow. The Pew study indicates that 62 percent of the media coverage of this President has been negative, while a scant 5 percent has been positive.

Compare that to two other presidents who were somewhat polarizing in their initial days in the White House—Bill Clinton and George W. Bush. Both had more negative coverage than positive, but the numbers were relatively close. According to the research, Clinton had 28 percent negative media stories to 27 percent positive, while Bush had 28 percent negative to 22 percent positive.

Majority of Americans say social media negatively affect the way things are going in the country today

% of U.S. adults who say social media have a ___ effect on the way things are going in this country today

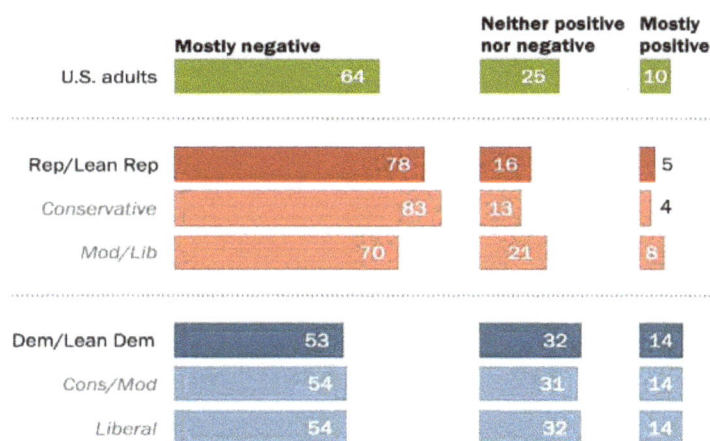

	Mostly negative	Neither positive nor negative	Mostly positive
U.S. adults	64	25	10
Rep/Lean Rep	78	16	5
Conservative	83	13	4
Mod/Lib	70	21	8
Dem/Lean Dem	53	32	14
Cons/Mod	54	31	14
Liberal	54	32	14

Note: Those who did not give an answer are not shown.
Source: Survey of U.S. adults conducted July 13-19, 2020.

PEW RESEARCH CENTER

That's nothing like what former President Obama received from a media that practically fawned over him on a daily basis. His coverage—42 percent *positive* to 20 percent negative.

"Compared with the first 60 days of the Clinton, Bush and Obama presidencies, news outlets' evaluations of Trump's start in office were far more negative and less positive," a summary of the report states. "About six-in-ten news stories about Trump's first 60 days (62%) carried an overall negative assessment of his words or actions."

"That is about three times more negative than for Obama (20%) and roughly twice that of Bush and Clinton (28% each)."

"Coverage was also far less positive, with just 5% of stories conveying an overall positive assessment of the president and the administration," the study continues. "This is in sharp contrast to Obama's first days in 2009, when 42% of the stories offered an overall positive assessment."

Another recent study out of Harvard indicated that during his first 100 days in office, 93 percent of the mainstream media's coverage toward President Trump was negative. Next time Trump is complaining about unfair media coverage, understand this—he's absolutely right.

Can Any Sapient Being Deny Trump Labeling Fake News as "Fake News?"

"No!" they cannot, and the majority of content outlined by the Media Research Center (MRC) shows why.

Going back to the 2016 presidential election fake news that Bozell and Graham captured, CNN commentator Sally Kohn lit some warning flares of her own. Even if you couldn't vote for Hillary, "the woman who's running with the impeccable and vast record of experience, if that's not enough for people, at least stopping us from being Nazi Germany would hopefully get Democrats and others to turn out." CNN anchor Alisyn Camerota left the Nazi smear unchallenged. Three days later on CNN, Kohn drove the hyperbole into Fantasyland. She worried: "When Trump institutes internment camps and suspends habeas; we'll all look back and feel pretty bad."

The Nazi smears were all the rage for the outraged! *New York Times* columnist David Brooks cracked on Meet the Press: "If we're going to get Trump, we might as well get the Nuremberg rallies to go with it!"

CNN host Erin Burnett badgered Florida's Republican governor, Rick Scott. "The current president of Mexico—two former presidents of Mexico—have compared him to Hitler," she said. "Vicente Fox, former president, specifically said, 'He reminds me of Hitler.' It's direct. It's not an allusion. It's a direct thing. 'He reminds me of Hitler.' Do they have a point?"

By March 15, 2016, Trump had won nineteen of the first twenty-nine state primaries or caucuses and his opponents were dropping like flies.

By May 13, as Trump closed in on the Republican nomination, NPR's On the Media host Bob Garfield lost control of his metaphors and, for a moment, his mind. Trump's "supposedly courageous candor is contaminated with the most cowardly hate speech—racism, xenophobia, misogyny, incitement, breathtaking ignorance on issues, both foreign and domestic, and a nuclear recklessness, reminiscent of a raving meth-head, with a machete on an episode of Cops."

Trump was no longer a joke. He was a threat, and once the leftists convinced themselves Trump was a national menace, it wasn't long before some of them started talking up violence. The *Huffington Post* published an article by Jesse Benn on June 6, 2016, headlined "Sorry, Liberals, a Violent Response to Trump Is as Logical as Any." Benn argued: "In the face of media, politicians, and GOP primary voters normalizing Trump as a presidential candidate—whatever your personal beliefs regarding violent resistance—there's an inherent value in forestalling Trump's normalization. Violent resistance accomplishes this."

Benn wasn't kidding. After a radical leftist gunned down Congressman Steve Scalise and several others in June 2017, Benn tweeted the shooter some advice: "For violent resistance to work, it'd need to be organized. Individual acts can be understandable, but likely counterproductive ineffective."

Then there was the army of amateur psychiatrists. On June 8, 2016, CBS contributor Nancy Giles insisted to MSNBC host Lawrence O'Donnell that Trump was "clinically insane." O'Donnell agreed. "You're not alone," he responded. "There's a lot of clinicians who have been speculating about that." Unsurprisingly for O'Donnell, he didn't produce a single name.

Legendary *Washington Post* reporter Carl Bernstein kept dropping the political F-word on Trump, as in this CNN interview snippet on October 21, 2016: "This campaign is now about a neo-fascist—I keep coming back to that—sociopath.... He is setting himself up as the head of ... a real neo-fascist movement.... Is there going to be remnants of a neo-fascist movement that he leads in this country after this election? It's a dangerous thing. We're in a dangerous place."

Media Bias Basics

Over the years, the Media Research Center has catalogued the views of journalists on the subject of bias. A number of journalists have admitted that the majority of their brethren approach the news from a liberal angle.

Four years later, NPR's Juan Williams talked about the tilt to Barack Obama on Fox News Sunday: "If you were going to events during the primaries, what you saw was that the executive editors and the top people at the networks were all rushing to Obama events, bringing their children, celebrating it."

Surveys of journalists' self-reported voting habits show them backing the Democratic candidate in every presidential election since 1964, including landslide losers George McGovern, Walter Mondale and Michael Dukakis. In 2004, a poll conducted by the University of Connecticut found journalists backed John Kerry over George W. Bush by a greater than two-to-one margin.

Compared to their audiences, journalists are far more likely to say they are Democrats or liberals, and they espouse liberal positions on a wide variety of issues. A 2004 poll by the Pew Research Center for The People & The Press found five times more journalists described themselves as "liberal" as said they were "conservative."

In increasing numbers, the viewing audiences recognize the media's liberal tilt. Gallup polls have consistently found that three times as many see the media as "too liberal" as see a media that is "too conservative." A 2005 survey conducted for the *American Journalism Review* found nearly two-thirds of the public disagreed with the statement, "The news media try to report the news without bias," and 42 percent of adults disagreed strongly.

A number of journalists have admitted that the majority of their brethren approach the news from a liberal angle. During the 2004 presidential campaign, for example, *Newsweek's* Evan Thomas predicted that sympathetic media coverage would boost Kerry's vote by "maybe 15 points," which he later revised to five points. In 2005, ex-CBS News President Van Gordon Sauter confessed he stopped watching his old network: "The unremitting liberal orientation finally became too much for me."

Many journalists continue to deny the liberal bias that taints their profession. During the height of CBS's forged memo scandal during the 2004 campaign, Dan Rather insisted that the problem wasn't his bias, it was his anybody who criticized him. "People who are so passionately partisan politically or ideologically committed basically say, 'Because he won't report it our way, we're going to hang something bad around his neck and choke him with it, check him out of existence if we can, if not make him feel great pain,'" Rather told *USA Today* in September 2004. "They know that I'm fiercely independent and that's what drives them up a wall."

The Media Research Center (MRC) continuously reports on instances of the liberal bias in the mainstream media. Daily Bias Alerts offer a regular roundup of the latest instances of biased reporting, their NewsBusters blog allows Web users to post their own reactions. MRC's Media Reality Check reports showcase important stories that the news media have distorted or ignored, and several times each year the MRC publishes its Special Reports offering in-depth documentation of the media's bias on specific issues.

The Media Bubble is Real—And Worse Than You Think

Heterodox Academy leader Musa al-Gharbi shared his April 2017 viewpoint diverse report "The Media Bubble is Real—And Worse Than You Think" with Heterodox Academy's 3,000 plus academic membership as follows:

Journalistic outlets face many of the same challenges as academic institutions. Like the academy (especially social research fields), most newsrooms skew decisively left. According to the American Journalism Project—one of the longest-running and most comprehensive studies of U.S. journalists (conducted every ten years since 1972)—only about 7% of contemporary journalists are Republicans.

This is a major decrease as compared to previous studies, suggesting that much like U.S. institutions of higher learning, there has been a significant and fairly rapid ideological shift in newsrooms since the 90s. The American Journalism report also shows that, like the academy, journalism is also suffering a legitimacy crisis driven, in part, by the perceived distance between reporters and the publics they are supposed to serve.

A recent study by Jack Shafer and Tucker Doherty, published by Politico, demonstrates just how vast this divide has grown:

Where do journalists work, and how much has that changed in recent years? To determine this, Doherty excavated labor statistics and cross-referenced them against voting patterns and Census data to figure out just what the American media landscape looks like, and how much it has changed.

The results read like a revelation. The national media really does work in a bubble, something that wasn't true as recently as 2008. And the bubble is growing more extreme. Concentrated heavily along the coasts, the bubble is both geographic and political. If you're a working journalist, odds aren't just that you work in a pro-Clinton county—odds are that you reside in one of the nation's most pro-Clinton counties...

...The "media bubble" trope might feel overused by critics of journalism who want to sneer at reporters who live in Brooklyn or California and don't get the "real America" of southern Ohio or rural Kansas. But these numbers suggest it's no exaggeration: Not only is the bubble real, but it's more extreme than you might realize. And it's driven by deep industry trends.

The authors then go on to explain why the shift is happening. It turns out, the trend seems to be driven overwhelmingly by structural changes to the industry itself rather than by any type of overt or intentional bias on the part of reporters. Internet publishers are now adding workers at nearly twice the rate newspaper publishers are losing them.

This isn't just a shift in medium. It's also a shift in sociopolitics, and a radical one. Where newspaper jobs are spread nationwide, internet jobs are not: Today, 73 percent of all internet publishing jobs are concentrated in either the Boston-New York-Washington-Richmond corridor or the West Coast crescent that runs from Seattle to San Diego and on to Phoenix. The Chicago area, a traditional media center, captures 5 percent of the jobs, with a paltry 22 percent going to the rest of the country. And almost all the real growth of internet publishing is happening outside the heartland, in just a few urban counties, all places that voted for Clinton. So, when your conservative friends use "media" as a synonym for "coastal" and "liberal," they're not far off the mark.

Something akin to the *Times* ethos thrives in most major national newsrooms found on the Clinton coasts—CNN, CBS, the *Washington Post*, BuzzFeed, Politico and the rest. Their reporters, an admirable lot, can parachute into Appalachia or the rural Midwest on a monthly basis and still not shake their provincial sensibilities: Reporters tote their bubbles with them.

Unfortunately, as the authors explain in great detail, the structural changes driving these bubbles are likely to persist, or even accelerate, in coming years. So, what can be done to mitigate the sociocultural and epistemic costs of these changes?

The best medicine for journalistic myopia isn't re-education camps or a splurge of diversity hiring, though tiny doses of those two remedies wouldn't hurt. Journalists respond to their failings best when their vanity is punctured with proof that they blew a story that was right in front of them. If the burning humiliation of missing the biggest political story in a generation won't change newsrooms, nothing will.

Overall, this seems like a constructive approach—one also advocated in the *Times Higher Education* piece. However, one point of concern remains, namely, the extent to which most reporters actually perceive or acknowledge they did in fact, "blow the story."

Understanding the Liberal vs. Conservative Imbalance in Journalism

To get an idea of the imbalance, consider the cases of Quinn Norton, a libertarian technology writer, and Sarah Jeong, a progressive technology writer. After the *New York Times* announced that it was hiring Norton for its editorial page, it took just seven hours for progressives to get her fired. On Twitter and in an internal *Times* chat room (as HuffPost reported), Norton was attacked for having tweeted that she was friends with a neo-Nazi hacker whom she had covered.

She had always repudiated his ideology, calling him a "terrible person," but that wasn't enough to save her job. Six months later, in August 2018, when the *Times* hired Jeong for the editorial page, conservative activists unearthed tweets from Jeong, an Asian-American, denigrating white men as well as whites as a race. One used a hashtag "#CancelWhitePeople;" another predicted that whites would soon go extinct and said, "This was my plan all along." The *Times* stuck with its decision to hire her. (The paper recently announced that Jeong would no longer be part of its editorial board, though she will continue as a contributing writer.)

Conservative journalists criticized the *Times* for its double standard, but they didn't unite with the online activists demanding that Jeong be fired. The *Times*'s Bret Stephens wrote a column urging the paper to overlook the offensive tweets. Andrew Sullivan lambasted Jeong's bigotry and the progressive dogma that it's impossible to be racist against whites, but he, too, urged the *Times* not to fire her because media companies should not succumb to online mobs.

You might think that Sullivan's forbearance would win him some points with progressives, and perhaps even make them question their own enthusiasm for purges, but the column didn't play well even with Sullivan's colleagues at the *Times*. Brian Feldman, an associate editor, tweeted: "Andrew Sullivan's newest column is complete garbage and I'm embarrassed to be even tangentially associated with it." Not exactly collegial, but again, that's where we are.

Media Conservatives: An Endangered Species

When you add it up, 58.47% admit to being left of center. Along with that, another 37.12% claim to be "moderate."

What about the mythic "conservative" financial journalist? In fact, a mere 0.46% of financial journalists called themselves "very conservative," while just 3.94% said they were "somewhat conservative." That's a whopping 4.4% of the total that lean right-of-center.

That's a ratio of 13 "liberals" for every one "conservative." Whatever happened to ideological diversity? Please remember this as you watch the business news or read a financial story in the paper. You might want to take its message with a grain of salt. That's especially true if the piece seems unduly harsh on the free-market system and its many proven benefits. Or if it lauds socialism as an "answer" to society's ills.

This is an enormous problem for the media—perhaps bigger than they realize. A Rasmussen Reports survey in late October 2018 found that 45% of all likely voters in the midterm elections believed "that when most reporters write about a congressional race, they are trying to help the Democratic candidate."

Just 11% said the media would try to help the Republican. And only 35% said they thought reporters simply try to report the news in an unbiased way.

Rasumussen notes that this "helps explain why Democratic voters are much bigger fans of election news coverage" than others. They see it as favorable to their own beliefs. Perhaps that's why the 2016 presidential election results triggered an epic snowflake meltdown and liberal madness.

What Journalists Think/How Journalists Vote

Reporters should keep their personal opinions from influencing the news stories they write and produce. But journalists are only human. A reporter's political outlook is bound to sway the judgments he or she makes each day, such as what events are newsworthy, and on whom to rely for trustworthy information. It is therefore essential to know if the media truly represent a diverse range of viewpoints or are dominated by just one political philosophy.

Surveys over the past 50 years have consistently found that journalists—especially those at the highest ranks of their profession—are much more liberal than rest of America. They are more likely to vote liberal, more likely to describe themselves as liberal, and more likely to agree with the liberal position on policy matters than members of the general public. The Media Research Center has compiled the relevant data on journalist attitudes, as well as polling showing how the American public's recognition of the media's liberal bias has grown over the years.

These surveys of journalists were conducted by professional pollsters, academics, or news organizations, not by conservatives trying to score a political point against the press. That fact, along with the remarkable consistency of their findings, is powerful proof that liberals are far over-represented in the American media.

Adding Insult to Injury: Social Media

The conservative movement is facing a threat to its very existence—a new, insidious form of media censorship. Media bias has always been an enemy of the right. Liberal journalists relied on talking points and talking heads they agreed with for their stories. Conservatives were typically ignored or even targeted by old-school media monopolies.

But while conservatives were excluded, their organizations were still allowed to function and even flourish. The internet gave the right new tools to go around traditional media—websites, email, video, and social media. Conservatives' power online continued to grow as groups expanded their base of supporters and were even able to fundraise online.

Now, all of that is under threat by social media.

The left has become more radicalized, more obsessed with political correctness. They have taken the tools honed by the left for years on college campuses into the tech world. Disagreement is discouraged. Opponents are to be silenced or even banned. Opinions they don't like are termed "hate speech" and those they disagree with are called "bigots." The goal is to deny their opponents the chance to speak, also known as "deplatforming."

Tech companies awash in these so-called progressive worldviews are eager to placate the left. They push diversity initiatives internally that care little for opinion diversity. As a result, their workforces are filled with social justice activists promoting everything from the LGBT agenda to a war on gun rights. Conservatives in that world either go along to get along or find themselves marginalized and even fired.

Furthermore, as latter discussed in this book, anti-conservative bias using deplatforming is coming from major social media services such as Facebook and Twitter, as well as those platforms outright silencing important news that harms Democrats, like the Biden family influence peddling scandal.

Twitter and Facebook regularly place notices and/or restrictions on Trump's tweet and news of voter fraud on the allegation that the opinions and/or evidence expressed and presented are disputed or not yet confirmed. In the four years Trump has been the subject of dishonest and malicious conspiracy claims, particularly the Russia collusion (and so much more), far fewer restrictions, or none at all, are placed on Adam Schiff, other Democrat politicians, or mainstream media outlets peddling their own and/or unrestricted disinformation.

These double standards exist as you will see and are mostly the left's doing.

3 – The Problem With Journalists, Social Justice Warriors & Media Bias

Credit: USAToday.com

As John Tierney explains in his November 2019 *City Journal* article "Journalists Against Free Speech" the once unswerving defenders of the First Amendment, members of the press increasingly support restricting expression. Free speech is no longer sacred among young journalists who have absorbed the campus lessons about "hate speech"—defined more and more broadly—and they're breaking long-standing taboos as they bring "cancel culture" into professional newsrooms.

They're not yet in charge, but many of their editors are reacting like beleaguered college presidents, terrified of seeming insufficiently "woke." Most professional journalists, young and old, still pay lip service to the First Amendment, and they certainly believe that it protects *their* work, but they're increasingly eager for others to be "de-platformed" or "no-platformed," as today's censors like to put it—effectively silenced.

Even journalists are adopting these attitudes, as Robby Soave observed while reporting on young radicals in his book *Panic Attack*. A decade ago, when Soave was an undergraduate on the University of Michigan's student paper, his fellow editors stood in the Hentoff tradition: devout leftists but also free-speech absolutists.

Starting around 2013, though, Soave saw a change at Michigan and other schools. "The power dynamic switched on campus so that the anti-speech activists began dominating the discourse while those who believed in free speech became afraid to speak up," says Soave, now a writer for *Reason*.

"Campus newspapers, especially at elite institutions, have become increasingly sympathetic to the notion that speech isn't protected if it makes students feel unsafe. And now you're seeing these graduates going into professional journalism and demanding that their editors provide a safe workplace by not employing people whose views make them uncomfortable."

Journalists Are Becoming Zealous to Silence Their Ideological Rivals

Today, journalists are becoming zealous to silence their ideological rivals—and the fervor is mainly on the left. During the 1960s, the left-wing activists leading Berkeley's Free Speech movement fought for the rights of conservatives to speak on campus, but today's activists embrace the New Left's intellectual rationalizations for censorship.

To justify the protection of an ever-expanding array of victimized groups, theorists of intersectionality—the idea that subgroup identities, such as race, gender, and sexuality, overlap to make people more oppressed—have adapted Herbert Marcuse's neo-Marxist and Critical Theory notions of "repressive" and "liberating" tolerance."

In the essay "Repressive Tolerance" (1965), the German born American critical theorist Herbert Marcuse (1898-1979) of the Frankfurt School of political theorists argued that, under the conditions of advanced industrial capitalism, the only hope for realizing the original objectives of "liberalist" or "pure" toleration (as articulated by the British philosopher John Stuart Mill [1806-1873])— freeing the mind to rationally pursue the truth—was to practice a deliberately selective "liberating tolerance" that both targeted and enacted the repression alluded to in the essay's paradoxical title.

Simplified, this "liberating tolerance" would involve "the withdrawal of toleration of speech and assembly from groups and movements" on the Right, as opposed to the aggressive partisan promotion of speech, groups, and progressive movements on the Left. Younger journalists and the "so-called" progressive BLM and Antifa movements (whether they know it or not) practice liberating tolerance. That's why the term liberating tolerance is referred to by the SAPIENT Being as an oxymoron and illiberal because it represents *intolerance of the right* in favor of *tolerance of the left* and that by itself, suppresses First Amendment rights, and is also unsapient.

Dr. Greg Lukianoff, who has fought free-speech wars on campus for two decades as the head of the Foundation for Individual Rights in Education (FIRE), dates the ascendancy of the new censors to 2013, when student protesters at Brown University forced the cancellation of a speech by Raymond Kelly, the New York City police commissioner.

"For the first time, rather than being ashamed of this assault on free speech, most people on campus seemed to rally around the protesters," says Lukianoff, coauthor of *The Coddling of the American Mind*. "That's when we started hearing the language of medicalization, that free speech would cause medical harm. Outsiders dismissed this as a college phenomenon and predicted that these intolerant fragile kids would have to change when they hit the real world. But instead, they're changing the world."

'Progressive' Journalists Lead Campaigns to Get Conservative Journalists Fired

These mostly younger progressive journalists lead campaigns to get conservative journalists fired, banned from Twitter, and "de-monetized" on YouTube. They don't burn books, but they've successfully pressured Amazon to stop selling titles that they deem offensive. They encourage advertising boycotts designed to put ideological rivals out of business. They're loath to report forthrightly on left-wing censorship and violence, even when fellow journalists get attacked. They equate conservatives' speech with violence and rationalize leftists' actual violence as...speech.

It's a strange new world for those who remember liberal journalists like Nat Hentoff, the *Village Voice* writer who stood with the ACLU in defending the free-speech rights of Nazis, Klansmen, and others whose views he deplored—or who recall the days when the *Columbia Journalism Review* stood as an unswerving advocate for press freedom. While America has seen its share of politicians eager to limit speech, from John Adams and Woodrow Wilson (who both had journalists prosecuted for "sedition") to Donald Trump (who has made various unconstitutional threats), journalists on the left and the right have long shared a reverence for the First Amendment, if only out of self-interest.

When liberals supported campaign-finance laws restricting corporations' political messages during election campaigns, they insisted on exemptions for news organizations. One could fault them for being self-serving in this selective censorship, which the Supreme Court declared unconstitutional in its Citizens United decision, but at least they stood up for their profession's freedom.

Citizens United v. Federal Election Commission, 558 U.S. 310 (2010), was a landmark decision of the Supreme Court of the United States concerning campaign finance. The Court held that the free speech clause of the First Amendment prohibits the government from restricting independent expenditures for political communications by corporations, including nonprofit corporations, labor unions, and other associations.

A Generational Divide in Newsrooms and Social Media

The result is what Dean Baquet, the *New York Times* executive editor, recently called a "generational divide" in newsrooms. The progressive activism of younger journalists often leaves their older colleagues exasperated. "The paper is now written by 25-year-old gender studies majors," said one *Washington Post* veteran. She wouldn't speak for the record, though: as fragile and marginalized as these young progressives claim to be, they know how to make life miserable for unwoke colleagues.

If their publication is considering hiring a conservative, or if a colleague writes or tweets something that offends them, young progressives express their outrage on social media— sometimes publicly on Twitter, sometimes in internal chat rooms. The internal chat is supposed to be confidential, but comments often get leaked, stoking online outrage. These are examples of snowflake madness.

It takes remarkably little to start the cycle, as *New York Times* opinion writer Bari Weiss discovered. Weiss, already in disfavor among progressives for criticizing aspects of the #MeToo movement, got into trouble for celebrating the Olympic performance of gymnast Mirai Nagasu, the American-born daughter of Japanese immigrants. Weiss adapted a line from the Hamilton musical to tweet: "Immigrants: They get the job done." Weiss was promptly attacked for describing Nagasu as an immigrant, making her guilty of a progressive offense known as "othering."

"Today, journalists are becoming zealous to silence their ideological rivals with illiberalism—and the fervor is mainly on the left." Illiberalism describes an attitude that is close-minded, intolerant, and bigoted.

Social Justice Warriors Taking Over and Purging Newsrooms

In the wake of the protests and riots that erupted following the killing of George Floyd by a Minneapolis police officer, MRC's CNS News site Jarrett Stepman reports in June 2020 on "Social Justice Warriors Taking Over and Purging Newsrooms."

Stepman provides a revealing transformation has been occurring in the country's media landscape. This is now the message coming from the media: The narrative about how society should look at these police shooting incidents shall remain in accordance with the most radical, "woke" voices. Deviating opinions will not be tolerated. Words are violence!

That attitude was on full display in a dustup at America's leading liberal newspaper. Chaos at *The New York Times* began after it published an editorial by Sen. Tom Cotton, R-Ark., who argued that cities with police forces overwhelmed by looting and violence have the option, under the Federal Insurrection Act, to request aid from the military.

The article's headline was "Call in the Troops," which had been selected by *New York Times* editors. In it, Cotton explained how military force has been used to quell domestic unrest in the past, including those who attempted to obstruct desegregation at Little Rock's Central High School in Arkansas in 1957. Following the article's publication on June 3, *New York Times* reporters and editors protested publicly en masse. Many claimed that Cotton's opinions put their colleagues "in danger."

The same *New York Times* has also published Russian leader Vladimir Putin, a member of the Taliban, a long symposium glorifying the communist Russian Revolution of 1917, and even an excerpt of "Mein Kampf" in the 1940s (to demonstrate the philosophy of Hitler as the nation entered World War II).

Yet, an editorial by a U.S. senator, articulating views shared by more than half of registered voters and 37 percent of black voters, according to a Morning Consult poll, is beyond the pale and a literal threat to fellow Americans?

Instead of standing by the practice of publishing diverse opinions, *The New York Times* appended a lengthy editor's note to Cotton's column, saying that the piece "fell short of our standards and should not have been published."

However, the note didn't list any serious fact-based inaccuracies and only nitpicked at Cotton's characterizations of the protests. It concluded by saying that the tone of the piece was "needlessly harsh."

I challenge anyone reading the piece to check out this week's lineup of *New York Times* editorials and columns and not find one that's harsh. A recent Paul Krugman editorial column, for instance, insinuated that President Donald Trump is provoking a race war and that the president is "clearly itching for an excuse to use force." It didn't end there, however. The editorial-page editor, James Bennet, was effectively forced to step down and resigned from the position.

Whatever else can be said of the merits of Cotton's piece or of whatever else is published generally in *The New York Times*, it's increasingly clear that newsrooms of the most prominent liberal publications are being taken over by the most radical voices, who demand that they maintain an increasingly rigid ideological line in how they cover—and comment on—the news of the day.

Most of America's Leading "Mainstream" Media Outlets Lean to the Left

The fact is, most of America's leading "mainstream" media outlets have leaned to the left—in some cases, the far left—of the average American for a long time. Generations, really.

The difference, however, is that in the past they at least attempted to thread the needle of nudging the country leftward without outright devolving into cheerleading for the Democratic Party or leading with activism at the expense of at least some measure of objectivity.

Wesley Lowery—a correspondent for "60 in 6," a short-form spinoff of CBS' "60 Minutes" for the Quibi short-form streaming service—wrote of this turning point in journalism on Twitter:

"American view-from-nowhere, 'objectivity'-obsessed, both-sides journalism is a failed experiment. We need to fundamentally reset the norms of our field. The old way must go. We need to rebuild our industry as one that operates from a place of moral clarity."

That old dynamic of objectivity is crumbling, as newsrooms are now being turned entirely over to the whims of the most activist social justice warriors, who demand political conformity with a strident push toward the left's current cultural and political aims.

It's a process that has already taken place on America's college campuses for several generations, as aggressive left-wing activists push the mostly liberal faculty and staff to be more aggressively left-wing. But campus politics are spilling over into the rest of society.

Nikole Hannah-Jones, the lead architect of the Pulitzer Prize-winning—but factually challenged—"1619 Project," actually did a good job of revealing and elucidating what's happening in our leading newspapers' newsrooms.

She said in an interview with CNN on Sunday that outlets need to abandon the adherence to "evenhandedness, both-sideism," and that an article offering the views of someone like Cotton should only occur in a news piece "where we can check the facts, where we can push back," so readers wouldn't receive what she called "misinformation."

We can't let people decide for themselves what to believe, after all, without social justice warriors—I mean, reporters—guiding the way and leading us along. People might start to form opinions of their own. The horror and free speech madness!

Hannah-Jones then said, "Our role as journalists is to give people correct information so they can make decisions," but clearly demonstrated that she thinks the role of journalists is subtle and not-so-subtle activism, rather than simply reporting the news.

So, the mask is coming off for media outlets, big and small, that are now revealing that they are ultimately tools of the political left, rather than objective guardians of truth, as they often portray themselves.

The recent actions of many prominent media outlets simply reveal and highlight what many Americans already know; namely, that they have an agenda beyond simply publishing "all the news that's fit to print," as the *Times'* motto insists.

It's a clarifying moment—or at least it should be—for Americans who have been under the illusion that they can simply trust, without question, what they see in even the most prominent and established publications.

Newspapers & Print Media Ideology Scores

It turns out there is quantitative proof academia, Hollywood, and the media actually are dominated by liberals and graphic evidence is provided by an article titled "These Three Charts Confirm Conservatives' Worst Fears About American Culture" by Andy Kiersz and Hunter Walker in November 2014.

In a data set provided to Business Insider, the non-partisan political analytics firm Crowdpac used information about federal campaign contributions dating back to 1980 to determine the political biases of various professions. Crowdpac found the entertainment industry, news media, and academia were among the most liberal professions in America.

Crowdpac CEO and co-founder Steve Hilton noted this data matches with perceptions about Hollywood and the media:

"In compiling all this data, and building these tools, we have the opportunity to shine some light on the political system and reveal some interesting insights and trends," Hilton said. "For example, our real data conforms with the claims that have been circulated about the extremely liberal profile of the entertainment and media sectors."

Indeed, a Gallup poll released in September 2020 found trust in the US news media is at an all-time low and 44% of Americans believe it is too liberal.

Crowdpac's data analysis technique gives a good objective measure of ideology. Rather than relying on self-reported views and opinions from surveys, the company looks at how individuals put their money where their mouth is by analyzing what kinds of candidates they give money to. Hilton said Crowdpac's overall goal is to provide people "good objective, non-partisan information about the candidates on their ballot" in order to "boost the number of small donors and reduce the influence of big money in politics."

Here's Crowdpac's results showing the number of donors working in newspapers and print media falling in each ideology score. The blue bars to the left indicate people in each industry who are more liberal, and the red bars to the right show those who are more conservative.

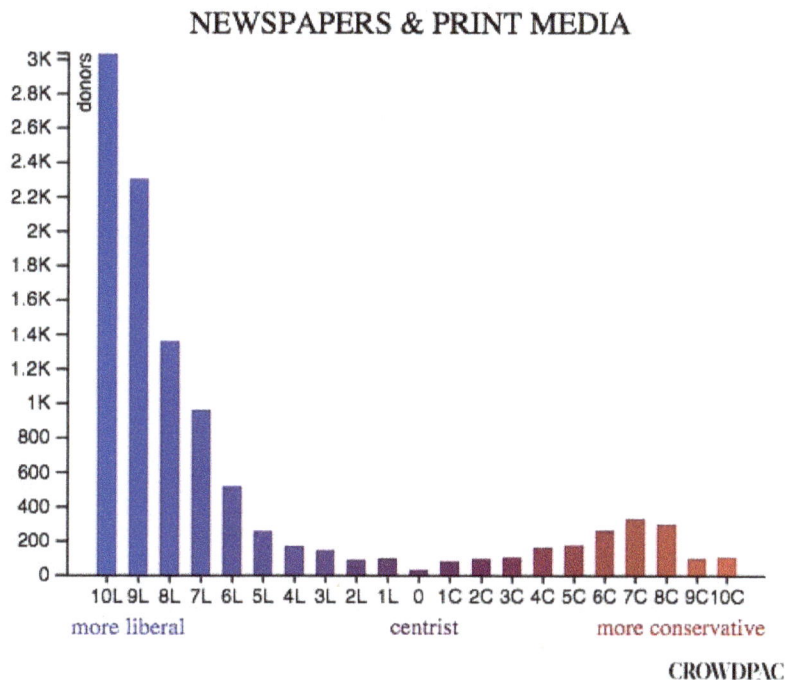

NEWSPAPERS & PRINT MEDIA

CROWDPAC

Liberal donors absolutely dominate conservative donors in the newspaper and print media industry. Crowdpac's data set, which includes donor records going back to 2004, includes 1,743 donors to the right of center, compared to 8,976 donors to the left of center. The liberal donors are also strongly concentrated on the far left of Crowdpac's spectrum.

Bari Weiss Quits *New York Times* After Bullying by Colleagues Over Views

Fox News reporters Brian Flood and Joseph A. Wulfsohn contributing reported in July 2020 regarding *New York Times* journalist Bari Weiss' resignation and the harassment and bullying she received from her illiberal peers that caused it. The Fox News segment titled "Bari Weiss quits *New York Times* after bullying by colleagues over views" reveals the rampant bias inside the Gray Lady.

in Weiss' own words, "They have called me a Nazi and a racist...and the lessons that ought to have followed the (2016) election...have not been learned. It is with sadness that I write to tell you that I am resigning from *The New York Times*."

Weiss published a scathing resignation letter that she sent to *Times* publisher A.G. Sulzberger on her personal website, noting she doesn't understand how toxic behavior is allowed inside the newsroom and "showing up for work as a centrist at an American newspaper should not require bravery."

Weiss joined the paper in 2017 to help offer a different perspective, as the *Times'* "failure to anticipate the outcome of the 2016 election meant that it didn't have a firm grasp of the country it covers," and fixing that issue was critical.

"But the lessons that ought to have followed the election—lessons about the importance of understanding other Americans, the necessity of resisting tribalism, and the centrality of the free exchange of ideas to a democratic society—have not been learned," Weiss wrote. "Instead, a new consensus has emerged in the press, but perhaps especially at this paper: that truth isn't a process of collective discovery, but an orthodoxy already known to an enlightened few whose job is to inform everyone else."

Weiss then wrote that "Twitter is not on the masthead of *The New York Times*," but social media acts as the ultimate editor.

"As the ethics and mores of that platform have become those of the paper, the paper itself has increasingly become a kind of performance space. Stories are chosen and told in a way to satisfy the narrowest of audiences, rather than to allow a curious public to read about the world and then draw their own conclusions. I was always taught that journalists were charged with writing the first rough draft of history," she wrote. "Now, history itself is one more ephemeral thing molded to fit the needs of a predetermined narrative."

In her resignation letter, Weiss noted that her own "forays into Wrongthink" have made her the subject of "constant bullying by colleagues" who disagree with her views.

"They have called me a Nazi and a racist," she wrote. "I have learned to brush off comments about how I'm 'writing about the Jews again.' Several colleagues perceived to be friendly with me were badgered by coworkers," Weiss added. "My work and my character are openly demeaned on company-wide Slack channels where masthead editors regularly weigh in."

Weiss then said she doesn't understand how Sulzberger has allowed such behavior inside the newsroom "in full view of the paper's entire staff and the public. I certainly can't square how you and other *Times* leaders have stood by while simultaneously praising me in private for my courage. Showing up for work as a centrist at an American newspaper should not require bravery," Weiss wrote. "Part of me wishes I could say that my experience was unique. But the truth is that intellectual curiosity—let alone risk-taking—is now a liability at the *Times*."

She continued: "Why edit something challenging to our readers, or write something bold only to go through the numbing process of making it ideologically kosher, when we can assure ourselves of job security (and clicks) by publishing our 4,000th op-ed arguing that Donald Trump is a unique danger to the country and the world? And so self-censorship has become the norm."

Weiss wrote in the scathing letter that rules at the paper "are applied with extreme selectivity" and work goes unscrutinized if it aligns with the new orthodoxy.

"Everyone else lives in fear of the digital thunderdome. Online venom is excused so long as it is directed at the proper targets," she wrote. "Op-eds that would have easily been published just two years ago would now get an editor or a writer in serious trouble, if not fired."

"The paper of record is, more and more, the record of those living in a distant galaxy, one whose concerns are profoundly removed from the lives of most people," Weiss wrote. "This is a galaxy in which, to choose just a few recent examples, the Soviet space program is lauded for its "diversity;" the doxxing of teenagers in the name of justice is condoned; and the worst caste systems in human history includes the United States alongside Nazi Germany."

Weiss said that despite her struggles to be accepted by colleagues, she believes they don't all hold these views. She speculated that *Times* employees are playing along and possibly "believe the ultimate goal is righteous," "believe that they will be granted protection if they nod along," "feel lucky to have a job in a contracting industry" or know that "standing up for principle at the paper does not win plaudits."

Weiss wrote that the *Times*' culture hurts "independent-minded young writers and editors paying close attention to what they'll have to do to advance in their careers" and explained how it will be seen by the next generation of journalists. The rules for advancement are:

- Rule One: Speak your mind at your own peril.
- Rule Two: Never risk commissioning a story that goes against the narrative.
- Rule Three: Never believe an editor or publisher who urges you to go against the grain.

"Eventually, the publisher will cave to the mob, the editor will get fired or reassigned, and you'll be hung out to dry," she wrote. Weiss added that "America is a great country that deserves a great newspaper," but doesn't feel the Gray Lady is currently providing that. She complimented some former colleagues, noting that "some of the most talented journalists in the world" still work for the paper she is walking away from.

Which is what makes the illiberal environment especially heartbreaking," Weiss wrote. "I can no longer do the work that you brought me here to do—the work that Adolph Ochs described in that famous 1896 statement: 'to make of the columns of *The New York Times* a forum for the consideration of all questions of public importance, and to that end to invite intelligent discussion from all shades of opinion.'"

The Southern Poverty Law Center Bullies and Silences Conservatives

One of the most sinister ways tech companies have stifled conservative speech has been by caving to pressure from anti-conservative groups, especially the Southern Poverty Law Center (SPLC) as MRC's *"CENSORED! How Online Media Companies Are Suppressing Conservative Speech"* guidebook points out.

The SPLC claims to fight "hate and bigotry" and promote "justice for the most vulnerable members of our society." In reality, it has used its position to attack conservative groups like the American Family Association (AFA) and the Family Research Council (FRC) alongside Ku Klux Klan and Black Panther groups. Most conservative groups targeted by the SPLC were categorized as being "Anti-Muslim" or "Anti-LGBT" for either criticizing Islamic terrorism or promoting traditional marriage.

The SPLC has a disturbing history with the conservative movement. In August 2012, a gunman entered the FRC headquarters to "kill as many people as possible" and wounded a security guard before being disarmed. The man told investigators he targeted FRC after finding it listed as an anti-LGBT "hate group" on the SPLC's "Hate Map," a literal map pinpointing the location of supposed "hate groups."

Despite the shooting and conservative complaints, FRC and other conservative groups remain on the SPLC's dangerous hate map.

News outlets and companies continue to trust SPLC claims in spite of the group's history. Social media organizations not only refuse to stand up to the SPLC's bullying, but they also consult the anti-conservative group for data and recommendations about so-called hate groups.

Liberal news outlet ProPublica published an expose claiming PayPal and Amazon were complicit in promoting "hate" by allowing organizations to raise money through their partnerships. ProPublica was founded with tens of millions from liberal donors Herb and Marion Sandler, who also funded Moveon.org. It has also been supported by liberal mega-donor George Soros' Open Society Institute.

The ProPublica story relied on data from both the SPLC and the ADL hate group lists. PayPal allows people and organizations to solicit donations through links, while Amazon allows people to either be affiliates which receive revenue from clicks on advertisements or AmazonSmile partners. Amazon donates 0.5 percent of the price of eligible purchases to charitable organizations which are AmazonSmile partners.

ProPublica senior reporting fellow Lauren Kirchner asked organizations if they disagree with being deemed a hate group, according to a version of the email obtained by the Daily Wire. American Freedom Defense Initiative (AFDI) leader Pamela Geller received a similar email.

Kirshner also asked the organizations to confirm whether they received money through PayPal and Amazon, and what the impact would be if they could no longer receive revenue from PayPal, Amazon, and others.

Days after the ProPublica report, Jihad Watch, the AFDI and ACT for America lost their ability to receive donations through PayPal. In the email Geller provided on her Facebook page, PayPal said it limited her account "due to the nature of your activities." The email told Geller to "remove all references to PayPal from your website," including "removing PayPal as a payment option, as well as the PayPal logo and/or shopping cart."

PayPal quickly reversed its decision to ban AFDI and Jihad Watch from raising money through their site. Their accounts were reportedly fully restored days later. ACT for America, however, was not as lucky. Its account was still suspended as of March 9, 2018.

The SPLC's "anti-LGBT" hate group list was also used to deprive organizations of the ability to register with AmazonSmile. The Ruth Institute and D. James Kennedy Ministries both said they were unable to register as AmazonSmile partners because of their SPLC designation.

A remarkably similar "hate group" list popped up as part of a project launched by Color of Change in August 2017. The self-described "racial justice organization" launched a campaign called Blood Money which tried to pressure credit card companies, PayPal, ApplePay and Amazon to cut ties with supposed "white supremacist, anti-Muslim, anti-LGBTQ, anti-Semitic, anti-immigrant" groups.

"These companies direct funds to the groups responsible for numerous hate crimes, murders and the radicalization of terrorists like Dylann Roof, Timothy McVeigh, Wade Michael Page and Anders Behring Breivik," the campaign outrageously claimed.

Its list includes the AFA, Center for Family and Human Rights, the David Horowitz Freedom Center, AFDI and the Ruth Institute. Blood Money's list records which companies each group conducts business through, and whether it has successfully pressured the companies into cutting ties with each group.

While Blood Money did not cite any sources for its data, the list was very similar to the SPLC's hate list. FastCompany speculated the Color of Change ripped off the SPLC list for its campaign.

The SPLC's hate list was also briefly used by GuideStar, a non-profit database, to label certain conservative organizations as "hate groups."

According to *The Washington Post*, GuideStar added "warning labels" on its website to each group targeted by the SPLC. Two days after 41 conservative leaders wrote a letter opposing GuideStar's decision to flag their organizations, GuideStar announced it was removing the warning labels because of "harassment and threats directed at our staff and leadership." "In the meantime," GuideStar said it "will make this information available to any user on request."

D. James Kennedy Ministries, which was impacted by both the AmazonSmile ban and the GuideStar designation, sued the SPLC because of its "false and illegal characterizations" that reportedly "have a chilling effect on the free exercise of religion and on religious free speech for all people of faith." The lawsuit was still ongoing as of March 2018.

The SPLC's hate list is the impetus behind actions at companies including Facebook and Google too.

4 – Today's Media Elites: A Byproduct of Campus Illiberalism

From a November 2018 article from *Investor's Business Daily* regarding media bias, the once unswerving defenders of the First Amendment, members of the press increasingly support restricting expression. Free speech is no longer sacred among young journalists who have absorbed the campus lessons about "hate speech"—defined more and more broadly—and they're breaking long-standing taboos as they bring "cancel culture" into professional newsrooms.

The SAPIENT Being's World of Writing Warriors (WOWW) Program aims to reverse this trend by promoting freedom of speech, viewpoint diversity and intellectual humility to campus newsrooms, media, and journalists.

Researchers from Arizona State University and Texas A&M University questioned 462 financial journalists around the country. They followed up with 18 additional interviews. The journalists worked for the *Wall Street Journal*, the *New York Times*, *Washington Post*, Associated Press, and a number of other newspapers.

What they found surprised them. Even the supposedly hard-nosed financial reporters were overwhelmingly liberal. Of the 462 people surveyed, 17.63% called themselves "very liberal," while 40.84% described themselves as "somewhat liberal."

Illiberalism & Campus Ideological Battlegrounds

The new campus illiberalism is more than intolerance, it suppresses freedom of speech, restricts viewpoint diversity, and knows no intellectual humility. *Webster's Dictionary* defines illiberalism as "opposition to or lack of liberalism." In popular usage, the word is used to describe an attitude that is close-minded, intolerant, and bigoted. Illiberalism is the breeding ground for fake news and false narratives.

The pursuit of knowledge and the maintenance of a free and democratic society require the cultivation and practice of the virtues of intellectual humility, openness of mind, and, above all, love of truth. These virtues will manifest themselves and be strengthened by one's willingness to listen attentively and respectfully to intelligent people who challenge one's beliefs and who represent causes one disagrees with and points of view one does not share.

That's why all of us should seek respectfully to engage with people who challenge our views. And we should oppose efforts to silence those with whom we disagree—especially on college and university campuses. As John Stuart Mill taught, a recognition of the possibility that we may be in error is a good reason to listen to and honestly consider—and not merely to tolerate grudgingly—points of view that we do not share, and even perspectives that we find shocking or scandalous.

None of us is infallible. Whether you are a person of the left, the right, or the center, there are reasonable people of goodwill who do not share your fundamental convictions. This does not mean that all opinions are equally valid (especially in this day and age) or that all speakers are equally worth listening to. It certainly does not mean that there is no truth to be discovered. Nor does it mean that you are necessarily wrong. But they are not necessarily wrong either.

All of us should be willing—even eager—to engage with anyone who is prepared to do business in the currency of truth-seeking discourse by offering reasons, marshaling evidence, and making arguments. The more important the subject under discussion, the more willing we should be to listen and engage—especially if the person with whom we are in conversation will challenge our deeply held—even our most cherished and identity-forming—beliefs.

The Closing of the Collegiate Mind Fuels Illiberalism

Way back in 1987, Allan Bloom's *Closing of the American Mind: How Higher Education Has Failed Democracy and Impoverished the Souls of Today's Students* saw the illiberalism problem early on.

In order to understand what's been going on at some of our college campuses, it's necessary to explore the ideology that provides the impetus for a lot of the protesters who violently obstruct events, pull fire alarms, assault professors and even other students, and the impetus for administrators who all too often humor these protesters. It's called illiberalism.

Here's an example: Psychologist Lisa Feldman Barrett of Northeastern University published an essay in *The New York Times* suggesting that words should be seen as physical violence because they can cause stress and stress causes physical harm. Thus, Feldman suggested it is reasonable scientifically speaking to ban or restrict speech you do not like at your school.

This is both inane and dangerous and a statement fully encamped in the idiocracy. That's because it leads to the final illogical step, words you don't like deserve to be fought physically—better known as "words are violence."

At the Conservative Political Action Conference (CPAC) in 2019, President Trump made a promise to protect free speech on college campuses across the country. Conservative activist Hayden Williams joined him on stage as an example of the need for protected free speech.

While assisting the University of California at Berkeley's Turning Point USA chapter, Williams was punched in the face by an individual who *did not agree* with him. The President announced he would soon sign an executive order requiring colleges to take measures to protect our Constitutional right to free speech if they want to continue receiving federal money.

Williams is not the only person whose rights has been violated on a college campus. Several colleges have cancelled or banned Conservative speakers like Ben Shapiro and Milo Yiannopulos. The Foundation for Individual Rights in Education (FIRE) tracks disinvitation attempts across all campuses noting whether the action was from the Right or the Left. Since 2000, they have recorded 379 instances, with nearly 25% of those occurring from 2016-2018 alone. In those two years, 82% of disinvitations have been because of the Left's doing.

Organizations like Speech First and Alliance Defending Freedom are fighting against these injustices by representing students who have been mistreated. Even the Department of Justice has weighed in on several of these cases. They are ensuring that students will be able to think and speak freely for many generations to come. President Trump's executive order would aid in that fight.

Similar Experiences of the Academy's Intimidation of Conservative POV Abound

From the *Christian Science Monitor*, here's an article about what happened in July 2009 when freelance journalist and journalism student Dan Lawton at the University of Oregon wrote an article concerning the inclusiveness of conservative thought on campus. In his own words:

After my article on political diversity was published, I received numerous e-mails from students at other schools who spoke of similar experiences. As a result of my research and personal experience, I can now say without reservation that the lack of ideological diversity on college campuses is a dangerous threat to free and open discourse in academia. Sadly, there are few perfect solutions.

One proposal considered by universities is endowing a chair of conservative thought to lure a high-profile conservative scholar to campus. However, this has the potential to exacerbate partisan tensions by sanctioning an explicitly ideological position.

A more draconian option is to enact a political litmus test and mandate that Republicans fill a certain number of positions but doing so would exclude many qualified professors and be unfairly discriminatory.

The fact is that political diversity, like many diversity efforts, is something that cannot be created through edict, but only by a concerted effort on the behalf of those in power. While hiring on the basis of party affiliation isn't the answer to reducing political discrimination, denying that political beliefs influence pedagogy is simply naive.

Faculties in ideological departments should examine the body of work of a candidate to see if it fills a shortcoming. In a department of journalism or political science, a professor with a right-leaning perspective would not only provide a balance in curriculum, but a potential mentor to conservative students who feel isolated in their beliefs. At left-leaning universities, such professors should be aggressively pursued.

Above all, deans, provosts, and professors must not allow their aversion to conservative ideas to manifest so contemptuously. Political disagreement is crucial to vibrant discourse, but not in the form of caricatures, slights, or mockery.

Students should never come under personal attack from faculty members for straying from the party line. The fact that they do shows how easily political partisanship can corrupt the elements of higher education that should be valued the most.

Universities Are Becoming Increasingly Hostile to Diverse Ideas

A recent study by the American Association of Colleges and Universities (AACU) of 24,000 college students and 9,000 faculty and staff members found that only 18 per cent of the faculty and staff strongly agreed that it was "safe to hold unpopular positions on campus."

There is a difference between an opinion and an argument. An opinion is an expression of preference; it does not require any support (although it is stronger with support). An opinion is only the first part of an argument and to be complete, arguments should have three parts: an assertion, reasoning, and evidence (easily remembered with the mnemonic ARE).

We live in a climate ripe for noise: Media outlets and 24-hour news cycles mean that everyone with access to a computer has access to a megaphone to broadcast their views. Never before in human history has an opinion had the opportunity to reach so many so quickly regardless of its accuracy or appropriateness. This is a huge problem!

Educators are well positioned to provide a counterweight to this loudest-is-best approach. Speaking in a classroom or school environment is different from speaking in the outside world. Schools and classrooms strive to be safe places where students can exchange ideas, try out opinions and receive feedback on their ideas without fear or intimidation.

Children, of course, often come to school with opinions or prejudices they have learned in their homes or from the media. This means that it is also possible for schools to become places of intolerance and fear, especially for students who voice minority opinions.

Schools must work to be sites of social transformation where teachers and young people find ways to communicate effectively. However, due to the negative effects of postmodernism and its illiberal influence of cancel culture, which becomes increasingly difficult.

Postmodernism and Its Influence

While encompassing a wide variety of approaches and disciplines, postmodernism (modern, "progressive," far-left liberalism) is generally defined by an attitude of skepticism, irony, or rejection of the grand narratives and ideologies of modernism, often calling into question various assumptions of Enlightenment rationality.

Consequently, common targets of postmodern critique include universalist notions of objective reality, morality, truth, human nature, reason, science, language, and social progress.

Postmodern thinkers frequently call attention to the contingent or socially conditioned nature of knowledge claims and value systems, situating them as products of particular political, historical, or cultural discourses and hierarchies. Accordingly, postmodern thought is broadly characterized by tendencies to self-referentiality, epistemological and moral relativism, pluralism, and irreverence.

Postmodern critical approaches gained purchase in the 1980s and 1990s and have been adopted in a variety of academic and theoretical disciplines, including cultural studies, philosophy of science, economics, linguistics, architecture, feminist theory, and literary criticism, as well as art movements in fields such as literature, contemporary art, and music.

Postmodernism is often associated with schools of thought such as deconstruction, post-structuralism, and institutional critique, as well as philosophers such as Jean-François Lyotard, Jacques Derrida, and Fredric Jameson.

The SAPIENT Being has detected a correlation between the influence of Progressivism on campus and the growth of fake news off campus and encourages further study to determine if there is a cause-and-effect relationship to this variable.

'Fake News' Stories of the Trump Years Students Believe In

Journalists bristle when President Trump criticizes them as "fake news," and they complain that such criticism erodes the public's faith in the news media as an independent watchdog on the powerful.

But Trump's critiques wouldn't have nearly as much impact if news organizations actually acted like careful, professional, independent purveyors of fact. Instead, they too often behave as sloppy partisans, carelessly jumping on one false story after another if they think it will prove their larger narrative that the President is unfit for office.

Sometimes, the "fake news" is about a small detail that suggests a broader pattern: the *Time* magazine pool reporter who wrongly claimed on Twitter that Trump had removed a bust of Martin Luther King, Jr., from the Oval Office, perhaps hinting at a racial animus. In fact, the bust was right there, obscured from view by a Secret Service agent and a door.

Or it can be sheer sloppiness: ABC adorned two of its 2019 weekend newscasts with footage supposedly showing Kurds being bombed to oblivion after the President announced U.S. troops would leave Syria. The problem? The footage was taken at a Kentucky gun range two years earlier and had nothing to do with Trump, Syria, or the Kurds.

There's also the fraudulent headline that exposes recklessness in pursuit of imagined wrongdoing. Case in point: In June 2017, a CNN.com story claimed the Senate Intelligence Committee was investigating the head of a massive Russian investment fund who had supposedly met with Anthony Scaramucci (then a Trump insider who would briefly serve as White House Communications Director. The story speculated that the two might have discussed the new administration lifting Russian sanctions.

But the next day, visitors to CNN's Web page found a giant "Editor's Note," explaining that the story "did not meet CNN's editorial standards and has been retracted.... CNN apologizes to Mr. Scaramucci." In the aftermath, the CNN reporter, Thomas Frank, along with assistant managing editor Eric Lichtblau and investigative reporting editor Lex Haris resigned on June 26.

Over the past three years, the examples of factual sloppiness have piled up. And there seems little doubt that there's an agenda afoot—after all, how many of these embarrassing corrections have involved the retraction of a pro-Trump story?

MRC's NewsBusters has tracked it all during the first forty months of the Trump presidency with a special report titled, "The Eight Worst 'Fake News' Stories of the Trump Years" compiled by Rich Noyes in May 2020 along with a team of MRC staffers. Here are their choices for the eight worst "fake news" stories of the Trump era, all pushed by supposedly mainstream journalists operating under the highest levels of professionalism. Judge for yourself:

1. The Imaginary Pee Tape

Ten days before Trump's inauguration, CNN tried to rain on his big moment by unveiling "exclusive" information that top intelligence officials, including then-FBI Director James Comey, had briefed the President-elect about a 35-page dossier crammed with supposedly damaging information. As is often the case in Washington, the least-likely/most-gossipy parts circulated the most widely, including the highly implausible claim that Trump, on a visit to Russia, had hired prostitutes to urinate on a bed President Obama had used during an earlier visit.

Of course, no news organization could confirm any of this, but it became a salacious bit of anti-Trump dirt that kept finding its way onto the airwaves. The high-water mark for this below-the-belt charge came in April 2018 when Comey, a year after he was fired from the FBI, used a book tour to publicize this smear all over again. He found a willing audience in the Trump-hating press; an MRC study found CNN talked about the non-existent "pee tapes" 77 times in a mere five-day period.

It was nothing but vicious nonsense. A later report from the Justice Department's Inspector General debunked the myth of a Russian "pee tape," and found that "the FBI knew early in 2017 that it was a highly dubious story and kept Donald Trump in the dark."

2. Fake News About a Flynn Deal with Mueller

During live "Special Report" coverage on December 1, 2017, ABC News chief investigative Brian Ross made the jaw-dropping claim that former National Security Advisor Michael Flynn would testify that during the 2016 campaign, then-candidate Donald Trump had "ordered him—directed him to make contact with the Russians, which contradicts all that Donald Trump has said to this point."

If true, that would conceivably put the President in legal jeopardy; within minutes, Ross's report was being parroted across the media and the stock market fell more than 300 points. But it turned out that Ross had committed one of the biggest blunders of his career: as Ross clarified hours later, Trump made the alleged request of Flynn not as a candidate, but during the transition—which made it merely an act of foreign policy, not collusion.

ABC suspended Ross for one month without pay and barred him from covering President Trump in the future. He has since left the network.

3. CNN's Botched WikiLeaks E-Mail 'Exclusive'

A few days later, on December 8, 2017, CNN.com published an early-morning story by correspondents Manu Raju and Jeremy Herb claiming Trump's campaign team received an e-mail from WikiLeaks on September 4, 2016 with "a decryption key and website address for hacked WikiLeaks documents" that would not be publicly revealed until September 13.

Was this finally some proof of the collusion that anti-Trump media have been searching for? That morning and into the afternoon, all of CNN's programs proudly touted a "Breaking News" banner with a "CNN Exclusive" that read the following: "Emails Reveal Effort to Give Trump Campaign WikiLeaks Documents."

It turned out, the e-mail actually went out on September 14, *2016*, after the information was available to anyone.

That afternoon, after hours of breathless hype, CNN issued an on-air correction read by Raju. The reporters however, faced no disciplinary action because, according to a spokeswoman, they "followed the editorial standards process." Some process!

4. Donald Trump, Secret Russian Agent

After the President, at a post-summit press conference, refused to contradict Russian President Vladimir Putin's denials of election meddling, journalists leaped to offering wild theories that the performance was evidence the Trump was a Russian agent. "We don't know if Putin is his handler, his hero or his co-conspirator, but it's obviously where his loyalty lies," *New York Times* columnist Michelle Goldberg declared on ABC's This Week on July 22, 2018.

CNN's Brian Stelter hosts the weekly Reliable Sources, a show that's supposed to encourage responsible journalism. Yet he used his program to tout the crazy conspiracies: "Trump's odd behavior with Vladimir Putin is compelling so many people to ask: 'What does Putin have on Trump? Has Trump been compromised?' All of those people, those experts, those reporters, they are looking at the fact pattern and seeing something strange, even sinister."

The next morning, former *Time* managing editor Walter Isaacson wandered away from reality on MSNBC's Morning Joe: "It's as if Donald Trump has been weaponized over the years by Vladimir Putin to go in and do Putin's bidding....It is astonishing how he has become such an effective and destructive virus created by Vladimir Putin."

A few days earlier, CNN's Don Lemon, used his network's airwaves to float the notion Trump was guilty of treason: "Article III in Section Three of the Constitution says this, 'treason against the United States shall consist only in levying war against them or in adhering to their enemies, giving them aid and comfort.'" Lemon asked historian Douglas Brinkley to agree: "Do you believe the President's actions fall anywhere within that definition?"

Such venomous speculation only harms the media's claims that they are a fact-based institution.

5. Liberal TV Nets Trumpet Phony CNN "Exclusive"

On July 26, 2018, CNN's Jim Sciutto and Carl Bernstein appeared on Cuomo PrimeTime to drop the "exclusive" bombshell claim that Michael Cohen would tell federal investigators that President Trump knew of the infamous Trump Tower meeting before it took place. It was exactly the sort of smoking gun that Trump-haters in the media had been yearning for since the Russia investigation began, and it quickly filled up liberal airwaves.

Cable news went nearly wall-to-wall, while the broadcast networks churned out a combined 28 and a half minutes touting the story on just their July 27 morning and evening news programs. Savannah Guthrie breathlessly opened NBC's Today: "Breaking overnight, bombshell. President Trump's longtime lawyer ready to deliver the goods...." ABC's Good Morning America heralded them as "stunning new claims," as Justice correspondent Pierre Thomas intoned that "these explosive new allegations are further evidence of the growing rift between President Trump and his former attorney...."

The only problem was it was all fiction leaked anonymously to CNN and other networks by Cohen's lawyer (and longtime Clinton lawyer and loyalist) Lanny Davis. The facts came out in late August after Axios reported that Cohen actually did not know if Trump had any knowledge of the meeting. Days later, Buzzfeed exposed that Davis was CNN's secret source—even after Davis had gone on CNN to assert he was not the source. The broadcast networks that had loudly promoted the fake "bombshell" in July published minor "updates" on their web sites but didn't say a word on their airwaves.

6. O'Donnell's Reckless Deutsche Bank Scoop

MSNBC host Lawrence O'Donnell began the August 27, 2019 edition of his 10pm ET Last Word program by teasing 9pm host Rachel Maddow as her show was concluding. "I may have some information," he promised, pertaining to Donald Trump's business dealings with Germany's Deutsche Bank.

While O'Donnell acknowledged that his "information" came from only a single source, and that neither he nor anyone at NBC News had confirmed it, he inexplicably chose to air his inflammatory allegation on live television: "This single source close to Deutsche Bank has told me that Donald Trump's loan documents there show that he has co-signers. That's how he was able to obtain those loans. And that the co-signers are Russian oligarchs.... That would explain, it seems to me, every kind word Donald Trump has ever said about Russia and Vladimir Putin, if true, and I stress the 'if true' part of this."

The next morning, an MSNBC producer acknowledged that not only had no one at NBC even seen the documents, O'Donnell's single source hadn't seen them, either. That's some "source."

Once again, a journalist's eagerness for a smoking gun to implicate the President led them to abandon any pretense of professionalism. With no confirmation from anyone else in the media, O'Donnell sheepishly abandoned his claims the next day, announcing on Twitter: "Last night I made an error in judgment by reporting an item about the president's finances that didn't go through our rigorous verification and standards process. I shouldn't have reported it and I was wrong to discuss it on the air."

7. Blaming Trump for Racist Mass Killings

Grotesquely seeking to exploit horrific tragedies for political advantage, some in the media actually accused the President of inspiring or otherwise supporting brutal mass killings in 2019. "The President needs to at some point look in the mirror and understand that the rhetoric.... gives permission to the craziest people in America," ABC's Matthew Dowd charged after a synagogue shooting that left eleven dead in April of that year.

After a horrible shooting in El Paso, Texas in which the gunman singled out Latinos, killing 23, TV viewers once again heard journalists aim the blame at President Trump. "If you're a white supremacist, you find the President's words possibly inspirational, possibly comforting," CNN's Nia Malika Henderson claimed on August 5. A few hours later, MSNBC host Nicolle Wallace falsely stated: "You now have a President, as you said, talking about exterminating Latinos."

Those seeking to blame Trump personally for the evil acts of others found support in a March 2019 *Washington Post* analysis that claimed, according to the headline, that "counties that hosted a 2016 Trump rally saw a 226 percent increase in hate crimes." The problem: a pair of Harvard researchers trying to duplicate the study found political rallies had no effect on hate crimes. In fact, using the same methodology would actually show "Clinton rallies contribute to an even greater increase in hate incidents than Trump rallies." Oops!

8. The Coronavirus "Hoax" Hoax

As the coronavirus spread in the U.S., so too did the fake news that President Trump had called the disease a "hoax," when in reality he used those words to talk about Democrats' attempt to exploit the crisis.

The butchering of reality began just a couple of hours after the President spoke at a February 28, 2020 political rally, with Politico's bogus headline: "Trump rallies his base to treat coronavirus as a 'hoax.'" That earned Politico a "false" rating from CheckYourFact.com the next day. The left-leaning fact-checker Snopes.com soon agreed, writing on March 2: "Despite creating some confusion with his remarks, Trump did not call the coronavirus itself a hoax."

But those pesky facts wouldn't stop some in the liberal media from pushing the phony version they preferred. On March 11, MSNBC's Joy Reid misled viewers when she claimed, "the Trump administration has struggled to present a coherent and unified message about the coronavirus outbreak, careening from downplaying it, with Trump tossing it off as a political hoax, to just seemingly scrambling."

Three days later, CNN's Boris Sanchez wrongly claimed the President has "suggested that this coronavirus epidemic—pandemic is a hoax perpetrated by Democrats."

As late as April 7, NBC's Tom Costello even bungled the liberal media's fantasy version of what Trump supposedly said. Talking about a memo written by White House advisor Peter Navarro, Costello asserted: "He wrote that, again, on January 29, at the time that the President was suggesting this was all a hoax." Actually, that would have been a month before the President said the words that have been so dishonestly distorted.

Fake news madness!

5 – Media Polarization and the 2020 Election: A Nation Divided

---

Ideology adds another layer to party-line divides of most trusted and distrusted news sources

% who _trust_ each source for political and election news (first five shown)

Democrat/Lean Dem				Republican/Lean Rep			
LIBERAL		MODERATE/ CONSERVATIVE		MODERATE/ LIBERAL		**CONSERVATIVE**	
CNN	70%	CNN	65%	Fox News	51%	Fox News	75%
New York Times	66	ABC News	63	ABC News	47	Hannity (radio)	43
PBS	66	NBC News	61	CBS News	42	Limbaugh (radio)	38
NPR	63	CBS News	60	NBC News	41	ABC News	24
NBC News	61	PBS	48	CNN	36	CBS News	23

% who _distrust_ each source for political and election news (first five shown)

Democrat/Lean Dem				Republican/Lean Rep			
LIBERAL		MODERATE/ CONSERVATIVE		MODERATE/ LIBERAL		**CONSERVATIVE**	
Fox News	77%	Fox News	48%	CNN	43%	CNN	67%
Limbaugh (radio)	55	Limbaugh (radio)	34	MSNBC	32	MSNBC	57
Breitbart	53	Hannity (radio)	28	HuffPost	30	New York Times	50
Hannity (radio)	50	Breitbart	22	BuzzFeed	29	NBC News	50
NY Post	27	BuzzFeed	20	Fox News	29	CBS News	48

Note: Order of outlets does not necessarily indicate statistically significant differences.
Source: Survey of U.S. adults conducted Oct. 29-Nov. 11, 2019.
"U.S. Media Polarization and the 2020 Election: A Nation Divided"

PEW RESEARCH CENTER

The Pew Research Center is a nonpartisan fact tank that informs the public about the issues, attitudes and trends shaping the world. It does not take policy positions. The Center conducts public opinion polling, demographic research, content analysis and other data-driven social science research. It studies U.S. politics and policy; journalism and media; internet, science and technology; religion and public life; Hispanic trends; global attitudes and trends; and U.S. social and demographic trends.

As the news media landscape continues to evolve, Pew research has shown, Americans' news habits are changing. In Pew's own words: In this study, we take a snapshot of the news outlets people rely on and trust for news about politics and the upcoming national elections. We examine responses based on party identification to see whether Republicans and Democrats are turning to similar, or different, sources of information.

To do this, they surveyed 12,043 U.S. adults in October and November of 2019 and asked whether they had heard of or used any of 30 media sources, chosen so that respondents were asked about a range of news media across different platforms. Everyone who took part is a member of Pew Research Center's American Trends Panel (ATP), an online survey panel that is recruited through national, random sampling of residential addresses.

Recruiting their panelists by phone or mail ensures that nearly all U.S. adults have a chance of selection. This gives Pew confidence that any sample can represent the whole population. To further ensure that each survey reflects a balanced cross section of the nation, the data are weighted to match the U.S. adult population by gender, race, ethnicity, partisan affiliation, education, and other categories.

As the U.S. enters a heated 2020 presidential election year, a new Pew Research Center report finds that Republicans and Democrats place their trust in two nearly inverse news media environments.

Overall, Republicans and Republican-leaning independents view many heavily relied on sources across a range of platforms as untrustworthy. At the same time, Democrats and independents who lean Democratic see most of those sources as credible and rely on them to a far greater degree, according to the survey of 12,043 U.S. adults conducted Oct. 29–Nov. 11, 2019, on Pew Research Center's American Trends Panel.

These divides are even more pronounced between conservative Republicans and liberal Democrats. Moreover, evidence suggests that partisan polarization in the use and trust of media sources has widened in the past five years. A comparison to a similar study by the Center of web using U.S. adults in 2014 finds that Republicans have grown increasingly alienated from most of the more established sources, while Democrats' confidence in them remains stable, and in some cases, has strengthened.

Democrats Express More Trust of Most News Sources; Republicans Express More Distrust

The study asked about use of, trust in, and distrust of 30 different news sources for political and election news. While it is impossible to represent the entire crowded media space, the outlets, which range from network television news to Rush Limbaugh to the *New York Times* to the *Washington Examiner* to HuffPost, were selected to represent popular media brands across a range of platforms.

Greater portions of Republicans express distrust than express trust of 20 of the 30 sources asked about. Only seven outlets generate more trust than distrust among Republicans—including Fox News and the talk radio programs of hosts Sean Hannity and Rush Limbaugh.

For Democrats, the numbers are almost reversed. Greater portions of Democrats express trust than express distrust in 22 of the 30 sources asked about. Only eight generate more distrust than trust—including Fox News, Sean Hannity and Rush Limbaugh.

Another way to look at the diverging partisan views of media credibility: Almost half of the sources included in this report (13) are trusted by at least 33% of Democrats, but only two are trusted by at least 33% of Republicans. Republicans' lower trust in a variety of measured news sources coincides with their infrequent use. Overall, only one source, Fox News, was used by at least one-third of Republicans for political and election news in the past week. There are five different sources from which at least one-third of Democrats received political or election news in the last week (CNN, NBC News, ABC News, CBS News and MSNBC).

And in what epitomizes this era of polarized news, none of the 30 sources is trusted by more than 50% of all U.S. adults.

The Fox News phenomenon In the more compact Republican media ecosystem, one outlet towers above all others: Fox News. It would be hard to overstate its connection as a trusted go-to source of political news for Republicans. About two-thirds (65%) of Republicans and Republican leaners say they trust Fox News as a source. Additionally, 60% say they got political or election news there in the past week.

However, Fox News is nowhere near the leader board of fake news journalism as are the Democrats and Democratic leaners choices are.

Among Democrats and Democratic leaners, CNN (67%) is about as trusted a source of information as Fox News is among Republicans. The cable network is also Democrats' most commonly turned to source for political and election news, with about half (53%) saying they got news there in the past week.

The big difference is that while no other source comes close to rivaling Fox News' appeal to Republicans, a number of sources other than CNN are also highly trusted and frequently used by Democrats. The partisan gaps become even more dramatic when looking at the parties' ideological poles –conservative Republicans and liberal Democrats.

About two-thirds of liberal Democrats (66%) trust *The New York Times*, for example. In comparison, just 10% of conservative Republicans trust the *Times*, while 50% outright distrust it. Rush Limbaugh, meanwhile, is the third-most trusted source among conservative Republicans (38%) but tied for the second-most distrusted source among liberal Democrats (55%).

Liberal Democrats are Democrats and independents who lean toward the Democratic Party who say they are liberal or very liberal. Conservative Republicans are Republicans or Republican leaners who say they are conservative or very conservative.

At the same time, the gap is less pronounced among the more moderate segments in each party. For example, three-quarters of conservative Republicans trust Fox News, while just about half (51%) of moderate or liberal Republicans do. Conversely, moderate, and conservative Democrats are more than twice as likely as liberal Democrats to trust Fox News (32% vs. 12%).

There is also evidence that suggests that these partisan divides have grown over the past five years, particularly with more Republicans voicing distrust in a number of sources. A comparison to a similar study of web-using U.S. adults conducted by the Center in 2014 finds that Republicans' distrust increased for 15 of the 20 sources asked about in both years—with notable growth in Republicans' distrust of CNN, *The Washington Post*, and *The New York Times*.

Democrats' levels of trust and distrust in media sources have changed considerably less than Republicans' during this time span. Even accounting for the modest methodological differences Ideology adds another layer to party-line divides of most trusted and distrusted news sources who trust each source for political and election news.

What these trends indicate is that Republicans seem to understand that fake news and liberal bias is prevalent in MSM that Democrats don't—or perhaps Democrats are engaging in confirmation bias based on their pre-existing viewpoints that their news sources reconfirm. If the opposite were true and most news sources leaned right and Republicans respected and approved of more news sources, they too could be engaging in confirmation bias. But that's not the case.

All in all, it's not that partisans live in entirely separate media bubbles when it comes to political news. There is some overlap in news sources but determining the full extent of that overlap can be difficult to gauge. One factor is that getting news from a source does not always mean trusting that source. Indeed, the data reveals that while 24% of Republicans got news from CNN in the past week, roughly four-in-ten who did (39%) say they distrust the outlet. And of the 23% of Democrats who got political news from Fox News in the past week, nearly three-in-ten (27%) distrust it.

Democrats Report Much Higher Levels of Trust in a Number of News Sources Than Republicans

One of the clearest differences between Americans on opposing sides of the political aisle is that despite the overwhelming evidence and proof of fake news (as this book covers in great detail), large portions of Democrats express trust in a far greater number of fake news sources than do Republicans.

This analysis asked individuals about 30 specific news sources across different platforms, selected on a range of measures including audience size, topic areas covered and relevance to political news. Respondents were shown grids of sources and asked to click on those they had heard of. Among the outlets respondents had heard of, they were asked to then click on those they trusted and then those they distrusted for political and election news. It's worth noting that trust and distrust figures are somewhat dependent on how much of the population has heard of the source. Outlets with low awareness among the public, for example, would also necessarily have smaller portions who could express trust or distrust.

Almost half (13) of the 30 sources asked about are trusted by at least 33% of Democrats, and six are trusted by at least 50%. Among Democrats and Democratic leaners, CNN sits at the top, trusted by two-thirds (67%) of Democrats. That is followed by the three commercial broadcast networks, all closely bunched together: NBC News (61% of Democrats), ABC News (60%) and CBS News (59%).

Large differences in news sources trusted by Democrats and Republicans % who trust each source for political and election news (sources trusted by 33% or more shown).

Also trusted by at least 50% of Democrats are the public television outlet PBS (56%) and *The New York Times* (53%). Next come the United Kingdom-based public media outlet BBC (48%), the cable channel MSNBC (48%) and *The Washington Post* (47%). Public radio outlet NPR and *Time* magazine are each trusted by 46% of Democrats.

Conversely, after the 65% of Republicans and Republican leaners who trust Fox News as a source, trust levels drop precipitously. The only other source trusted by as many as one-third of Republicans is ABC (33% of Republicans), followed closely by CBS, NBC and the Sean Hannity radio show (all at 30%). Even though the three broadcast networks rank among Republicans' top five most-trusted sources, only about half as many Republicans as Democrats trust them.

Similarly, the percentage of Republicans who trust *The New York Times* (15%) and *The Washington Post* (13%) is about a third of the share of Democrats who do. Trust measures for the full list of sources can be found in the sortable tables, but in all, 18 sources are trusted by fewer than 20% of Republicans, compared with 13 trusted by fewer than 20% of Democrats.

How Were Respondents Asked About 30 Sources?

Respondents were shown grids of 30 news outlets and asked to select the ones that they had heard of. If they had heard of an outlet, they were asked if they trusted it for political and election news. If they didn't say that they trust an outlet, they were then asked if they distrusted it. Finally, respondents were asked if they had gotten political or election news in the past week from any of the outlets they had heard about.

It is one thing to not express trust in an outlet; voicing outright distrust is another matter. Hefty party-line differences come through when looking at levels of distrust as well. Only four of the 30 sources in this study are distrusted by one-third or more Democrats and Democratic leaners. At the top of the list by a wide margin is Fox News, distrusted by 61% of Democrats for political and election news.

Other sources distrusted by a third or more of Democrats are Rush Limbaugh (43%), the Sean Hannity radio show (38%) and Breitbart (36%). Here is it worth noting that only between 40% and 50% of Democrats have heard of those sources, which means the vast majority who could weigh in express distrust.

Beyond these news outlets, there is little Democratic distrust to go around. Fewer than 10% of Democrats distrust the three major commercial broadcast networks, the two U.S. public media sources (NPR and PBS), the two weekly news magazines (*Newsweek* and *Time* magazine) or the four daily newspapers with a national reach. These numbers are another way of reflecting Democrats' confidence in many sources in this study.

Let me repeat my previous analysis: What these trends indicate is that Republicans seem to understand fake news and liberal bias is so prevalent in MSM that Democrats don't—or perhaps Democrats are engaging in confirmation bias based on their pre-existing viewpoints that their news sources reconfirm. If the opposite were true and most news sources leaned right and Republicans respected and approved of more news sources, they too could be engaging in confirmation bias. But that's not the case.

Among Republicans and Republican leaners, distrust of media sources is more common. Eight sources—twice as many as the Democrats' total—are distrusted by at least one-third of Republicans. At the top of the list is CNN, which is distrusted by 58% of Republicans. Then come MSNBC (distrusted by 47%), *The New York Times* (42%), NBC (40%), *The Washington Post* (39%), CBS (37%), ABC (37%) and HuffPost (34%).

Ideology Reveals Largest Gaps in Trust Occur Between Conservatives and Liberals

The extent of partisan media polarization—the fundamental divergence over the credibility of news sources—may be most clearly reflected by looking at trust and distrust together. Of the 30 sources examined in this study, there are seven that Republicans (and those who lean Republican) trust more than they distrust for political and election news, 20 are distrusted by more Republicans than trusted, and three receive a mixed verdict.

The numbers are close to reversed: 22 sources are trusted by more Democrats than distrusted, while eight are distrusted by more Democrats than trusted.

Of the sources trusted by more Republicans than distrusted, Fox News stands out. More than three times as many Republicans trust it as distrust it for political and election news (65% of Republicans vs. 19% who express distrust). The Sean Hannity radio show is trusted by three times as many Republicans as those who distrust it (30% of Republicans trust it vs. 10% who distrust it). Rush Limbaugh is trusted by 27% of Republicans and distrusted by 14%.

Other sources trusted by more Republicans than distrusted include several long-established news outlets where the ratio of trust to distrust is narrower. PBS is trusted by 27% of Republicans and distrusted by 20%, the BBC is trusted by 21% and distrusted by 16%, and *The Wall Street Journal* is trusted by 24% and distrusted by 19%.

Not only are Democrats much more likely to express more trust than distrust of most sources, but the ratio is also often much wider. Given the undeniable facts about fake news, this is a disturbing trend. Among the Democrats' sources with the largest margins between trust and distrust are PBS (56% trust vs. 4% distrust), NPR (46% vs. 2%), NBC (61% vs. 6%), CBS (59% vs. 6%), ABC (60% vs. 7%), BBC (48% vs. 5%), *The New York Times* (53% vs. 6%), *The Washington Post* (47% vs. 7%) and CNN (67% vs. 10%).

Within that group, both The *Washington Post* and *The New York Times* are among the outlets with the greatest distrust-to-trust ratio among Republicans. Also highly distrusted among

Republicans are HuffPost (4% of Republicans trust and 34% distrust) and BuzzFeed at 3% trust to 29% distrust.

The much smaller group of sources distrusted by more Democrats than trusted includes Breitbart, Rush Limbaugh and the Sean Hannity radio show. Each of these is trusted by about 1% of Democrats and distrusted by about a third or more. One other outlet that fares poorly among Democrats is Fox News (23% trust to 61% distrust).

Americans Are Divided by Party in the Sources They Turn to For Political News

Amid this deep polarization, a few sources stand out across parties. PBS, the BBC and the *Wall Street Journal* are the three outlets trusted more than distrusted by both Republicans and Democrats. At the other end of the spectrum, three outlets are distrusted by more in each party than trusted: the *Washington Examiner*, the *New York Post*, and BuzzFeed.

1. NPR
2. PBS
3. BBC
4. NBC News
5. CBS News
6. ABC News
7. *New York Times*
8. Time
9. *Washington Post*
10. CNN
11. *Newsweek*
12. Politico
13. MSNBC
14. *Wall Street Journal*
15. *USA Today*
16. Univision
17. *The Guardian*
18. *Business Insider*
19. *The Hill*
20. Vox
21. HuffPost
22. Vice
23. *New York Post*
24. BuzzFeed
25. *Washington Examiner*
26. Fox News
27. Daily Caller
28. Breitbart
29. Limbaugh (radio)
30. Hannity (radio)

Why does the study include more outlets with left-leaning audiences than right-leaning audiences?

Pew selected these outlets based on a number of factors, including their audience size and platform type, but not based on the ideological orientation of their audiences, which they didn't measure until later in the research process. Using this method, they ended up with 17 outlets whose audiences are left-leaning, six outlets whose audiences are right-leaning and seven outlets with mixed audiences.

One factor that may be at play here is that Republicans have a more compact media ecosystem. They rely to a large degree on a small number of outlets and view many established brands as not trustworthy. If this smaller sample were due to choice, this would be a troubling trend, but the most plausible reason is there are far fewer conservative news sources to choose from. Democrats, on the other hand, rely on a wider number of outlets.

What Can Readers Take Away From This Study?

It's often tempting to use studies like this one to "rank" media outlets against one another in terms of trust or distrust, but that wasn't the purpose of this research. Instead, Pew wanted to offer insight into the news sources partisans rely on for political news, and the degree to which there is common ground or division. That's especially important in an election year like 2020.

Overall, these findings reveal sharp divides in the use and trust of political news sources. They don't reveal completely separate media bubbles. There are some news sources that both Democrats and Republicans turn to, but even those areas of overlap can be hard to fully gauge since using a news source doesn't always mean people trust it.

In summary, more Democrats and Democratic-leaning independents trust than distrust most of the 30 outlets in the study, but the reverse is true among Republicans and GOP leaners. And while Democrats' trust in many of these outlets has remained stable or in some cases increased since 2014, Republicans have become more alienated from some of them, widening an already substantial partisan gap.

Beyond the Red vs. Blue Political Divide: Independents

A growing number of Americans are choosing not to identify with either political party, and the center of the political spectrum is increasingly diverse. Rather than being moderate, many of these independents hold extremely strong ideological positions on issues such as the role of government, immigration, the environment and social issues. But they combine these views in ways that defy liberal or conservative orthodoxy.

It's also helpful to expose the relationship between American's individual political ideologies and their political parties, keeping in mind that in the last century, American voters were more likely to be a conservative Democrat and/or a liberal Republican.

An oxymoron you, say? Hardly! It's true they existed in significant numbers in the 20th century but less so today in the 21st century.

Today, there are two core Republican groups, compared with three in 2005, to some extent reflecting a decline in GOP party affiliation. However, Democrats have not made gains in party identification. Rather, there has been a sharp rise in the percentage of independents—from 30% in 2005 to 37% in 2011.

While Republicans trail the Democrats in party affiliation, they enjoy advantages in other areas: The two core GOP groups are more homogenous—demographically and ideologically—than are the three core Democratic groups. And socioeconomic differences are more apparent on the left: Nearly half of Solid Liberals (49%) are college graduates, compared with 27% of New Coalition Democrats and just 13% of Hard-Pressed Democrats.

The Political Typology Study by the Pew Research Center

These are the principal findings of the 2011 political typology study by the Pew Research Center for the People & the Press, which sorts Americans into cohesive groups based on values, political beliefs, and party affiliation. The latest study is based on two surveys with a combined sample of 3,029 adults, conducted Feb. 22-Mar. 14, 2011 and a smaller callback survey conducted April 7-10, 2011 with 1,432 of the same respondents.

The most visible shift in the political landscape since Pew Research's previous political typology in early 2005 is the emergence of a single bloc of across-the-board conservatives. The long-standing divide between economic, pro-business conservatives and social conservatives has blurred into the 21st century.

During the Obama presidency, Staunch Conservatives took extremely conservative positions on nearly all issues –on the size and role of government, on economics, foreign policy, social issues, and moral concerns. Most agreed with the Tea Party and even more very strongly disapproved of Barack Obama's job performance. A second core group of Republicans—Main Street Republicans—are also conservative, but less consistently so.

On the left, Solid Liberals express diametrically opposing views from the Staunch Conservatives on virtually every issue. While Solid Liberals are predominantly white, minorities make up greater shares of New Coalition Democrats—who include nearly equal numbers of whites, African Americans, and Hispanics—and Hard-Pressed Democrats, who are about a third African American. Unlike Solid Liberals, both of these last two groups are highly religious and socially conservative. New Coalition Democrats are distinguished by their upbeat attitudes in the face of economic struggles.

But the three groups in the center of the political typology have little in common, aside from their avoidance of partisan labels. Libertarians and Post-Moderns are largely white, well-educated, and affluent.

They also share a relatively secular outlook on some social issues, including homosexuality and abortion. But Republican-oriented Libertarians are far more critical of government, less supportive of environmental regulations, and more supportive of business than are Post-Moderns, most of whom lean Democratic.

Independents Played a Determinative Role in the Last Four National Elections

Today, there are three disparate groups of independents: Libertarians, Disaffecteds, and Post Moderns, compared with two in 2005.

Disaffecteds, one group of independents, are financially stressed and cynical about politics. Most lean to the Republican Party, though they differ from the core Republican groups in their support for increased government aid to the poor.

The new and revised typologies find a deep and continuing divide between the two parties, as well as differences within both partisan coalitions, and the nature of the partisan divide has changed substantially over time and it's good to know these trends as they relate to political persuasions and their impact from fake news.

Media Biased Against Conservative Research & Think Tanks

A new study in the *Journal of Media Economics* shows the media is biased against right-leaning think tanks. Wayne Dunham, an economist in the Anti-Trust Division of the Department of Justice, concluded that the media "had a much higher propensity to associate ideological frames with think tanks associated with the right or conservative side of the political spectrum."

For example, an article may cite a study from the "conservative Heritage Foundation" while citing another study from the "Urban Institute" with no ideological qualifier indicating the Urban Institute is a "liberal" think tank.

The study measured 25,000 references to think tanks by six major newspapers and the Associated Press over an 18-year period. Dunham used 12 think tanks in his measurement, including the Heritage Foundation and American Enterprise Institute on the right, and the Brookings Institution, RAND Corporation and the Urban Institute on the left.

"This data show that conservative think tanks are ideologically framed 10 times more frequently than liberal think tanks," said Dunham. There are several factors that "suggest a liberal media bias."

Attaching an ideological label to a think tank is a subtle way of making its conclusion seem less credible. By doing this selectively, journalists have a powerful influence on the public perception of conservative think tanks.

AllSides Media Bias Chart

The AllSides Media Bias Chart below helps identify different perspectives so you can get the full picture of the range of media bias and their ideological niche. However, please keep in mind that the viewership of the two left leaning categories exceeds the viewership of the right leaning categories by at least a ratio of 9:1 meaning the left and far left reach is nine times greater.

Only Fox News on the right and far right has a huge reach by comparison to its smaller right and far right competitors. Nonetheless, the majority of left and far left news organizations have substantially larger reaches like CNN, MSNBC, ABC, NBC and CBS than the second-tier conservative outlets.

Overall and in general, the SAPIENT Being agrees with the AllSides L-L-C-R-R ratings with the following exceptions:

- *Epoch Times* is a Centrist newspaper (excluding their right leaning opinion and special reports sections), not a far Right one as shown. If their opinion and special reports were shown (they are not), they would be in the Right (but not far Right) category.

- Bloomberg, *USA Today*, Reuters, *Christian Science Monitor*, and *The Hill* are not Centrist and should reside in the Leans Left column. After these corrections, there are few Centrist news organizations that remain.

Per AllSides, knowing the political bias of media outlets allows you to consume a balanced news diet and avoid manipulation and fake news. Everyone is biased, but hidden bias misleads and divides us. The AllSides Media Bias Chart is based on their full and growing list of over 800 media bias ratings.

Unless otherwise noted, AllSides rates only online content, not TV, radio, or broadcast content. Their chart helps to free you from filter bubbles so you can consider multiple perspectives.

AllSides™ Media Bias Chart

All ratings are based on online content only — not TV, print, or radio content.
Ratings do not reflect accuracy or credibility; they reflect perspective only.

L	L	C	R	R
ALTERNET	abc	AP news only	The American Conservative	THE AMERICAN SPECTATOR
BuzzFeed NEWS	The Atlantic	BBC	THE DISPATCH	BREITBART B
CNN opinion	CBS	Bloomberg	FOX NEWS online news only	THE BLAZE
DEMOCRACY NOW!	CNN news only	The CHRISTIAN SCIENCE MONITOR	MarketWatch	CBN
THE DAILY BEAST	The Economist	npr news only	Newsmax news only	THE DAILY CALLER
HUFFPOST	the guardian	REUTERS	NEW YORK POST news only	Daily Mail
The Intercept_	NBC	REAL CLEAR POLITICS	The Post Millennial.	DAILY WIRE
JACOBIN	The New York news only Times	THE HILL	reason	THE EPOCH TIMES
MotherJones		USA TODAY	THE WALL STREET opinion JOURNAL	FOX NEWS opinion
msnbc	npr opinion	THE WALL STREET JOURNAL news only	Examiner	FEDERALIST
Newsweek	POLITICO		The Washington Times	NATIONAL REVIEW
THE NEW YORKER	PROPUBLICA			NEW YORK POST opinion
The New York opinion Times	TIME			Newsmax opinion
Nation.	The Washington Post			OAN
SLATE	YAHOO! NEWS			
Vox				

L LEFT   L LEAN LEFT   C CENTER   R LEAN RIGHT   R RIGHT

AllSides Media Bias Ratings are based on multi-partisan, scientific analysis.
Visit AllSides.com to view hundreds of media bias ratings.   Version 2 | AllSides 2020

6 – Not So Hidden Agenda and Collusion of Fake News Media

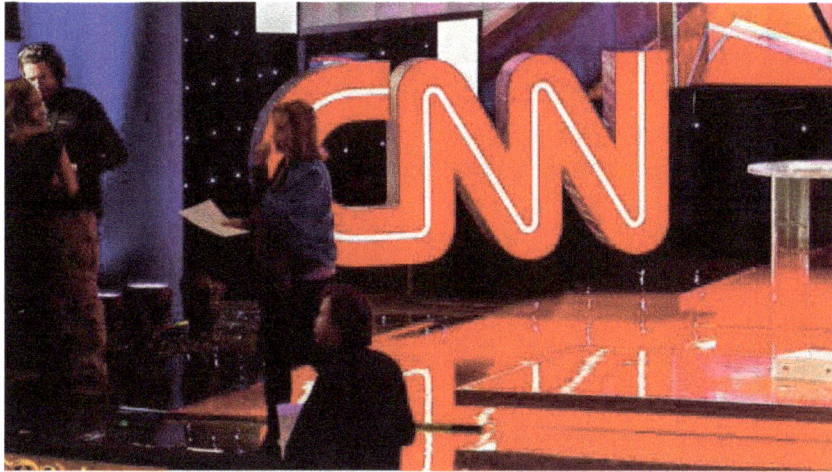

Credit: CNN

As Jim Morrison, singer of the 60's rock band The Doors, proclaimed, "Whoever controls the media, controls the mind," and with mainstream media losing its power in recent years from countless new websites, blogs, YouTube channels and Facebook pages functioning as news outlets—the monopoly that major media companies had on the control of information for decades was collapsing. Today, anyone with a Facebook page can post an article, a picture, or a video, and in a matter of minutes it can be seen by just as many people as something broadcast on the national news by a major television network.

The media oligarchy could no longer control what information the public was consistently fed, or what information was purposefully ignored. Many people started to see this new 'fake news' scare as a veiled attempt at censorship and a bold move to try and take back control of the distribution of media, which is why Mark Dice wrote the 2017 best seller: *The True Story of Fake News: How Mainstream Media Manipulates Millions,* which this chapter utilizes considerable content from as follows:

The *New York Post* ran an article titled, "The War on 'Fake News' Is All About Censoring Real News," which said, "Scrambling for an explanation for Donald Trump's victory, many in the media and on the left have settled on the idea that his supporters were consumers of 'fake news'—gullible rubes living in an alternate reality made Trump president," and noted that this new 'fake news' scare itself was fake news, and there was a growing backlash from conservatives who saw this witch hunt for what it was.

Just a few weeks later *The New York Times* admitted, "'Fake news' as short hand will almost surely be returned upon the media tenfold," as conservatives began to throw them back in the face of the mainstream media. One outlet published an article cautioning against the growing fake news panic titled, "Stop Calling Everything 'Fake News'" and pointed out, "Two months ago, almost no one was talking about fake news."

A Google Trends search for the term shows that it barely registered before October 2016. Now you can hardly turn on the real news without hearing it." The backlash was getting so bad that even President-Elect Donald Trump, in a now-famous outburst, called CNN "fake news" at his first press conference of 2017. Some people in the audience could be heard applauding him and "You are fake news" became an instant meme.

The SAPIENT Being's Definition of Fake News

Fake News has many definitions and is a broad term. However, at the SAPIENT Being, the term collectively includes media bias manifested in many different ways in mainstream journalism, social media, and illiberal establishments that in principle and practice are antithetical to an intellectually vibrant and viewpoint diverse sapient being mindset.

Per Andrew Klavan's edited definition, fake news can be further defined as follows:

Mainstream American news is ALL fake because the major news outlets are so consistently biased toward the left that whether any given story they report is factual or not, their overall reportage is essentially liberal, progressivism, or leftist propaganda. They can counter the right-wing slant of Fox News, but it's futile—because left-wing ABC, CBS, NBC, MSNBC and CNN have, combined, almost ten times the viewers.

Only seven percent of American journalists identify as Republican and the rest claim that despite the fact they're all Democrats, they can be objective. As previously noted, psychologists and the Heterodox Academy have shown that when people associate almost exclusively with those who agree with them, they suffer from groupthink, viewpoint orthodoxy, and confirmation bias—and lose their ability to see events clearly and objectively.

As Dice notes: With this sudden concern about fake news affecting our election, studies were conducted which actually proved fake news didn't swing the election or have any measurable effect on how people voted in 2016 (but not the same scenario in 2020).

New York University and Stanford reported that only eight percent of people were actually duped by fake news in 2016. Of those eight percent who supposedly believed some fake news articles were real, it's highly unlikely those stories actually swayed their opinions at all about a candidate, and instead only reflected what they already believed. *Columbia Journal Review* conducted a study and found, "The fake news audience is real, but it's also really small."

They also pointed out that, "the fake news audience does not exist in a filter bubble. Visitors to fake news sites visited real news sites just as often as visitors to real news sites visited other real news sites. In fact, sometimes fake news audiences visited real news sites more often." They even asked, "Is fake news a fake problem?" and concluded their report saying that their findings, "call into question the scope of the fake news problem."

In 2016, most voters got their news from TV and actual news websites, not from random stories posted on unknown websites. "Our data suggest that social media were not the most important source of election news and even the most widely circulated news stories were seen by only a small fraction of Americans," the researchers said.

The 2016 Election Agenda and Meltdown

Democrats were so shocked at Hillary's defeat that they couldn't come to grips with the fact that despite all the polls and media coverage painting a picture that Trump would surely lose—he didn't. With headlines like "Think Trump has a chance to snag GOP nomination? Analysis gives him just 1%," and "Our pollster polls model gives Hillary Clinton a 98.1% chance of winning the presidency," and Hillary supporters thought her victory would be a sure thing. In a now-famous clip, Bill Maher's audience burst out in laughter at Ann Coulter on his HBO show when she predicted Donald Trump had the best chance of winning early on in the race.

Instead of accepting the facts and learning from them that voters wanted a non-politician in the White House for a change, and that they wanted the illegal immigration problem fixed, Obamacare overhauled, and a conservative Supreme Court Justice to replace Antonin Scalia who had recently died—Democrats and MSM started playing the blame game, and their reasons for Hillary's defeat kept getting longer and more bizarre by the day.

First, they pointed the finger at FBI director James Comey for amending his testimony about the investigation into Hillary Clinton's email scandal when classified material sent from her was later found on Anthony Weiner's computer (then-husband of Huma Abedin, her campaign's vice chairman). Then they blamed white supremacists and the KKK, or the "whitelash" against a black president as CNN's Van Jones famously cried about on election night.

They went on to blame Islamophobia, xenophobia, and sexism, saying that people just didn't want a "woman president." But then they produced their most creative excuse ever. An excuse that would serve as a massive umbrella under which all other excuses could be tied together into one grand unified excuse: "Fake News."

Even Facebook CEO Mark Zuckerberg admitted back in 2016, "To think it influenced the election in any way is a pretty crazy idea." He surprisingly confirmed what rational people understood that Hillary supporters underestimated the amount of support for Donald Trump. "I do think there is a certain profound lack of empathy in asserting that the only reason someone could have voted the way they did is they saw some fake news. If you believe that, then I don't think you have internalized the message the Trump supporters are trying to send in this election," Zuckerberg said.

Facebook's chief operating officer Sheryl Sandberg agreed. When she was asked if 'fake news' played a big role in the 2016 election, she answered, "Well, there have been claims that it swayed the election, and we don't think it swayed the election, but we take those claims seriously."

Even MSNBC's Joe Scarborough, a RINO Republican who hates Donald Trump, admitted, "When you look at this 'fake news,' and you see what happened up at Harvard and you hear everybody writing articles saying millennials cost Hillary Clinton the election, and dogs with three legs cost Hillary Clinton the election, and comets passing in the night—Hillary Clinton cost Hillary Clinton the election. Hillary Clinton's campaign staff cost Hillary Clinton the election."

He continued, "Listen, if you care about Democrats digging out of the hole that they have put themselves in now, you've got to ask yourself—what have Democrats done to so offend Americans that they only have 11 governorships, they've lost control of the Senate, they've lost control of the House, they lost 900 legislative seats over the past six (Obama) years." He concluded, "It wasn't fake news. It was something much, much bigger."

His cohost Mika Brzezinski responded, "Ugh, I don't think people are ready to hear that, Joe," and of course, they weren't or that Donald Trump ran a more effective campaign. Liberals were sinking deeper into a depression, unable to handle the reality that Donald Trump beat Hillary Clinton on election night 2016 and would soon be sworn in as our next president. Trump Derangement Syndrome (TDS) had arrived!

Mainstream Fake News Media vs. Donald Trump

As Dice explains from his personal experience in *The True Story of Fake News: How Mainstream Media Manipulates Millions:* Like never before, the mainstream media kept making mountains out of molehills and using their platforms to influence public opinion by framing everything Donald Trump did and said in a negative light.

Their constant criticism and nitpicking were soon difficult to distinguish from satire or parody because much of it was so absurd, but unfortunately millions of Americans couldn't help but get swept up in their manufactured controversies. Anti-Trump hatred would soon grow to extremes few could have imagined as the constant disinformation was whipping people into a frenzy (and continues to this day).

Conservatives fought back and started fact checking the liberal media like hawks, and every time CNN or another major 'news' organization would report a false or absurdly biased story, Trump supporters would shout from the rooftops about it and use each instance to mock the diminishing credibility of mainstream media.

Liberals pushed back even harder and began labeling conservative websites, YouTube channels, and social media personalities not just as "fake news," but as "extremists" and "racists" who post "hate speech."

Facebook began implementing "fact checkers" and issuing warnings when people would post links to certain stories or websites, as well as outright banning links to some or labeling them "spam" when someone tried to share them. The major social media platforms also implemented stricter terms of service and vowed to crack down on people posting "hateful content," which in reality is often just mild criticism of certain liberal policies or ideologies that Big Tech disagrees with.

YouTube began demonetizing (removing advertisements from) videos covering certain topics they deemed "not advertiser-friendly," thus preventing 'YouTubers' like Dice from making money off them, which for many people is a part-time or full-time job and how they pay their bills.

This was just the beginning of a censorship tsunami that was heading their way. Liberals would begin going after the advertisers on conservative websites and TV shows to pressure them to pull their sponsorships. Google began scrutinizing websites and YouTube channels which use their Ad Sense system to generate revenue. Anti-feminist videos, videos criticizing radical LGBT activists, or ones calling to stop illegal immigration, or the massive influx of Muslim refugees were now being stripped of advertisers in droves.

YouTube wasn't just for posting funny cat videos or online tutorials anymore. It had become a powerful platform for distributing news and commentary. The 'YouTube stars' weren't just entertainers, beauty vloggers and gamers anymore, but news commentators and anti-social justice warrior activists.

Many found that social media platforms weren't just useful for communicating with friends and family, but the technology could also easily be used as a massive publishing outlet allowing literally anyone to be able to have their content seen and heard by just as many people as a major newspaper or television network, and with little or no cost at all.

The news and tech conglomerates figured if they could remove the financial incentives for this rapidly growing industry of alternative media platforms and personalities, they could dramatically discourage people from putting out content and commentary, and thus reduce the growing number of conservative voices online whose audience kept growing by the day as more people abandoned mainstream media and were turning to new independent outlets and online personalities for their news and commentary.

Viewpoint Diversity in the Newsroom is Essential

Many of America's news and media organizations have fallen into a narrow orthodoxy in what is acceptable to report and discuss regarding public policy and political positions. Now is the time for all of us who value the pursuit of truth and knowledge to support a new heterodoxy that welcomes, supports, and encourages a diversity of viewpoints.

If you're looking for demographic diversity in the newsroom, there are countless articles about this important topic—but search for viewpoint diversity in the newsroom as an equally important topic and locating any content is almost as difficult as finding Bigfoot. However, W. Joseph Campbell, the author of the 2017 book *Getting It Wrong: Debunking the Greatest Myths in American Journalism* has some important points and expert references to add to this section about this very important issue that he wrote about in 2016 with the help from others as follows:

Amid the media's self-flagellation and agonized introspection in the days since Donald Trump's stunning election victory—days that brought such astonishing turns as the *New York Times* all but begging subscribers not to quit the newspaper—I have thought often of an ombudsman's column published eight years ago, soon after Barack Obama won the presidency (in 2008).

The ombudsman, or in-house critic, was Deborah Howell of the *Washington Post*, who wrote:

"I'll bet that most *Post* journalists voted for Obama. I did. There are centrists at *The Post* as well. But the conservatives I know here feel so outnumbered that they don't even want to be quoted by name in a memo."

The column stuck with me not only because of Howell's evident candor in describing conservatives in the newsroom—you could almost see them cowering—but because viewpoint diversity remains largely elusive in mainstream American journalism.

Howell was right in 2008, and her analysis rings true today: Leading U.S. news outlets have done little to address a failing that has been evident for years.

As John Kass, a conservative columnist for the *Chicago Tribune* wrote, "It's no secret that most of American journalism is liberal in its politics. The diversity they prize has nothing to do with diversity of thought."

The viewpoint-diversity deficit was highlighted anew in Trump's electoral victory over Democratic nominee Hillary Clinton, an outcome that gave journalists what Joshua Benton of the Nieman Journalism Lab called "the shock of their professional lives."

The shock was of 1948 proportions, the year when President Harry S. Truman defied broad expectations that he would handily lose the election to Republican Thomas Dewey. This year, as Nate Silver of the FiveThirtyEight data blog observed, "most campaign coverage was premised on the idea that Clinton was all but certain to become the next president."

The outcome revealed how inadequately journalists had prepared their audiences for a Trump victory.

Granted, the viewpoint-diversity deficit in leading American newsrooms hasn't been much measured. That such surveys have been rare is hardly reason to pretend the deficit is imaginary. Or that it can be justified by arguing, "Well, conservatives have Fox News," the cable outlet.

Few media self-critiques following Trump's victory were as brutally discerning—or as revealing of the viewpoint-diversity deficit—as the essay Will Rahn wrote for CBS News. Rahn, managing director of political coverage for CBS News Digital, did not refer specifically to viewpoint diversity in his essay. But he said as much, writing:

"Journalists love mocking Trump supporters. We insult their appearances. We dismiss them as racists and sexists. We emote on Twitter about how this or that comment, or policy makes us feel one way or the other, and yet we reject their feelings as invalid. It's a profound failure of empathy in the service of endless posturing."

Rahn further wrote of journalists:

"We must become more impartial, not less so. We have to abandon our easy culture of tantrums and recrimination. We have to stop writing these know-it-all, 140-character sermons on social media and admit that, as a class, journalists have a shamefully limited understanding of the country we cover. … There's a fleeting fun to gang-ups and groupthink. But it's not worth what we are losing in the process."

The periodic Wikileaks disclosures during the fall campaign that revealed fawning interactions of journalists and the Clinton campaign further confirmed that the deficit in viewpoint diversity is no evanescent problem. And it's not of recent vintage.

Howell's column in 2008 quoted Tom Rosenstiel, then the director of the Washington-based Project for Excellence in Journalism as saying that "conservatives are right that journalism has too many liberals and not enough conservatives. It's inconceivable that that is irrelevant." Rosenstiel added: "More conservatives in newsrooms will bring about better journalism."

In this year's election (2020) and in 2016, journalists openly challenged or flouted professional norms of impartiality and detachment in reporting, saying the incendiary character of Trump's views and remarks was so egregious that they were left with no choice.

In 2016, the *Columbia Journalism Review* fairly rejoiced in what it saw as a latter-day "Murrow Moment" for journalists, a reference to the mythical 1954 television program when Edward R. Murrow took on the red-baiting Republican senator, Joseph R. McCarthy.

The journalism review said "we … are witnessing a change from existing practice of steadfast detachment, and the context in which journalists are reacting is not unlike that of Murrow: The candidate's comments fall outside acceptable societal norms, and critical journalists are not alone in speaking up."

Research on Media Bias: It's Real and the Data Don't Lie

The rest of this chapter's content is from John Perazzo' s October 2008 article "In the Tank: A Statistical Analysis of Media Bias."

As outlined by Perazzo: The overwhelming data doesn't lie—but there are many deniers that do and others that ignore MSM bias and focus on inconsequential non-mainstream media site (NMSM). The leftwing bias of the American mass media is pervasive and quantifiable in so many ways as we shall read below.

Since the 1980s, studies have consistently shown that the professionals who constitute America's mainstream news media—reporters, editors, anchors, publishers, correspondents, bureau chiefs, and executives at the nation's major newspapers, magazines, and broadcast networks—are preponderantly left-oriented and Democrat.

These studies have excluded commentators, editorialists, and opinion columnists—all of whom make it clear that they are giving their opinions and analyses of the news as they view it. Rather, the focus of the research has been on those individuals whose ostensible duty is to present the relevant facts impartially and comprehensively to the readers, listeners, and viewers.

What Media Believe About a Wide Array of Social, Ethical, and Political Issues

A useful way of gauging the news media's political and ideological makeup is to examine what the professionals in that industry believe about a wide array of social, ethical, and political issues. For example, research shows that:

- Fully 81% of news media professionals favor affirmative action in employment and academia.

- Some 71% agree that the "government should work to ensure that everyone has a job."

- 75% agree that the "government should work to reduce the income gap between rich and poor."

- 56% say that the United States has exploited the nations of the Third World.

- 57% say that America's disproportionate consumption of the world's natural resources is "immoral."

- Nearly half agree that "the very structure of our society causes people to feel alienated."

- Only 30% agree that "private enterprise is fair to workers."

How Media Have Supported Democrat or Liberal/Left Candidates and Causes

It is equally illuminating to examine the degree to which members of the news media have supported Democrat or liberal/left candidates and causes, both at the ballot box and with their checkbooks:

- In 1964, 94% of media professionals voted for Democrat Lyndon Johnson over Republican Barry Goldwater.

- In 1968, 86% voted for Democrat Hubert Humphrey over Republican Richard Nixon.

- In 1972, 81% voted for Democrat George McGovern over the incumbent Nixon.

- In 1976, 81% voted for Democrat Jimmy Carter over Republican Gerald Ford.

- In 1980, twice as many cast their ballots for Carter rather than for Republican Ronald Reagan.

- In 1984, 58% supported Democrat Walter Mondale, whom Reagan defeated in the biggest landslide in presidential election history.

- In 1988, White House correspondents from various major newspapers, television networks, magazines, and news services supported Democrat Michael Dukakis over Republican George H.W. Bush by a ratio of 12-to-1.

- In 1992, those same correspondents supported Democrat Bill Clinton over the incumbent Bush by a ratio of 9 to 2.

- Among Washington bureau chiefs and congressional correspondents, the disparity was 89% vs. 7%, in Clinton's favor.

- In a 2004 poll of campaign journalists, those based outside of Washington, DC supported Democrat John Kerry over Republican George W. Bush by a ratio of 3-to-1. Those based inside the Beltway favored Kerry by a 12-to-1 ratio.

- In a 2008 survey of 144 journalists nationwide, journalists were 8 times likelier to make campaign contributions to Democrats than to Republicans.

- A 2008 *Investor's Business Daily* study put the campaign donation ratio at 11.5-to-1, in favor of Democrats. In terms of total dollars given, the ratio was 15-to-1.

It is exceedingly rare to find, even in the most heavily partisan voting districts in the United States, such pronounced imbalances in terms of votes cast or dollars earmarked for one party or the other.

How News-Media Professionals Identify Themselves

The figures cited above are entirely consistent with how news-media professionals identify themselves in terms of their political party affiliations and ideological leanings:

- In a 1988 survey of business reporters, 54% of respondents identified themselves as Democrats, 9% as Republicans.

- In a 1992 poll of journalists working for newspapers, magazines, radio, and television, 44% called themselves Democrats, 16% Republicans.

- In a 1996 poll of 1,037 reporters at 61 newspapers, 61% identified themselves as Democrats, 15% as Republicans.

- In a 2001 Kaiser Family Foundation poll, media professionals were nearly 7 times likelier to call themselves Democrats rather than Republicans.

- A 2014 study by Indiana University's School of Journalism found that just 7.1% of all journalists identified themselves as Republicans, vs, 28.1% who self-identified as Democrats and 50.2% who said they were Independents.

How News-Media Professionals Rate Themselves on the Left-to-Right Political Spectrum

We see similar ratios in studies where news people are asked to rate themselves on the left-to-right political spectrum:

- In a 1981 study of 240 journalists nationwide, 65% identified themselves as liberals, 17% as conservatives.

- In a 1983 study of news reporters, executives, and staffers, 32% identified themselves as liberals, 11% as conservatives.

- In a 1992 study of more than 1,400 journalists, 44% identified themselves as liberals, 22% as conservatives.

- In a 1996 study of Washington bureau chiefs and congressional correspondents, 61% identified themselves as liberals, 9% as conservatives.

- In a 1996 study of 1,037 journalists, the respondents identified themselves as liberals 4 times more frequently than as conservatives. Among journalists working for newspapers with circulations exceeding 50,000, the ratio of liberals to conservatives was 5.4 to 1.

- In a 2004 Pew Research Center study of journalists and media executives, the ratio of self-identified liberals to conservatives was 4.9 to 1.

- In a 2007 Pew Research Center study of journalists and news executives, the ratio was 4 liberals for each conservative.

Bias in the news media manifests itself most powerfully not in the form of outright, intentional lies, but is most often a function of what reporters choose *not* to tell their audience, i.e., the facts they purposely omit so as to avoid contradicting the political narrative they wish to advance. As media researchers Tim Groseclose and Jeffrey Milo put it: "For every sin of commission…we believe that there are hundreds, and maybe thousands, of sins of omission—cases where a journalist chose facts or stories that only one side of the political spectrum is likely to mention."

By no means is such activity the result of an organized campaign or conspiracy. Media expert Bernard Goldberg says: "No, we don't sit around in dark corners and plan strategies on how we're going to slant the news. We don't have to. It comes naturally to most reporters." Goldberg explains that "a lot of news people … got into journalism in the first place" so they could: (a) "change the world and make it a better place," and (b) use their positions as platforms from which to "show compassion," which "makes us feel good about ourselves."

Expanding further upon this point, Goldberg quotes researcher Robert Lichter of the nonpartisan Center for Media and Public Affairs, who said that journalists increasingly "see themselves as society's designated saviors," striving to "awaken the national conscience and force public action." Or as ABC News anchor Peter Jennings admitted to the *Boston Globe* in July 2001: "Those of us who went into journalism in the '50s or '60s, it was sort of a liberal thing to do: Save the world."

The Dangerous Liberal Ideas for Censorship in the United States

Almost everywhere you turn today, politicians are telling the public to "get used to the new normal" after the pandemic as covered in Jonathan Turley's May 2020 article in *The Hill* titled "The Dangerous Liberal Ideas For Censorship in the United States."

Turley explains: The most chilling suggestion comes from the politicians and academics who have called for the censorship of social media and the internet. The only thing spreading faster than the coronavirus has been censorship and the loud calls for more restrictions on free speech. The *Atlantic* recently published an article by Harvard Law School professor Jack Goldsmith and University of Arizona law professor Andrew Keane Woods calling for Chinese style censorship of the internet.

They declared that "in the great debate of the past two decades about freedom versus control of the network, China was largely right and the United States was largely wrong" as "significant monitoring and speech control are inevitable components of a mature and flourishing internet, and governments must play a large role in such practices to ensure that the internet is compatible with society norms and values."

The justification for that is the danger of "fake news" about coronavirus risks and cures. Yet this is only the latest rationalization for rolling back free speech rights. For years, Democratic leaders in Congress called for censorship of "fake news" on social media sites. Twitter, Facebook, and YouTube have all engaged in increasing levels of censorship and have a well-known reputation for targeting conservative speech.

Hillary Clinton has demanded that political speech be regulated to avoid the "manipulation of information" and stated that Facebook founder Mark Zuckerberg "should pay a price for what he is doing to our democracy" by refusing to remove any opposition postings. In Europe, free speech rights are in a free fall, and countries such as France and Germany are imposing legal penalties designed to censor speech across the world.

Many of us in the free speech community have warned about the growing insatiable appetite for censorship in the West. Yet we have been losing the fight, and free speech opponents are now capitalizing on the opportunity presented by the pandemic. Representative Adam Schiff sent a message to the executives of Google, Twitter, and YouTube demanding censorship of anything deemed "misinformation" and "false information."

Yet YouTube did exactly that a few days earlier by removing two videos of California doctors who called for the easing of state lockdown orders. The doctors argued that the coronavirus is not as dangerous as suggested and that some deaths associated with the pandemic are not accurate. There is ample reason to contest their views but, instead, YouTube banned the two videos to keep others from reaching their own conclusions.

Facebook will not only remove posts it considers misinformation about the coronavirus but will issue warnings to those who "like" such postings. Facebook said that it wants to protect people from dangerous remedies and false data. Ironically, the World Health Organization praised Sweden for its rejection of the very restrictions criticized by the two doctors. The group declared that Sweden is a "model" country despite its rejection of lockdown measures being protested in the United States.

Moreover, many mainstream media sources have reported information that is now known to be false from the lack of any benefits of wearing masks to the failure in trials of drugs like Remdesivir to the shortage of thousands of ventilators. Despite those being wrong, related opposing views were often treated as either fringe or false positions. Fake news madness!

This subjectivity of censorship is why the cure is worse than the illness. The best cure for bad speech is more speech rather than regulation. The fact is that the pandemic, as Clinton reminded voters, is a "terrible crisis to waste." Yet the waste for some would be to emerge from the pandemic with free speech still alive.

7 – The Destructive Influence & Power of Fake News Media

Credit: DailyDot.com

Fake news stories have been around for centuries, although they had usually just been called disinformation, propaganda, yellow journalism, conspiracy theories, or hoaxes; but this modern incarnation was different. All of a sudden it was supposedly everywhere, and just cost Hillary Clinton the election.

As Mark Dice points out in *The True Story of Fake News: How Mainstream Media Manipulates Millions*: Just one week after the 2016 presidential election, when tens of millions of Hillary supporters were still in absolute shock that Donald Trump actually beat her—and while many Trump supporters were in a similar state of surprise since he was the long-awaited anti-establishment underdog and populist—the term "fake news" became the talk of the town and quickly turned into one of the most loaded and controversial labels in America.

The mainstream media often steers the public conversation by giving constant coverage to certain stories which reinforce the ideologies they are trying to promote, which fits within The SAPIENT Being's definition of fake news. They'll often choose an isolated incident that's making news in the local community where it happened, and while it has no real national significance, the major networks will 'coincidentally' determine it should be one of the top stories in the country and then sensationalize it, so the incident then becomes a widely talked about topic.

Agenda Setting by Fake News Media

These stories often include rare police brutality incidents involving a white police officer and a black suspect. But when it's a white officer and a white victim, or a black officer and a white victim, the incidents remain local stories and don't get national attention. Similarly, if a celebrity happens to call a gay or transgender person a derogatory name, then the big networks all have panels of pundits complain about it for hours, days, or even weeks on end to emphasize how 'hateful' and 'dangerous' such language is.

When these mountains out of molehills are turned into the top stories on the evening news of the Big Three broadcast networks (ABC, NBC, CBS) it doesn't take a professional media analyst to see a pattern and realize there is coordination among these companies behind the scenes to decide which topics will be the "top stories."

It's statistically impossible that the Big Three would regularly choose the same little-known local stories from the newswires to all report on nationally. Many events of the day warrant being the top stories on all networks, but most do not and shouldn't make it any further than their local news channels, yet they regularly get the national spotlight, and always when they fit the current agenda of the time.

The technical term for what they're doing is called agenda-setting. They magnify selected stories and topics through their constant coverage and endless panel discussions about every little detail. Talking for hours on end about the stories creates a self-fulfilling prophecy by building certain instances into major issues, and by treating them as if they are major issues when they are not and getting people to talk and think about them so much, they then become major issues.

As television became part of everyone's lives, a study was conducted during the 1968 presidential election called the Chapel Hill Study, which showed the strong correlation between what people thought were the most important election issues and what the national news media repeatedly reported were the most important issues.

It basically showed that instead of just reporting on the news, the networks were actually influencing what people thought was news. Since then, hundreds of studies into the agenda-setting power of the mainstream media have been conducted which consistently show the immense power the industry has to shape public opinion and not only influence what people think about, but how they think about it.

Aside from agenda-setting, the major networks also frame topics in a certain light trying to influence how they are perceived. Through their carefully selected panelists and pointed questions, they can easily paint a person or issue in a positive light or a negative one.

For example, during the height of the Black Lives Matter protests in 2016 and 2020, the liberal media always portrayed the protests (and riots) as a civil rights movement on par with Martin Luther King of the 1950s and 60s, consisting of people who were fighting against an 'epidemic 'of white police officers shooting 'innocent' black men. In reality, the vast majority of black men shot and killed by police are armed and dangerous thugs with criminal histories, but those facts are ignored, and the incidents are always framed as another 'innocent' black man who has been 'murdered' by police because 'they're all racists.'

The media likes to take rare and isolated instances of officer involved shootings and magnify them to give the appearance that there is a nation-wide epidemic of 'racist' police officers who are gunning down innocent young black men, thus adding fuel to the fire of black power groups and further straining race relations in America.

People like Trayvon Martin, Michael Brown and George Floyd are turned into celebrities from the nonstop coverage. Their names even trend on Twitter on the birthdays and the anniversaries of their deaths. Leftist organizations had signs, T-shirts, and murals made with their faces on them which people wore to protests and they are revered as if they're Martin Luther King or Tupac Shakur.

CNN and MSNBC love to give airtime to any Republican who expresses sympathy for a liberal cause. Congressmen who are completely unknown outside of their own small districts are held up as examples of a "growing trend" of "resistance " against conservatives when they speak out against members of their own party, when in reality, most of the time they're just an eccentric member of the House of Representatives with no national influence at all.

Career and Content Intimidation by Liberal Publishers and Fake News Media

Kyle Smith's October 2014 *New York Post* article "Ex-CBS Reporter's Book Reveals How Liberal Media Protects Obama" shows how difficult it can be to get to the truth. Using Sharyl Attkisson's 2015 memoir/exposé of senior media and government officials in the Obama administration titled *Stonewalled: My Fight for Truth Against the Forces of Obstruction, Intimidation, and Harassment in Obama's Washington*, it can be close to impossible to get at the truth.

Attkisson unloads on her colleagues in big-time TV news for their cowardice and cheerleading for the Obama administration while unmasking the corruption, misdirection and outright lying of today's Washington political machine. Attkisson is an unreasonable woman. Important people have told her so.

When the longtime CBS reporter asked for details about reinforcements sent to the Benghazi compound during the Sept. 11, 2012 terrorist attack, White House national security spokesman Tommy Vietor replied to her, "I give up, Sharyl… I'll work with more reasonable folks that follow up, I guess."

Another White House flack, Eric Schultz, didn't like being pressed for answers about the Fast and Furious scandal in which American agents directed guns into the arms of Mexican drug lords. "Goddammit, Sharyl!" he screamed at her. "*The Washington Post* is reasonable, the *LA Times* is reasonable, *The New York Times* is reasonable. You're the only one who's not reasonable!"

Harper's was similarly roiled by internal rebellion and online fury for publishing articles by John Hockenberry, the NPR host who lost his job over sexual harassment accusations, and by Katie Roiphe, whose criticism of #MeToo was controversial even before the magazine published it. Rumors about the pending article prompted Nicole Cliffe, a columnist at Slate, to call for freelance writers to boycott *Harper's* unless it killed Roiphe's piece; Cliffe even offered to compensate them for any money they lost by withdrawing their articles. Her preemptive strike didn't stop publication of the Roiphe article, but it did inspire at least one company to withdraw an ad from *Harper's*.

The Atlantic faced a campaign to fire Kevin Williamson shortly after he was hired away from *National Review*. Writers at the *New Republic*, the *New York Times*, Slate, Vox, the Daily Beast, and other outlets called him unfit for the job. They were particularly appalled by an earlier podcast in which Williamson, in a spirit of provocation, said that women who have abortions deserved the same punishment as those who commit first-degree murder, even if that meant hanging.

The Atlantic initially stood by him, and Ta-Nehisi Coates, one of its star progressive writers, even praised Williamson's work and said that he'd advised hiring him. But the online dragging and internal discontent soon led to his exit. At a staff meeting (a video of which was leaked to *HuffPost*) after Williamson's firing, Coates apologized to his colleagues. "I feel like I kind of failed you guys," he said.

A more immediate danger is self-censorship by writers fearful of being fired or blacklisted and by editors fearful of online rage, staff revolts, and advertising boycotts. After the cowardly firing of Kevin Williamson, *The Atlantic* (to its credit) published a dissent from that decision by Conor Friedersdorf, in which he worried about the chilling effect it would have on the magazine's writers and editors, and how their fear of taking chances would ultimately hurt readers.

But all editors and publishers can take a couple of basic steps. One is to concentrate on hiring journalists committed to the most important kind of diversity—viewpoint diversity with a wide range of ideas open for vigorous debate. The other step is even simpler: stop capitulating. Ignore the online speech police, and don't reward the staff censors, either. Instead of feeling their pain or acceding to their demands, give them a copy of Nat Hentoff's *Free Speech for Me— but Not for Thee.*

These are just some of the dangers at every unsapient publication that bows to the new censors. Resisting them won't be easy if journalism keeps going the way of a *1984* type fake news scenario, but in the 21st century setting. If they still don't get it—if they still don't see that free speech is their profession's paramount principle—tactfully suggest that their talents would be better suited to another line of work.

Republican Ideas Are Frequently Caricatured and Rarely Presented Fairly

From the July 2009 *Christian Science Monitor* article "Republican Ideas Are Frequently Caricatured and Rarely Presented Fairly," below is a relevant article about what happened when freelance journalist and journalism student Dan Lawton at the University of Oregon posed a simple question. In his own words, Lawton explains:

Nearly all my professors are Democrats. Isn't that a problem? That's a sure sign that universities should address the lack of ideological diversity. When I began examining the political affiliation of faculty at the University of Oregon, the lone conservative professor I spoke with cautioned that I would "make a lot of people unhappy."

Though I mostly brushed off his warning—assuming that academia would be interested in such discourse—I was careful to frame my research for a column for the school newspaper diplomatically.

The University of Oregon (UO), where I study journalism, invested millions annually in a diversity program that explicitly included "political affiliation" as a component. Yet, out of the 111 registered Oregon voters in the departments of journalism, law, political science, economics, and sociology, there were only *two* registered Republicans.

A number of conservative students told me they felt Republican ideas were frequently caricatured and rarely presented fairly. Did the dearth of conservative professors on campus and apparent marginalization of ideas on the right belie the university's commitment to providing a marketplace of ideas?

In my column, published in the campus newspaper *The Oregon Daily Emerald* June 1, I suggested that such a disparity hurt UO. I argued that the lifeblood of higher education was subjecting students to diverse viewpoints and the university needed to work on attracting more conservative professors.

I also suggested that students working on right-leaning ideas may have difficulty finding faculty mentors. I couldn't imagine, for instance, that journalism that supported the Iraq war or gun rights would be met with much enthusiasm.

What I didn't realize is that journalism that examined the dominance of liberal ideas on campus would be addressed with hostility.

A professor who confronted me declared that he was "personally offended" by my column. He railed that his political viewpoints never affected his teaching and suggested that if I wanted a faculty with Republicans I should have attended a university in the South. "If you like conservatism you can certainly attend the University of Texas and you can walk past the statue of Jefferson Davis every day on your way to class," he wrote in an e-mail.

Lawton was shocked by such a comment, which seemed an attempt to link Republicans with racist orthodoxy. When he wrote back expressing his offense, the professor neither apologized nor clarified his remarks. Instead, he reiterated them on the record. Was such a brazen expression of partisanship representative of the faculty as a whole?

Lawton continues: I decided to speak with him in person in the hope of finding common ground. He was eager to chat, and after five minutes our dialogue bloomed into a lively discussion. As we hammered away at the issue, one of his colleagues with whom he shared an office grew visibly agitated. Then, while I was in mid-sentence, she exploded:

"You think you're so [expletive] cute with your little column," she told me. "I read your piece and all you want is attention. You're just like Bill O'Reilly. You just want to get up on your [expletive] soapbox and have people look at you!" she screamed.

Lawton continues: From the disgust with which she attacked me; you would have thought I had advocated Nazism. She quickly grew so emotional that she had to leave the room. But before she departed, he added: "You understand that my column was basically a prophesy."

And so, by simply suggesting right-leaning ideas weren't welcome on campus and in response to the faculty tying Lawton's viewpoints to racism and addressing him with profanity-laced insults, the ideological bubble on campus is a tough one to penetrate with sapience.

Per Lawton: "What's so remarkable is that I hadn't actually advocated Republican ideas or conservative ideas. In fact, I'm not a conservative, nor a Republican. I simply believe in the concept of diversity—a primarily liberal idea—and think that we suffer when we don't include ideas we find unappealing."

So Called 'Impartial' Algorithms Disproportionately Impact Conservative Material

Borrowing a politics and policy article written by Ben Shapiro for the *National Review*, it's becoming more evident that media companies' so called 'impartial' algorithms disproportionately impact conservative material. Ben Shapiro is the editor in chief of the Daily Wire and writes the following.

The biggest names in social media are cracking down on news. In particular, they're cracking down disproportionately on conservative news. That's not necessarily out of malice; it's probably due to the fact that our major social-media sites are staffed thoroughly with non-conservatives who have no objective frame of reference when it comes to the news business.

Thus, Google biases its algorithm to prevent people from searching for guns online in shopping; temporarily attached fact-checks from leftist sites like Snopes and PolitiFact to conservative websites but not leftist ones; showed more pro-Clinton results than pro-Trump results in news searches; and, of course, fired tech James Damore for the sin of examining social science in the debate over the wage gap. Google's bias is as obvious as the "doodles" it chooses for its logos, which routinely feature left-wing icons and issues.

YouTube has demonetized videos from conservatives while leaving similar videos up for members of the Left. Prager University has watched innocuous videos titled "Why America Must Lead," "The Ten Commandments: Do Not Murder," and "Why Did America Fight the Korean War" demonetized (i.e., barred from accepting advertisements) at YouTube's hands. Prager's lawyer explains, "Google and YouTube use restricted mode filtering not to protect younger or sensitive viewers from 'inappropriate' video content, but as a political gag mechanism to silence Prager U."

Facebook was slammed for ignoring conservative stories and outlets in its trending news; now Facebook has shifted its algorithm to downgrade supposedly "partisan" news, which has the effect of undercutting newer sites that are perceived as more partisan, while leaving brand names with greater public knowledge relatively unscathed.

Facebook's tactics haven't just hit conservative Web brands—they've destroyed the profit margins for smaller start-ups like LittleThings, a four-year-old site that fired 100 employees this week after the algorithm shift reportedly destroyed 75 percent of the site's organic reach (the number of people who see a site's content without paid distribution).

And Twitter has banned nasty accounts perceived as right-wing while ignoring similar activity from the Left. James O'Keefe recently exposed the practice of "shadowbanning," in which Twitter hides particular content or mutes particular hashtags for political purposes. That's no coincidence: Twitter head Jack Dorsey is an ardent leftist who has campaigned with radicals like DeRay Mckesson, and whose company relies on the input of an Orwellian Trust and Safety Council staffed thoroughly with left-wing interest groups.

Banned Prager U Videos by Google/YouTube

Per Prager University in July of 2020: "Big Tech is censoring Prager U again. Facebook announced that they will be limiting Prager U's reach to our own followers, and Twitter locked us out of our account."

Prager U, founded by Dennis Prager in 2011, is a not-for-profit organization that helps millions understand the values that shaped America and provides millions of Americans and people around the world with the intellectual ammunition they need to advocate for limited government, individual responsibility, and economic freedom.

Per Prager: "Why are they censoring them? Because they dared to show America a different point of view. This time the flashpoint is a collection of frontline medical doctors' testimonials about their successful use of Hydroxychloroquine (HCQ) in treating their COVID-19 patients."

Here's what's happening to Prager U per their statement:

- Twitter locked us out of our account.
- Facebook is censoring our reach to our own followers.
- Instagram is removing our posts.
- YouTube and LinkedIn deleted our videos.

Prager U does not give medical advice. But they make sure you hear alternative voices the media either refuses to cover, or falsely discredits, so that you can hear all sides and make your own decisions. If you support free speech, you'll support Prager U and their hundreds of 5-minute videos on the hot issues for the last decade that have been viewed by more than 4 billion viewers and 70 million followers.

Yes, and just as impressive as McDonald's hamburgers served—that's billions and counting, but in 2020 it lost its 2017 suit against Google/YouTube, claiming the platform had violated its First Amendment rights by unlawfully censoring its educational videos and discriminating against its right to freedom of speech. A court ruled in YouTube's favor, saying private companies like YouTube and its parent company Google are not bound by the First Amendment.

The lawsuit cites more than 50 Prager U videos which have either been "restricted" or "demonetized" by Google/YouTube. The Prager U videos range on various subjects presenting a conservative point of view and include a video by noted Harvard Law professor Alan Dershowitz on the founding of Israel. Prager U previously compiled a complete list of their restricted videos here, which includes: "Why America Must Lead," "The Ten Commandments: Do Not Murder," "Why Did America Fight the Korean War," and "The World's Most Persecuted Minority: Christians."

In correspondence cited in the filing, Google/YouTube made it clear that the censorship of certain videos was because they were deemed "inappropriate" for younger audiences.

"Watch any one of our videos and you'll immediately realize that Google/YouTube censorship is entirely ideologically driven. For the record, our videos are presented by some of the finest minds in the Western world, including four Pulitzer Prize winners, former prime ministers, and professors from the most prestigious universities in America," stated Prager U founder Dennis Prager.

Prager added, "They are engaging in an arbitrary and capricious use of their 'restricted mode' and 'demonetization' to restrict non-left political thought. Their censorship is profoundly damaging because Google and YouTube own and control the largest forum for public participation in video-based speech in not only California, but the United States, and the world."

The Total Number of People Who Currently Use YouTube Exceeds 1.3 Billion

Google and YouTube advertise YouTube to the public as a forum intended to defend and protect free speech where members of the general public may express and exchange their ideas. They have represented that their platforms and services are intended to effectuate the exercise of free speech among the public. According to Google and YouTube: "voices matter." YouTube states that it is "committed to fostering a community where everyone's voice can be heard."

"However," said Eric George of Browne George Ross, the firm representing Prager U, "Google and YouTube use restricted mode filtering not to protect younger or sensitive viewers from 'inappropriate' video content, but as a political gag mechanism to silence Prager U. Google and YouTube do this not because they have identified video content that violates their guidelines or is otherwise inappropriate for younger viewers, but because Prager U is a conservative nonprofit organization that is associated with and espouses the views of leading conservative speakers and scholars."

"This is speech discrimination plain and simple, censorship based entirely on unspecified ideological objection to the message or on the perceived identity and political viewpoint of the speaker," said former California Governor Pete Wilson of Browne George Ross. "Google and YouTube's use of restricted mode filtering to silence Prager U violates its fundamental First Amendment rights under both the California and United States Constitutions. It constitutes unlawful discrimination under California law, is a misleading and unfair business practice, and breaches the warranty of good faith and fair dealing implied in Google and YouTube's own Terms of Use and 'Community Guidelines.'"

"There is absolutely nothing 'inappropriate' about the content of the Prager U videos censored by Google and YouTube; the videos do not contain any profanity, nudity or otherwise inappropriate 'mature' content and they fully comply with the letter of YouTube's Terms of Use and Community Guidelines," said Marissa Streit, Prager U's chief executive officer who has engaged in a year-long-effort to try and persuade Google to stop censoring Prager U content. Streit continues, "It's clear that someone doesn't like what we teach and so they intend on stopping us from teaching it. Can you imagine what the world would look like if Google is allowed to continue to arbitrarily censor ideas they simply don't agree with?"

"This is not a left/right issue. It is a free speech issue, which is why prominent liberals, such as Harvard law professor Alan Dershowitz, are supporting our lawsuit," Prager concluded.

The List of 21 Educational Videos From Prager U That YouTube is Restricting

Rachel del Guidice of The Daily Signal put together a quick summary list in October 2016 and here it is for your consideration and judgement. To watch each 5-minute video, follow the link in the Appendix under Prager U:

1. **Are the Police Racist?** This video explores the debate that the police are targeting African American communities.

2. **Why Don't Feminists Fight for Muslim Women?** Why do feminists claim to be champions of women's rights everywhere, but do not fight for women facing oppression in Muslim countries? This video attempts to answer that question.

3. **Why Did America Fight the Korean War?** Due to just slashing its military budget, why did America choose to get involved in this fight?

4. **Who's More Pro-Choice: Europe or America?** This video examines the fact that western Europeans are much more conservative about abortion than American progressives.

5. **What ISIS Wants:** What is the Islamic State? Where did it come from? What does it want? This video examines all these questions and more.

6. **Why Are There Still Palestinian Refugees?** Israel is a nation of refugees, and especially refugees from Arab countries. This video examines why.

7. **Are 1 in 5 Women Raped at College?** According to many gender activists, academics, and politicians, college campuses can be promoters of a "rape culture."

8. **Islamic Terror: What Muslim Americans Can Do:** This video examines how American Muslims can lead a winning fight toward radical Islam.

9. **Did Bush Lie About Iraq?** This video clarifies the belief that President George W. Bush lied his way into the war in Iraq.

10. **Who NOT to Vote For:** Without naming parties or names, this video talks about what one should keep in mind when heading to the ballot box.

11. **Do Not Murder:** Out of all the 10 Commandments, one would think that "do not murder" would be the most self-explanatory of all. Prager U President Dennis Prager examines why this is not the case.

12. **Is America Racist?** This video discusses President Barack Obama's claim that "racism is in our DNA."

13. **Israel: The World's Most Moral Army:** Is the Israeli military "a paragon of morality and wartime ethics" or "an oppressive force that targets innocent Palestinian civilians and commits war crimes as a matter of policy?" Col. Richard Kemp, a commander of British Forces in Afghanistan, answers this question.

14. **Radical Islam: The Most Dangerous Ideology:** In the earlier part of the 20th century, the answer to this question was fascism. Raymond Ibrahim, author of *The Al Qaeda Reader*, examines why the answer to this question today is radical Islam.

15. **The Most Important Question About Abortion:** Dennis Prager, president of Prager U, discusses the most critical question of this debate.

16. **Why Do People Become Islamic Extremists?** This video examines what drives a person to become an Islamic extremist and even a suicide bomber.

17. **Don't Judge Blacks Differently:** How come the election of this nation's first African American president did not usher in a "new era of racial harmony"? This video examines why.

18. **What is the University Diversity Scam?** Are colleges places of "racism, sexism, and homophobia?" This video talks about why some believe this to be college culture today.

19. **He Wants You:** This video discusses the differences between how men and women perceive each other.

20. **Israel's Legal Founding:** When Israel was founded in 1948, it was approved by the United Nations. With this being the case, why do Israel's enemies relentlessly attack this nation's existence?

21. **Pakistan: Can Sharia and Freedom Coexist?** Is it possible for freedom to coexist in a country based on "religious Sharia Islamic law?"

The Bias in Social Media Has Profound Impact on News Consumption

For users, exposure to news stories isn't based on market forces—it's not that these companies provide results precisely tailored to user desires. Information is disseminated to users based on a combination of their history *and* the whims of the companies at issue.

So, for example, Facebook's new news algorithm is explicitly designed to minimize "passively reading articles or watching videos," and instead to maximize "people's well-being," and to encourage "meaningful interactions between people." Mark Zuckerberg wrote, in rather frightening fashion, "There's too much sensationalism, misinformation and polarization in the world today." Thus, he concluded, Facebook should favor content that is "broadly trusted."

How does Facebook determine whether a source is "broadly trusted"? They ask users if they are familiar with a news source and then whether they trust that news source. Presumably, Left-wingers won't trust *National Review*, and right-wingers won't trust the *Huffington Post*—but activists on the left are more common on Facebook than activists on the right, so the Right will be more easily damaged.

Facebook's new algorithmic change also means that stories that generate controversy are disfavored, while those that encourage positive interaction are favored. News with partisan implications is likely to suffer the most—and that's the news people are most interested in. In fighting against the brawl that is daily politics, Facebook is defanging the new media altogether, and handing power back to institutional sources with brand value.

America has become more polarized in many ways. But the rise of the new media is a necessary corrective to the dominance of a thoroughly left-wing "objective" media.

That model was supported, in large measure, by the freedom of social media—and by the freedom of the ad-based model that turned traffic into cash flow. Now that social media are reestablishing themselves as the gatekeepers, they're actually *exacerbating* the news bubble by preventing Democrats from seeing conservative content, and even preventing conservatives from seeing conservative content so long as it's been downvoted by Democrats. All of which means that the ad-based model has started to shrivel for news outlets, encouraging them to turn toward a subscription-based model—where, not surprisingly, legacy media have the upper hand.

The great irony here, of course, is that conservatives aren't the ones threatening to regulate social media—that's the Democrats. Conservatives may be the targets, but they're not the threat.

Nevertheless, the market of ideas will not be quashed so easily. Already, competitors are eyeing the crackdown by social-media companies and sensing an opening. The default Democrats at social-media giants may attempt to choke off the traffic and income valve for those with whom they disagree, but so long as the Internet remains a free market, they're unlikely to succeed in the long term. They're only likely to earn the scorn and ire of a huge percentage of Americans who feel that they're being censored.

8 – Social and Mainstream Media's Anti-Conservative Bias

Credit: The Hill

Conservatives have complained for years about biased treatment on social media, in particular Facebook, too. Things got so bad in 2016, that they sought a meeting with Facebook founder Mark Zuckerberg. In April of 2018, a group of more than 60 conservatives issued a joint demand to Facebook and other social media and search sites that they "rectify their credibility with the conservative movement" by explaining why they sometimes remove innocuous material and delete legitimate accounts.

Among those signing included former Attorney General Edwin Meese and Family Research Council President Tony Perkins.

A study by The Western Journal found: "After Facebook's January algorithm changes, pages associated with members of both major parties saw a significant decrease in interactions with readers, but the Facebook pages of Republican members of the House and Senate were impacted measurably more than those of their Democrat counterparts."

Right-of-center critics have lodged similar complaints about Google's search engine, which seems to favor liberal-left news sites when bringing up the results of a search. In some ways, Google, a pervasive search utility, has less of a defense for its alleged bias than either Facebook or Twitter, which are basically luxury communication apps.

No surprise, the apparent bias has riled up President Trump, who's own 80 million plus Twitter account and is the subject of a movement to have it removed, starting in 2017. When that didn't work, Twitter restricted Trump accounts over 'harmful' virus claim and Facebook used left leaning fact checkers to remove his Facebook campaign ads stating Biden would raise taxes.

Misinformation Has Become Pervasive in the Information Age

It's a paradox. Misinformation has become so pervasive in the information age that some say we're living in a 'post-truth' world. The Oxford Dictionary defines post-truth as "Relating to or denoting circumstances in which objective facts are less influential in shaping public opinion than appeals to emotion and personal belief."

The constant flow of media that is carefully crafted from multibillion-dollar corporate conglomerates has gotten constructing a post-truth world down to a science. Millions of people are mesmerized by an endless amount of information that bombards us constantly; wanting our attention, wanting us to believe something, wanting us to buy something, and wanting us to be something. It's hard to tune it out and think for ourselves sometimes, and it seems that fewer people are even thinking at all.

Thankfully, however, many are waking up to this mass manipulation and have seen the new systems of media production and distribution as they were constructed, and remember what society was like before this information overload engulfed our world. The many victims of fake news are taking a stand like Nick Sandmann.

In January 2020, the cable news network CNN reached a settlement with Nick Sandmann, a Covington Catholic High School student who sued the news outlet for $275 million saying it defamed him over coverage of a viral video that took place in January 2019 when he was filmed with Nathan Phillips, a Native American in Washington D.C. A video shows Sandmann and Phillips standing close to each other in a crowd. Nick stares at Phillips as Phillips plays the drum. The situation unfolded after the March for Life on Jan. 18 which Sandmann and his classmates attended. Phillips was attending the Indigenous Peoples March.

As reported by Julia Fair of the Cincinnati Enquirer in August 2020, the Sandmann lawsuit against CNN stated: "CNN brought down the full force of its corporate power, influence, and wealth on Nicholas by falsely attacking, vilifying, and bullying him despite the fact that he was a minor child."

In January 2020, CNN settled for an undisclosed account and so did the *Washington Post* in July 2020. More lawsuits like this one might be filed but most never see a courtroom because the odds of winning are seen as insurmountable due to the financial resources mainstream and social media have to squash, or in this rare case, settle. A David versus a Goliath scenario is extremely intimidating.

Influencing People Instead of Informing Them

Owners of major media companies see the power their empires hold and often choose to use their outlets to influence people instead of informing them. From activist journalists to senior editors to CEOs, many in the big media companies can't help but impose their personal political ideology on the world by using the infrastructure they have at their disposal.

By building mountains out of molehills, through lying by omission, agenda-setting, framing stories and issues in a certain light, and by manipulating what is spread through social media by either limiting its reach or artificially amplifying it—the major media and tech companies influence the way people think and tell us how to act.

The shift from print journalism to websites and Facebook pages doesn't just pose a danger to the distribution and verification of news, but it also puts our historical records at risk as well.

Headlines and articles can now be changed without notice and information can vanish down a memory hole with little to no trace of its existence. With digital forgeries getting more sophisticated, how will we be able to verify that a document is actually authentic, especially if there are no physical documents anymore? Most people don't backup their own files locally anymore on external hard drives, and instead rely on cloud services. Many people don't even own software anymore, and instead pay monthly subscription fees for applications like Photoshop, Microsoft Office, and others.

Paperback books and magazines have become less and less popular since the creation of e-books and tablets, opening the door to dangers of remote deletion, alteration, or even device failure if an iPad or Kindle is dropped and breaks. Someone even gave a Ted Talk claiming that paper dictionaries aren't needed any more since they're too old fashioned, which is a dangerous road to go down. Society is on a strange course, making us more vulnerable to fake news, not less, and many question whether there is even a solution at all.

Is There a Cure for Fake News?

Microsoft's social media researcher Danah Boyd said, "No amount of 'fixing' Facebook or Google will address the underlying factors shaping the culture and information wars in which America is currently enmeshed." She continues, "The short version of it all is that we have a cultural problem, one that is shaped by disconnects in values, relationships, and social fabric. Our media, our tools, and our politics are being leveraged to help breed polarization by countless actors who can leverage these systems for personal, economic, and ideological gain."

As a clear and present danger of this phenomena, in 2016 the fake news media narrative was more an unequivocal declaration: Donald Trump must not win. As well all know, he did, and the overwhelming main stream media (MSM) predicted he would lose. And lose big! How could they get it so wrong? And how could one man be the number one obsession and enemy of fake news? Most of the rest of this chapter's content is from the 2019 best seller by L. Brent Bozell and Tim Graham titled *Unmasked* and it explains why in detail below:

Journalists are the smartest people in the room, so smart that they can't possibly be expected to just report the news. Thus, they grant themselves license to package it and analyze it with an intelligence only they seem to possess. They profess to believe in the power of facts, but what they really believe in is their power to proclaim facts. Facts exist to be bent to their will to further their narrative and agenda.

For those reasons, it was clear from the start that Donald Trump was itching for a fight with the media. He was going to put the entire profession on trial in the court of public opinion, and he did that by introducing two words that became part of the political lexicon: "fake news." The media were aghast that they would be so rudely challenged and dismissed as such.

Perhaps they had a point. It was certainly unfair to paint an entire institution with this broad, ugly brush. But when Trump unmasked one truly fake news story after another, the self-righteous press met the evidence with stony silence. The institution was guilty of aiding and abetting fake news. It still is.

Conservative POV Censorship vs. Social Media Companies' Pro-Liberal Bias

From the Media Research Center's guidebook, *CENSORED! How Online Media Companies Are Suppressing Conservative Speech*, like it or not, social media is the communication form of the future—not just in the U.S., but worldwide. Just Facebook and Twitter combined reach 1.8 billion people. More than two-thirds of all Americans (68 percent) use Facebook. YouTube is pushing out TV as the most popular place to watch video. Google is the No. 1 search engine in both the U.S. and the world.

War is being declared on the conservative movement in this space and conservatives are losing—badly. If the right is silenced, billions of people will be cut off from conservative ideas and conservative media.

It's the new battleground of media bias. But it's worse. That bias is not a war of ideas. It's a war against ideas. It's a clear effort to censor the conservative worldview from the public conversation.

The Media Research Center has undertaken an extensive study of the problem at major tech companies—Twitter, Facebook, Google and YouTube—and the results are far more troubling than most conservatives realize. Here are some of the key findings:

Twitter Leads in Censorship:

Project Veritas recently caught Twitter staffers admitting on hidden camera that they had been censoring conservatives through a technique known as shadow banning, where users think their content is getting seen widely, but it's not. The staffers had justified it by claiming the accounts had been automated if they had words such as "America" and "God." In 2016, Twitter had attempted to manipulate election-related tweets using the hashtags "PodestaEmails" and "#DNCLeak." The site also restricts pro-life ads from Live Action and even Rep. Marsha Blackburn (R-Tenn.), but allows Planned Parenthood advertisements.

Facebook's Trending Feed Has Been Hiding Conservative Topics:

A 2016 Gizmodo story had warned of Facebook's bias. It had detailed claims by former employees that Facebook's news curators had been instructed to hide conservative content from the "trending" section, which supposedly only features news users find compelling. Topics that had been blacklisted included Mitt Romney, the Conservative Political Action Conference (CPAC) and Rand Paul. On the other hand, the term "Black Lives Matter" had also been placed into the trending section even though it was not actually trending. Facebook had also banned at least one far-right European organization but had not released information on any specific statements made by the group that warranted the ban.

Google Search Aids Democrats:

Google and YouTube's corporate chairman Eric Schmidt had assisted Hillary Clinton's presidential campaign. The company's search engine had deployed a similar bias in favor of Democrats. One study had found 2016 campaign searches were biased in favor of Hillary Clinton. Even the liberal website Slate had revealed the search engine's results had favored both Clinton and Democratic candidates. Google also had fired engineer James Damore for criticizing the company's "Ideological Echo Chamber." The company had claimed he had been fired for "advancing harmful gender stereotypes in our workplace." Damore is suing Google, saying it mistreats whites, males and conservatives.

YouTube Is Shutting Down Conservative Videos:

Google's YouTube site had created its own problems with conservative content. YouTube moderators must take their cues from the rest of Google—from shutting down entire conservative channels "by mistake" to removing videos that promote right-wing political views. YouTube's special Creators for Change section is devoted to people using their "voices for social change" and even highlights the work of a 9/11 truther. The site's very own YouTube page and Twitter account celebrate progressive attitudes, including uploading videos about "inspiring" gay and trans people and sharing the platform's support for DACA.

Tech Firms Are Relying on Groups That Hate Conservatives:

Top tech firms like Google, YouTube and Twitter partner with leftist groups attempting to censor conservatives. These include the Southern Poverty Law Center (SPLC) and the Anti-Defamation League (ADL). Both groups claim to combat "hate," but treat standard conservative beliefs in faith and family as examples of that hatred. George Soros funded ProPublica is using information from both radical leftist organizations to attack conservative groups such as Jihad Watch and ACT for America, bullying PayPal and other services to shut down their funding sources. The SPLC's "anti-LGBT" list had also been used to prevent organizations from partnering with AmazonSmile to raise funds.

Liberal Twitter Advisors Outnumber Conservatives 12-to-1:

Twelve of the 25 U.S. members of Twitter's Trust and Safety Council—which helps guide its policies—are liberal, and only one is conservative. Anti-conservative groups like GLAAD and the ADL are part of the board. There is no well-known conservative group represented.

Tech Companies Rely on Anti-Conservative Fact-Checkers:

Facebook and Google both had partnered with fact-checking organizations in order to combat "fake news." Facebook's short-lived disputed flagger program had allowed Snopes, PolitiFact and ABC News to discern what is and is not real news. Google's fact-checkers had accused conservative sources of making claims that did not appear in their articles and disproportionately "fact-checked" conservative sources. On Facebook, a satire site, the Babylon Bee, had been flagged by Snopes for its article clearly mocking CNN for its bias. YouTube also had announced a partnership with Wikipedia in order to debunk videos deemed to be conspiracy theories, even though Wikipedia has been criticized for its liberal bias.

How 'Social Media' Became 'Anti-Social Media'

Quoting directly from the *Investor's Business Daily* article "How 'Social Media' Became 'Anti-Social Media': Twitter's and Facebook's Reckoning" article in July 2017: Twitter might soon have the government breathing down its neck for "shadow-banning" conservatives, while Facebook's market value has plunged more than $130 billion in just two days back then as the once-dominant social media site's growth goes flat amid charges of bias. Is this the beginning of the end of the social media boom?

A report by Vice Media, which can hardly be considered right of center, found that Twitter appeared to suppress certain accounts of conservative groups, individuals, and politicians.

As previously mentioned, it's called "shadow banning," in which Twitter engages in subtle blocking of conservative accounts on the site's search function. It amounts to making one side of the political debate—mainly, conservatives and libertarians—far less visible in searches than the liberal and progressive side.

The report said: "The Republican Party chair Ronna McDaniel, several conservative Republican congressmen, and Donald Trump Jr.'s spokesman no longer appear in the auto-populated drop-down search box on Twitter, Vice News has learned. It's a shift that diminishes their reach on the platform—and it's the same one being deployed against prominent racists to limit their visibility."

None of the above are racists and for those who state otherwise—please *prove* it.

Meanwhile, "Democrats are not being 'shadow banned' in the same way," the report said. "Not a single member of the 78-person Progressive Caucus faces the same situation in Twitter's search." In other words, once again a progressive-dominated tech-site biases its service towards the left-side of the political spectrum to the detriment of the conservative-libertarian right. It's not just Twitter, of course. Facebook is having problems now for the same reason: It treats Republicans and conservatives differently than Democrats and leftists on its site.

Of course, conservatives don't have to have Facebook or Twitter accounts. But then, if those two social media define themselves as politically oriented sites, the rules change somewhat.

That may be what Florida Republican Rep. Matt Gaetz was getting at as he was one of a number of well-known mainstream Republicans, including several other members of Congress and even the chair of the Republican National Committee, who had their accounts obscured by Twitter.

Section 230 of the Communications Decency Act

In response to those social media developments, Trump tweeted out: "Twitter shadow banning prominent Republicans. Not good. We will look into this discriminatory and illegal practice at once! Many complaints."

While the dangers of Trump's "war on the press" have been exaggerated—no matter how much he'd like to silence "fake news CNN" or the "failing *New York Times*," the courts won't suspend the First Amendment to please him—there is a danger of the federal government stifling speech on social media.

In the order, Trump asks government agencies to reinterpret the law in a way that would allow them to penalize companies for content decisions they deem politically biased. He has also threatened to push Congress to pass legislation to amend or revoke Section 230, a potentially existential threat to the companies' business models.

Per Trump, "I'm signing an Executive Order to protect and uphold the free speech and rights of the American people. Currently, social media giants like Twitter receive an unprecedented liability shield based on the theory that they are a neutral platform, which they are not."

This obvious anti-conservative bias is not healthy, not for our democracy or for the companies involved. Google, YouTube, Facebook, and Twitter should expect more trouble ahead. The SAPIENT Being's WOWW Program members have the opportunity to document and report on hundreds, perhaps thousands more anti-conservative bias incidences throughout social media. The sky (the cloud) is the limit!

That's especially true from those who feel "shadow-banned" or deceptively excluded from social media for expressing mainstream conservative political beliefs, while unhinged leftist critics on the same media routinely call their right-of-center foes "Hitler," "racist," "fascist," and even worse with impunity and zero facts to substantiate their claims.

It's time for the techie progressives that run the social media companies to clean up their act. If they don't, they face inevitable decline as a force in American culture. America's traditions of free speech, open debate and the marketplace of ideas deserve respect. Rank political bias against conservatives, libertarians and the Republican Party is not acceptable.

From Roger L. Simon's article in *The Epoch Times* in May 2020 titled "Twitter as Prototype of the New High-Tech Totalitarianism:" Trump is obviously using his bully pulpit to convince Twitter to play fair, to be an unbiased open forum as the Communications Decency Act envisioned. If they don't, he's threatened to shut them down. Neither is likely to happen.

Ultimately, this is a job for Congress to address. They should, and with considerable alacrity.

This censorship is often blamed on social media companies' progressive bias, which may well exist, but it's due at least in part simply to the greater external pressure from progressive activists and journalists. If progressives keep trying to de-platform their opponents—and if Twitter and Facebook and YouTube keep caving to the pressure—there'll be more bipartisan enthusiasm to restrict all speech on social media.

The *CJR* Blacklisting of So Called "Hate Mongers" and "Toxic Ideas"

As previously noted in Chapter 3 where John Tierney explains in his November 2019 *City Journal* article "Journalists Against Free Speech"—free speech should be of special interest to the *Columbia Journalism Review (CJR)*, which calls itself "the leading global voice on journalism news and commentary."

However, *CJR* sees the issue through a progressive filter. It not only criticized *The New York Review of Books* and *Harper's* for publishing articles by journalists fired for sexual harassment but also essentially advocated a blacklist: "The men who feel they have been unfairly treated following accusations of harassment or abuse are entitled to their perspective, but nothing demands that editors turn over the pages of their publications to these figures."

CJR applauded Facebook, Twitter, and YouTube for "stemming the flow of toxic ideas" by banning "hate-mongers like Milo Yiannopoulos and Alex Jones."

After the violence at Berkeley and Middlebury, *CJR* urged reporters covering campus unrest to "be wary of amplifying flashpoints that match Trump's own 'intolerant left' narrative," and it has been following its own advice.

CJR showed little interest in Antifa's censorious tactics until prompted recently by Quillette, the online magazine devoted to "dangerous ideas," which has run articles by journalists and academics on the culture wars over free speech.

Eoin Lenihan, a researcher in online extremism, reported in May 2019 on an analysis of the Twitter users who interact most heavily with Antifa sites. Most turned out to be journalists, including writers for the *Guardian*, the *New Republic*, and HuffPost as well for pro-Antifa publications.

Following a group closely on Twitter, of course, doesn't mean that one endorses its activity; journalists do need to track the subjects they cover. But these journalists seemed more devoted to promoting the cause than covering it impartially. "Of all 15 verified national-level journalists in our subset, we couldn't find a single article, by any of them, that was markedly critical of Antifa in any way," Lenihan wrote. "In all cases, their work in this area consisted primarily of downplaying Antifa violence while advancing Antifa talking points, and in some cases quoting Antifa extremists as if they were impartial experts."

CJR responded to Lenihan's article—but not by analyzing the press coverage of Antifa. Instead, it ran an article, "Right-Wing Publications Launder an Anti-Journalist Smear Campaign," by Jared Holt of Right-Wing Watch, a project of the liberal advocacy group People for the American Way.

Holt's article was a mix of ad hominem attacks, irrelevancies, and inaccuracies. Cathy Young, who wrote about the controversy for Arc Digital, concluded that every key point in his argument was wrong. Even worse was what Holt omitted. He didn't even address Lenihan's main conclusion: that press coverage of Antifa was biased—the issue that should have been most relevant to a journalism review.

Fake News Media Are Using Advertising Boycotts Unsapiently

Journalists have traditionally prided themselves on their independence from advertisers. Now the boycotters want to end that independence. If advertisers start being held accountable for content, their aversion to controversy will put pressure on media companies to churn out bland fare that won't risk offending anyone. "It's easy to imagine today's boycotts turning into tomorrow's blacklist," wrote Jack Shafer.

Instead of worrying about this threat to their autonomy, journalists at progressive and mainstream publications have promoted it. Activists announce boycotts regularly, but these rarely make an impact unless they get widespread public attention.

Sleeping Giants, an activist group leading the boycotts, has gotten lots of publicity (and web traffic) from largely uncritical articles heralding its leaders' pure motives. Margaret Sullivan, the *Washington Post*'s media columnist, acknowledged that there might be a problem if boycotters aimed at a provocative outlet like Gawker—a left-leaning site that meets her approval—but she couldn't bring herself to condemn the tactic. Quite the reverse: "To those who sympathize with Sleeping Giants' objections to online racism, sexism and hate-mongering—count me in this number—their efforts seem worthwhile, sometimes even noble."

Other journalists have explicitly endorsed the Tucker Carlson boycott, including Kevin Drum of *Mother Jones*, and Michelangelo Signorile of HuffPost. Some have even pitched in to pressure the advertisers directly. Jenna Amatulli, a reporter at HuffPost, published a list of the show's advertisers, complete with links to their contact information, and wrote that she had "reached out" for statements from each company—meaning, in effect, that she had personally threatened them with bad publicity.

No one wants to be named in a story accusing an advertiser of supporting "racism," "white nationalism," and "misogyny." Carlson's alleged sins were reported as established facts in HuffPost articles.

One Media Matters researcher, heroically profiled in the *Washington Post*, spent ten hours a day listening to recordings from 2006 to 2011 of Fox News Tucker Carlson's conversations with Bubba the Love Sponge, a shock-jock radio host. Media Matters published some of Carlson's cruder comments and followed up with new ones on subsequent days to keep the story alive and provide ammunition for activists demanding that corporations stop advertising on Carlson's Fox News show. The campaign succeeded in pressuring advertisers like Land Rover and IHOP to abandon the program, which runs fewer commercials than it did the previous year.

It's easy to see why progressive activists have made advertising boycotts one of their chief weapons against Fox, *Breitbart*, and other conservative outlets. What's harder to fathom is why so many journalists have cheered a tactic that's bad for their profession.

This kind of boycott is different from the traditional ones against companies accused of bad behavior like mistreating their workers or polluting the environment. In this case, companies are targeted not for the way they run their businesses but simply for advertising their wares. Jack Shafer, the longtime media critic, has been a lonely libertarian voice warning of the threat that this poses to journalism and public discourse. "I barely trust IHOP to make my breakfast," he wrote in *Politico*. "Why would I expect it to vet my cable news content for me?"

Bozell's Top 10 Anti-Trump Media Personalities

Who are the biggest Trump bashers in the press? When you consider that his coverage is regularly in the 90 percent negative range, you can conclude that just about everyone in the media qualifies except for conservative periodicals and radio talk shows, Internet and blog sites, and television outlets. Yet even on these platforms you'll find Never Trumper candidates. That includes the inaccurately pigeonholed Fox News.

For quality, it's just as daunting a proposition. How can you distinguish one ranting journalist from the next? The field looks a little like the beginning of the Boston Marathon, with a cast of thousands, all eager to burst to the front of the pack, elbowing aside the competition with that story (true or not, who cares) or, better yet, that sound bite (ditto) that will generate fist pumps and lazy copycatting from leftist agitators everywhere.

Yet amid the rabble there are some real standouts. This list is subjective, of course, but reflects what we believe and what our colleagues have suggested are those whose minds go into spontaneous combustion mode at the mere thought of Donald Trump as their commander in chief. Some of these so-called journalists are so left wing that they could stand on either side of the podium during a Nancy Pelosi-led press conference. It's not just those in the news business. This list begins with those who are meant to entertain with humor but cannot help frothing at the mouth instead.

1. Jim Acosta, CNN
2. Joe Scarborough & Mika Brzezinski, MSNBC
3. George Stephanopoulos, ABC
4. Every late-night talk-show host (except Jay Leno)
5. Chris Cuomo, CNN
6. Chris Matthews, MSNBC
7. Philip Rucker, *WAPO*
8. Jorge Ramos, Univision
9. Brian Stelter, CNN
10. Brian Williams, MSNBC

9 – 33 Examples of Twitter's Anti Conservative Bias

Credit: kusi.com "Jack Dorsey testifies regarding Section 230 of the Communications Decency Act."

President Donald Trump is right that social media companies have been targeting conservatives. Twitter, in particular, has been engaging in a relentless attack on the American political process by censoring conservatives. The social media giants have been shielded from such liability by Section 230 of the Communications Decency Act of 1996, legislation enacted in the salad days of the internet, when few anticipated how these companies would evolve into global monopolies and concerns were different.

Most recently, in May 2020, Twitter escalated its battle with President Trump by starting to fact check Trump's tweets nearly five months from a presidential election. Trump responded to Twitter's rulings by signing an executive order on May 28, 2020 that targets a law at the heart of the internet industry: Section 230 of the Communications Decency Act.

The Media Research Center released a report in 2018, which found that Twitter led in censoring the right. That hasn't changed. Project Veritas caught Twitter with hidden camera interviews admitting the process of shadow banning—which means content is hidden from users without the poster ever knowing it.

As previously noted, one engineer admitted that accounts were flagged as bots simply by searching for words such as "America" and "God." Twitter's rules have been influenced by liberal think tanks like the Anti-Defamation League and the Southern Poverty Law Center. Since then, Twitter has gotten worse and below are 33 examples of their high-tech totalitarianism courtesy of MRC's NewsBusters.

Twitter is the Prototype of High-Tech Totalitarianism

Abroad, China is the poster child for extreme total tech programs. By 2020, China's "social credit system" will monitor the behavior of each and every citizen, keeping tabs on everything from speeding tickets to social media posts critical of the state. Everyone will then be assigned their own unique "sincerity score;" a high score will be a requirement for anyone hoping to get the best housing, install the fastest Internet speeds, put their kids into the most prestigious schools, and land the most lucrative jobs.

Let that sink in as we begin to see in its earliest stages the beginnings of an American "social credit system" version courtesy of Big Tech.

1. Fact-Checking Trump's Tweets

A tweet from the president that discussed mail-in ballots was labeled as an "unsubstantiated claim" by Twitter. When Trump tweeted, "There is NO WAY (ZERO!) that Mail-In Ballots will be anything less than substantially fraudulent," a bright blue sentence was added by the social media platform at the bottom of the tweet. The link said, "Get the facts about mail-in ballots." The label led to a Twitter Events page, which said, "Trump makes unsubstantiated claim that mail-in ballots will lead to voter fraud."

The statement continued, "These claims are unsubstantiated, according to CNN, *Washington Post* and others. Experts say mail-in ballots are very rarely linked to voter fraud."

"From their bogus 'fact check' of @realDonaldTrump to their 'head of site integrity' displaying his clear hatred towards Republicans, Twitter's blatant bias has gone too far," tweeted Republican National Committee Chair Ronna McDaniel.

2. Censorship of Pro-Life Team Trump Videos

Twitter's warning and interstitial, or filter, used to keep viewers from unknowingly seeing inappropriate videos was applied to a Trump campaign pro-life promo. Following Trump's speech at the March for Life, his pro-life campaign video appeared to have been given an erroneous label/restriction by Twitter. The label was removed soon after Twitter admitted the error.

3. No Enforcement of Policy for Democrats

The bias against Trump has become so egregious that even *The Hill* and *The Washington Post* are calling it out. "According to emails reviewed by *The Hill*, the Trump campaign flagged new content on Twitter that it said had been deceptively edited," *The Hill*'s Jonathan Easly wrote March 16, 2020. One video in question was shared by Mike Bloomberg's former senior adviser Tim O'Brien and featured audio clips of Trump's words spliced together and taken out of context, set to a rising graph showing "Confirmed Coronavirus Cases in US." Former Vice President Joe Biden tweeted a video with similar language.

Even *The Post*'s video editor for The Fact Checker Meg Kelly wrote that Trump "never says that the virus itself is a hoax, and although the Biden camp included the word 'their,' the edit does not make clear to whom or what Trump is referring."

4. Labeling Simple Photos of Trump as "Sensitive Content"

NASCAR star Hailie Deegan posed for a picture with President Trump and First Lady Melania Trump at the Daytona 500. After she posted it to Twitter, some of her followers noted that the photo was covered by Twitter's "sensitive content" filter. Memer and influencer Carpe Donktum (known for his memes that have been retweeted by Trump) tweeted a screenshot of Deegan's post as it appeared on his feed.

5. Removing Trump's Twitter Account

President Trump's personal Twitter account had disappeared in 2017 and was nowhere to be found until it was restored 11 minutes later. The account reappeared without explanation until Twitter's official electoral and government relations account provided a bizarre explanation that it was "due to human error by a Twitter employee."

How Twitter Has Treated Other Conservatives:

6. Preventing a Pro-Life Election Ad

Before Twitter banned all political ads, it blocked a campaign ad by Rep. Marsha Blackburn (R-TN) for addressing the "sale" of aborted baby parts in the name of research. While she was allowed to tweet the ad, Twitter prohibited her from paying to promote the ad to a larger audience.

In the ad, Rep. Blackburn announced that she was running for U.S. Senate. To appeal to her conservative constituents, she cited her work fighting abortion.

7. Senator Mitch McConnell's Campaign Video

It should come as no surprise that the official campaign Twitter account for Sen. Mitch McConnell (R-KY) was suspended for sharing a video of the violent threats being made against the senator. Multiple people on Twitter were also suspended for sharing that video, including the Daily Wire's Ryan Saavedra. Twitter eventually overturned this decision but only after numerous complaints.

8. Candace Owens Censored

Conservative commentator Candace Owens had her Twitter account suspended for encouraging Americans to defy stay-at-home rules. A Twitter spokesperson said that Owens's tweet response to Democrat Michigan Gov. Gretchen Whitmer's stay-at-home policies encouraging the citizens of Michigan to "stand up" against Whitmer "violated the platform's COVID-19 misinformation policy, 'specifically around heightened-risk health claims,'" reported *The Hill*. Owens's tweet encouraged Michiganders to "Open your businesses" and "go to work."

9. Trump's Attorney Censored

Trump's attorney Rudy Giuliani's tweet said, "Hydroxychloroquine has been shown to have a 100% effective rate treating COVID-19. Yet Democrat Michigan Governor Gretchen Whitmer is threatening doctors who prescribe it. If Trump is for something- Democrats are against it. They're okay with people dying if it means opposing Trump." His tweet was in response to Whitmer, who challenged Trump in a press conference on March 26, 2020.

10. Turning Point Founder Charlie Kirk Censored

Turning Point USA founder Charlie Kirk tweeted a similar sentiment. He said, "Fact: Hydroxychloroquine has been shown to have a 100% effective rate treating COVID-19. Yet Democrat Gretchen Whitmer is threatening doctors who prescribe it. If Trump is for something—Democrats are against it. They're ok with people dying if it means opposing Trump. SICK!"

A Twitter spokesperson confirmed that both Guiliani's and Kirk's accounts were temporarily locked for violations of the Twitter rules in reference to COVID-19.

11. Fox News Host Laura Ingraham Censored

Fox News host Laura Ingraham (@IngrahamAngle) tweeted: "Lenox Hill in New York among many hospitals already using Hydroxychloroquine with very promising results. One patient was described as 'Lazarus' who was seriously ill from Covid-19, already released." After the liberal media demanded the tweet's removal, a Twitter spokesperson explained that the tweet was removed due to a violation of its new policy regarding tweeting about COVID-19.

12. Conservative Journalist Censored

New York Post journalist Jon Levine announced via tweet that "Twitter locked me out of my account last night over some of the Carlos Maza reporting," before adding that the platform later took back the decision. "A rep for the company tells me that their action against me was 'an error.'" But then Levine was suspended again almost immediately afterward, for the same tweets made about the former Vox reporter.

13. Conservative Actor and Trump Supporter Censored

Actor James Woods, noted for his conservative Twitter account, was locked out of Twitter more than once. Most recently he was suspended for sharing a picture of former Democratic gubernatorial candidate Andrew Gillum. Woods had initially tweeted, "Just remember, this could have been Florida's governor in the midst of the #WuhanCoronaVirus pandemic. Make sure you vote #Republican in November like your life depends on it. Because it does. #Trump2020Landslide."

14. Conservative Sites Locked Out

LifeSiteNews has been locked out of Twitter for "violating" its "rules" after tweeting an article about Jonathan "Jessica" Yaniv, a transgender activist who recently complained that gynecologists wouldn't see Yaniv as a patient, despite having male genitals.

15. Another Site Banned For "Platform Manipulation" Violations

The ZeroHedge founder reportedly, under the pseudonym Tyler Durden, asked, "Is This The Man Behind The Global Coronavirus Pandemic?" and theorized about the coronavirus's true origins. ZeroHedge was then suspended from Twitter. *Forbes* claimed that a spokesperson from Twitter indicated that "ZeroHedge was removed for violating its platform manipulation policy, which the social media giant describes as 'using Twitter to engage in bulk, aggressive or deceptive activity that misleads others and/or disrupts their experience.'" However, *The Daily Mail* cited a resurfaced research paper from the South China University of Technology, which may lend some credence to ZeroHedge's initial reporting.

ZeroHedge's Durden said that he was suspended from Twitter after Buzzfeed claimed that his blog had doxed a Chinese scientist whom Durden argues was a "public figure."

16. Failure to Enforce Consistently

Citing instances that "violate our abusive behavior policy," Twitter Safety announced that "Today, we permanently suspended Alex Jones and InfoWars from Twitter and Periscope." Not only was it enough to take down those accounts, but also, Twitter threatened to "take action" on "other accounts potentially associated with Alex Jones or InfoWars" if those accounts were "utilized in an attempt to circumvent their ban."

Meanwhile, comedian Kathy Griffin recently tweeted about assassinating the president, saying, "Syringe with nothing but air inside it would do the trick. F— TRUMP." Griffin also famously held up a bloody head that resembled Trump. She's still on the platform! Surprised?

17. Criticism of Bernie Sanders is "Sensitive Content"

A video posted by MRCTV, an arm of the Media Research Center, was censored as "sensitive content" by Twitter. "You may recall way back in 1961 they invaded Cuba, and everybody was totally convinced that Castro was the worst guy in the world," said Democratic presidential candidate Sen. Bernie Sanders (I-VT), at the beginning of the video. The clip was from an interview in the 1980s where Sanders defended Castro. It was contrasted with a news clip from CBS that showed people in the streets celebrating after Fidel Castro died in 2016.

18. 113 Prominent Conservatives Censored Between 2015-2019

Between 2015 and 2019, there have been at least 113 different cases of conservative, pro-Trump or anti-establishment figures on Twitter being punished for expressing their views, many of them well-known in their fields. Notable people have been suspended, banned, blocked from advertising, shadowbanned, and censored. While Twitter CEO Jack Dorsey testified in Congress in September 2020 that "Twitter does not use political ideology to make decisions," the evidence points in the opposite direction.

How Twitter Defends the Left:

19. Protecting Joe Biden

A meme, made to look like a fake ad from former Vice President Joe Biden's campaign, showed the candidate smiling with a beam of light coming from his chest. A statement that says, "His brain? No. His heart," sits to the left of the person. Trump's director of communications Tim Murtaugh allegedly tweeted the image, saying, "Is this fake? Can't trust Twitter, but this would seem to be the Biden campaign leaning in on the fact that ol' Joe has lost his fastball."

Murtaugh's tweet was removed, said tech magazine The Verge. At least 20 other accounts were allegedly suspended or had tweets allegedly removed, including actress and congressional candidate Mindy Robinson.

20. Promoting Liberal Values

Twitter CEO Jack Dorsey has been consistent in his left-wing political positions. "Dorsey, the billionaire CEO of Twitter and mobile-payment company Square, is giving $5 million to Humanity Forward" in order to "build the case for a universal basic income (UBI)," *Rolling Stone* reported.

Dorsey appeared on the May 21 episode of former presidential candidate Andrew Yang's "Yang Speaks" podcast where he explained the idea of UBI is "long overdue" and that now "the only way we can change policy is by experimenting and showing case studies of why this works."

21. Protecting Alexandria Ocasio-Cortez

An account that parodied Rep. Alexandria Ocasio-Cortez (D-NY) was suspended. The user, named Alexandria Ocasio Cortez Press Release, was "permanently suspended" because it was too similar to the congressional representative's account. According to the *Washington Examiner*, the man running the account, Michael Morrison, received an email explaining his permanent suspension and ominously saying, "This account will not be reinstated." Dorsey has expressed his support for the young Democratic Socialist in Congress previously.

22. Working With Planned Parenthood

David Daleiden, the undercover journalist for the Center for Medical Progress, reported that the organization had 19 tweets blocked on Twitter, at the advice of Planned Parenthood. The tweets that were blocked reported on the public testimony of Planned Parenthood in court proceedings. Planned Parenthood's attorneys told Twitter that the Center was live streaming the hearing. Twitter reinstated the tweets after the appeal explained that Planned Parenthood had falsely described the tweets as a "live-stream."

23. Preventing Discussion About Transgender Ideology

Twitter made it a rule that "misgendering or deadnaming of transgender individuals" was prohibited on its platform in 2018. Several people, including journalist Meghan Murphy, were banned, suspended, or blocked from the platform for statements like "Women aren't men." Dr. Ray Blanchard, who helped write the official psychological position on transgender identity, was temporarily blocked on May 12 for voicing his professional beliefs.

24. Protecting Former Rep. Katie Hill

The Daily Mail took a story that Red State's Jennifer Van Laar first broke about Rep. Katie Hill (D-CA) and ran it with a link in the story that led to graphic images of the politician with one of her staffers. Twitter then allegedly blocked the *Daily Mail*'s story, claiming, according to the Daily Wire's Ryan Saavedra, that "this link may be unsafe."

25. Protecting Liberal Journalists From "Learn to Code"

New York Post reporter Jon Levine alleged that some users were banned from Twitter for mocking recently laid-off journalists from liberal outlets Buzzfeed and HuffPost. Left-wing journalists once told working-class Americans to "learn to code" and adapt to a globalized economy. But now the shoe appears to be on the other foot, as some users tweeted the phrase "learn to code" at journalists who recently lost their jobs. The phrase was a response to journalists who told unemployed coal miners to switch their careers to tech, but journalists didn't like it when it was used back on them. Some users reported a Twitter claim that users were banned for tweeting this phrase at journalists under the terms of service rules against "targeted harassment," according to KnowYourMeme.

What Twitter Has Failed to Enforce:

26. Violence and Doxxing From Antifa

Smash Racism DC, a branch of Antifa, attacked Fox News host Tucker Carlson's house, reportedly threatened his wife, and doxed Carlson and his family on Twitter.

Twitter did not listen to Fox News' call for the doxxing tweets to be removed immediately. While the original Twitter posts no longer exist, the *National Review*'s Jack Crowe managed to document their contents. "Tucker Carlson has been spewing nonstop hate and lies about the migrant caravan. He also has close ties to white supremacists," one tweet said. "Activists protested tonight at Carlson's Washington DC area home. You can't hide from those you hurt, Tucker. #KnockKnockTucker"

"Racist scumbag, leave town," another tweet exclaimed.

27. Calls for Violence Against Children

A fake news story falsely accused Covington Catholic High School students (namely Nick Sandmann) of harassing a Native American activist. It outraged the internet since the video was later shown to edit out much of the encounter. The story was later corrected by some outlets, but the damage had been done. Twitter did not take down many of the threats or calls for violence against the students.

28. Chinese Propaganda and Misinformation

Twitter restrictions based on its COVID-19 rules haven't been handled in a consistent manner. The Chinese Embassy in France uploaded an absurd, lego-based propaganda video on April 30. The Ambassade de Chine en France's video "Once Upon a Virus…" featured numerous demonstrably untrue myths, acting as if the Chinese communist government and World Health Organization ("WHO") have both been forthcoming about the nature of the COVID-19 pandemic.

It wasn't fact-checked or removed.

The video featured a back-and-forth dialogue between several lego figurines and gave a false chronology of what happened from month to month. A masked lego figurine representing the Chinese regime as a responsible leader amidst the coronavirus appeared to be the foil to the ignorant and irresponsible Statue of Liberty LEGO figurine that represented America. The Statue of Liberty figurine's flaming torch curiously resembled Trump's signature hairstyle.

29. Terrorist Recruiter's Video

A video tweeted out by a pro-Palestine account, depicted a terrorist shooting up an Israeli shopping mall. The cartoon depicted a young man watching a security guard at an Israeli mall. The flag of Israel was perched atop the building. Disguised as a security guard, the young man sits on a bench across from the Israeli mall and waits. He then walks up, kills the security guard with his own club, and runs into the mall, shooting at shoppers. The video then ends with a focus on Arabic script, which in English translates to "The Intifada is continuing."

30. Anti-Hong Kong Protester Propaganda

Pinboard, the social bookmarking website run by developer Maciej Cegłowski, captured ads on Twitter from China Xinhua News which called for "a brake to be put on the blatant violence" in Hong Kong. The Twitter account for Pinboard noted "Xinhua, the agency buying these tweets, has literally referred to the Hong Kong protesters as 'cockroaches.'"

31. Noted Anti-Semite Rev. Louis Farrakhan

Noted anti-Semite Rev. Louis Farrakhan is still on Twitter and not fact checked. Reclaim The Net observed that Farrakhan, the controversial leader of the Nation of Islam, was "temporarily kicked off of Twitter." He was also "temporarily restricted" from Twitter when his account was completely booted. Shortly thereafter, however, his account was reinstated, and a Twitter spokesperson reportedly told Reclaim The Net that "The account was caught by our spam filter in error and has been reinstated."

32. China's Accusations Against the U.S. Go Unchecked

Twitter allegedly censored ZeroHedge for theorizing about the origin of the coronavirus, citing Twitter's Platform Manipulation policy, but since allowed what Buzzfeed called "Conspiracy Theories That The Coronavirus Didn't Originate In China" to remain online. Spokesperson & Deputy Director General, Information Department, Foreign Ministry of China Lijian Zhao tweeted a piece headlined "COVID-19: Further Evidence that the Virus Originated in the US". Later that day he speculated, "It might be US army who brought the epidemic to Wuhan."

2020 Election Censorship Insanity:

33. Twitter Goes After Trump and Campaign 325+ Times

MRC NewsBusters Corinne Weaver documented up to November 30, 2020 how Twitter has gone off the rails when it comes to censoring President Donald Trump and his campaign account. But meanwhile, Joe Biden and his campaign accounts remain untouched.

Twitter slapped labels on 63 Trump tweets since Nov. 23. When Trump tweeted: "Big Tech and the Fake News Media have partnered to Suppress. Freedom of the Press is gone, a thing of the past. That's why they refuse to report the real facts and figures of the 2020 Election or even, where's Hunter!" Twitter placed a label on the tweet, saying, "This claim about election fraud is disputed." However, nowhere in the tweet or in the accompanying video was election fraud mentioned. This tweet seemed more of a criticism of Big Tech rather than a statement implying electoral fraud.

Overall, since May 31, 2018, Trump and his campaign have been censored by Twitter 325 times. By comparison, neither former Vice President Joe Biden nor his campaign have been censored on the platform.

Twitter announced in an Oct. 9, 2020 blog, "Tweets with labels are already de-amplified through our own recommendation systems and these new prompts will give individuals more context on labeled Tweets so they can make more informed decisions on whether or not they want to amplify them to their followers." The company also stated that users who choose to retweet labeled tweets would receive a prompt "pointing them to credible information."

Labels varied based on the content of the tweet. Trump tweeted, "There is tremendous evidence of widespread voter fraud in that there is irrefutable proof that our Republican poll watchers and observers were not allowed to be present in poll counting rooms. Michigan, Pennsylvania, Georgia and others. Unconstitutional!" This tweet was marked with a label saying, "This claim about election fraud is disputed." In another tweet he said, "I won the Election!" The label under this tweet contested, "Official sources called this election differently."

A label was also placed on a tweet that mentioned the suspension of People's Pundit Daily editor Richard Baris. "Top US Pollster and Statistician Richard Baris—People's Pundit—SUSPENDED from Twitter for Reporting on Disputed Election—Political 'WrongThink' Not Allowed," tweeted Trump. The label said, "This claim about election fraud is disputed."

Some of the labels seemed arbitrarily applied. A video featuring White House Press Secretary Kayleigh McEnaney simply had the statement, "We want every *legal* vote to be counted." This tweet was given the label: "This claim about election fraud is disputed."

In a previous study, the president's Twitter account and the campaign account were found to have been censored 111 times. Tweets about the president's concern over mail-in voting, COVID-19, and the Black Lives Matter protests have been given "public interest notices."

The New Pandemic: Trump Derangement Syndrome

Documenting the severe reactions many people have to Donald Trump, a new medical term has emerged to describe it as noted in Joseph Epstein's humorous May 2020 *WSJ* Opinion section article titled "The New Pandemic: Trump Derangement Syndrome."

Symptoms include obsession with the president's hair and comparing him to Mao. It's been going around for some time and now appears to be in danger of spreading widely. I refer not to COVID-19, but to Donald-20, or, to use its pseudoscientific name, Trump Derangement Syndrome (TDS). Research has shown that TDS appears in five stages, each of advanced intensity. Perhaps there will be some value, if not promise of diminishment, in setting these parameters out for public awareness.

The cause of TDS is clear enough—Donald Trump, his looks, his manner, his nearly every utterance. So far there is no known cure. Ventilators are unnecessary in TDS, for people who progress beyond the first stage tend to vent quite vigorously on their own.

In Stage One, the afflicted has decided before 2016 that Donald Trump has serious, even strenuous, character flaws that disqualified him for the presidency or any other public office. Voting for him was never possible. For Stage One sufferers, a second Trump term could have effects that are frightening to contemplate. Stage One patients view the Trump presidency as a blotch in American political history.

In Stage Two, one dwells upon Donald Trump's looks. One has put a fair amount of thought into the architecture of his hairdo, wondering how much time each morning he must devote to its re-creation and whether he employs a stylist to help. One notices that the length of his neckties covers up his ample alderman as does the way he sits, leaning forward in his chair. Photographs of him in golf apparel are studied for what they reveal of the impressive breadth of his backside. The smugness of his smile is registered, the smallness of his hands always noted.

In Stage Three, one is ready to believe anything—anything pernicious or salacious, that is—about Mr. Trump and to reject anything he has done that might be good for the country, if only because he is the man who did it. One is ready to believe that he diets exclusively on the meat of endangered species, that there is something weirdly illicit about his relationship with Vladimir Putin, that he secretly admires Kim Jong Un's wardrobe. For Stage Three sufferers, nothing about President Trump can be totally disbelieved.

As for those of Donald Trump's policies that, coming from another president, one might be pleased about, these are rejected in Stage Three derangement syndrome. Israel shouldn't count on the allegiance of Mr. Trump. The revival of the American economy, before COVID-19 sent it cratering, was owing not to Mr. Trump but to President Obama. The lowering of black and Hispanic unemployment figures under the Trump administration is scarcely to be believed. Nor is the utility of his legislation reforming prisons or of his creating opportunity areas in black neighborhoods, if only because it happened under Donald Trump, who is, patients say, clearly a racist. In Stage Three derangement syndrome, if Donald Trump is for any specific policy, one is automatically against it; if he is against it, one is for it. Case not so much closed as never really opened.

In Stage Four, one imputes evil to Mr. Trump. One believes he became president of the United States to boost his hotel business. One is certain he has it in mind to create a dynasty, with Don Jr. and Jared Kushner waiting to succeed him as president-emperor. Even should Mr. Trump lose the forthcoming presidential election, Stage Four derangement syndrome sufferers believe he is unlikely to depart the White House willingly and is not beyond using military force to keep himself in power. Mussolini, Hitler, Stalin, Mao—for people with Stage Four derangement syndrome, Donald Trump is clearly a figure in their line.

In Stage Five TDS, one is weighted down with all the symptoms of the first four stages but brings to them an added choleric intensity of anger. At the mere mention of the name Donald Trump, unprintable expletives issue out of one's foam-flecked lips. One's skin flushes, veins appear on one's forehead, one's hands tremble, one loses all powers of speech.

Still, the nice thing about Trump Derangement Syndrome is that to prevent catching or spreading it, you don't have to wear a mask or always be washing your hands or practice social distancing. All you have to do is turn off your television set.

And that begs the question: What stage of TDS are you in?

10 –The MSM and Democratic Party's Collusion to Destroy Trump

Credit: @realDonaldTrump

If there was a Racketeer Influenced and Corrupt Organizations (RICO) type act for MSM collusion on fake news journalism directed at Trump, along with a fair and unbiased media trial jury to go along with it to determine how far MSM will go to dump Trump—a unanimous "guilty verdict" against MSM would be the uncontested outcome. Let's see why.

Few presidents have affected the perception of journalism like President Trump. A Pew survey found that Americans' confidence in news coverage is closely correlated to their opinion of Trump. Forty percent of Republicans who strongly approve of the president's job performance said that journalists have "very low" ethical standards, versus only 5 percent of Democrats.

As the overwhelming evidence from MRC proves, it's a simple cause and effect relationship when 90 plus percent of the new coverage of Trump is unjustifiably negative when it should be 90 plus percent positive based on the long list of Trump administration accomplishments, the moniker of "fake news" will forever haunt MSM.

CNN has had a stormy relationship with the new Trump administration since it took office, and early in his first term, three journalists resigned from CNN in June 2017 after the news network retracted an article alleging a Trump aide was under investigation by Congress.

The story was taken down following an internal investigation, with an apology to Anthony Scaramucci, an outspoken ally of the president. Scaramucci said it was not true, accusing the network of attacking President Donald Trump's friends.

Trump responded by taunting CNN in a tweet saying: "FAKE NEWS!" "Wow, CNN had to retract big story on 'Russia,' with 3 employees forced to resign," he posted. "What about all the other phony stories they do?"

Journalist Thomas Frank, investigative unit editor Eric Lictblau—a Pulitzer Prize winner—and Lex Harris, who oversaw the investigations unit, all resigned.

A spokesman for the network—which earlier said the story "did not meet CNN's editorial standards"—said: "In the aftermath of the retraction of a story published on CNN.com, CNN has accepted the resignations of the employees involved in the story's publication."

This is what TDS does to left leaning media and liberal journalists.

The Mainstream Media Is at the Point of No Return

A recent 2020 landmark poll of 20,000 citizens undertaken by the Knight Foundation and Gallup found that Americans' hope for and trust in an objective media is all but lost. They see not only an ever-growing partisanship in news reporting but a determination by the mainstream media to push a political agenda instead of honestly disseminating the news.

While generic faith in the media has been gradually declining over recent decades, the precipitous drop in trust and questions about what motivates the mainstream media can be traced to June 2015 and Donald Trump's entry into the presidential sweepstakes.

This latest poll is the most devastating indictment of the media in polling history. Some highlights:

- 84% of surveyed Americans lay either a moderate or a great deal of the blame for today's partisan hostility at the feet of the media.

- Further, 82% believe news outlets are either deliberately "misrepresenting the facts" or are "making them up entirely".

- This is further amplified as 79% of those surveyed say media outlets are trying to persuade people to adopt a certain opinion about an issue or an individual.

- Similarly, while the respondents in the poll believe that the media is "critical" or "very important" to democracy, 86% say they have witnessed either a fair amount or a great deal of bias in news reporting. Damningly, 78% feel that this bias is reflected in the spread of fake news which "is a major" problem" that exceeds all other in the mainstream media environment.

- By contrast, in 2007 62% of respondents in a Pew Research poll claimed to have witnessed either a fair amount or a great deal of bias in news reporting; in another Pew Research poll in 2012, that result increased slightly to 67% as compared to 86% today. How did the mainstream media sink to this abysmal level of distrust and disdain?

Donald Trump's entry into the presidential field in 2015 was a godsend to the mainstream media that had been hemorrhaging red ink for many years. The denizens of the mainstream media hierarchies knew that unremitting coverage of Trump, a global celebrity, would dramatically increase viewership, clicks on the internet and newspaper readership and thus their bottom line.

However, Donald Trump, during the campaign, continuously pointed out the left-wing bias and misreporting in the mainstream media and popularized a phrase that is now part of the American lexicon: fake news. With ridicule and mockery, he succeeded in making the media a potent campaign issue and a focal point of voter resentment.

While the vast majority of those in the mainstream media seethed at this disparagement, they, certain in the final outcome of the election, continued their unrestrained reporting and coverage of his every movement and utterance as their ratings and readership went through the roof.

No entity in the United States was more devastatingly affected by the 9.0 magnitude political earthquake that took place on November 8, 2016 than the mainstream media. Not only had they contributed mightily to the election of Donald Trump, a man they loathed, but they had willingly allowed him to make them the target of national derision and contempt.

The Single-Minded Determination of Mainstream Media to Seek Revenge

After the election, the anger and single-minded determination of the mainstream media to seek revenge and prove they could still remove or destroy a President was palpable.

The Bureau of Labor Statistics in their most recent National Occupational Employment and Wage Estimates Report claims 44,100 are currently employed as news analysts, reporters, and journalists. Yet, among the vast majority there is virtually no diversity of thought or political philosophy, as they associate among themselves to the exclusion of the rest of the populace, live in urban bubbles of like-minded and similarly educated elites, and view themselves as superior to the rabble in the rest of America. Thus, they inevitably are susceptible to a herd mentality when it comes to shaping and theoretically reporting the news as the groupthink mandates.

Since November 9, 2016, the groupthink has mandated that Donald Trump must be destroyed regardless of the fallout or potential destruction of trust and reliance in the mainstream media. While pursuing that desired outcome, the public over the course of 48 months has, as the current polls reveal, became increasingly aware of the tactics and dishonesty of the mainstream media.

It is now an unquestioned fact that the mainstream media, throwing away any pretense of objectivity, has overtly and unabashedly allied itself with the Democrat party and its dominant wing, the radical Marxists/socialists.

It is common knowledge that the media will not honestly report on or criticize avowed militant Marxist organizations Antifa or Black Lives Matter and their penchant for violence and determination to incite a societal upheaval. It is also becoming evident to an increasingly larger swath of the citizenry that the mainstream media is determined to deliberately foment unfounded fear and anxiety about the coronavirus epidemic.

However, in what is the most egregious example of media malpractice in American history, the mainstream media was and continues to be complicit in, as well as co-conspirators with, the Obama Administration in the greatest scandal in American history—the Russian collusion hoax—but are mostly silent and/or less eager to investigate into SpyGate. This is a reality that an increasing number of Americans are becoming acutely aware of.

Thus, more Americans on a daily basis have come to the conclusion that this credulous gaggle of mind-numbed robots are deliberately avoiding any honest reporting on any issue in order to further their political and retribution agenda, as well as promote Biden.

The mainstream media's obsession with revenge and proving they can destroy a presidency has brought them to the edge of the precipice and the point of no return as the devastating findings in the recent Gallup poll confirms. Particularly as these are the unvarnished opinions of an overwhelming majority of the American citizenry regardless of political affiliation.

John Sands, Director of Learning and Impact at the Knight Foundation commenting on this poll said: "We're starting to see more retrenchment among those who have already expressed deep concerns. Moving the dial on these attitudes becomes more and more difficult for media organizations. In other words, it will be nearly impossible for the mainstream media to ever recapture the faith and trust of the American people."

Democrats Obsessed With Impeachment From Fake and False News Sources

From a January 2020 article in *The Hill* by Bernard Goldberg titled "No rush to judgment on Trump—it's been ongoing since Election Day," he notes the battle cry of the Democratic Party arm of fake news media since Election Day has been, "Impeach! Impeach! Impeach!"

On Jan. 20, 2017, the *Washington Post* published an online story that ran under this headline: "The campaign to impeach President Trump has begun." The story was posted at 12:19 p.m., nine minutes after Donald Trump was sworn in as the 45th president of the United States.

First, Democrats were out to get the president for supposed violations of the Emoluments Clause to the U.S. Constitution. Then he had to go because he was a Russian asset. When that didn't pan out, he had to be impeached because they said he obstructed justice in the Mueller investigation. Someplace along the way, impeachment was the only answer to his payoff of hush money to a porn star, which Democrats said amounted to a violation of campaign finance laws.

As for the chat with the president of Ukraine: It was not a "perfect" phone call, as President Trump claims. It was a deeply flawed call—deeply flawed, like the impulsive man who made the call.

President Trump was clearly strong-arming the young president of Ukraine, a man who desperately needed U.S. military help to ward off the Russian army. And if he didn't investigate the Bidens, he might not get that aid.

But was that an impeachable offense? That depends—not so much on the facts of the matter but on whether you're a Democrat or a Republican. Virtually none of the jurors in the Senate entered the trial with an open mind, no matter what they're telling their allies in the mainstream media.

Why Are We Here?

As the Senate's impeachment trial opened on this matter, Jay Sekulow, a member of the president's legal team, stood before the 100 senators who decided the president's fate and asked a question everybody knew the answer to. "Why are we here?" Sekulow asked, rhetorically. "Are we here because of a phone call? Or are we here before this great body because, since the president was sworn into office, there was a desire to see him removed?"

As the old "Saturday Night Live" character Roseanne Roseannadanna used to say, "It's always something—if it's not one thing, it's another."

Every presidential misstep, to the president's partisan adversaries, was a threat to democracy; every gaffe put our national security at risk. If they could have gotten away with impeaching him because his neckties were too long, they would have tried. If being mean-spirited were an impeachable offense, if being petty, vulgar, and dishonest were considered "high crimes and misdemeanors," then he'd have to go.

But so was the decision to impeach the president a forgone conclusion. The decision was made right about the time he was declared winner of the 2016 presidential election. Donald Trump's real impeachable offense, as far as the anti-Trump "Resistance" is concerned, was defeating Hillary Clinton.

As the impeachment effort against President Donald Trump inevitably burns out on the ash heap of history, Democrats are being left to argue that if this president is left unchecked, if he's not removed from office, he'll "do it again." He'll pressure foreign governments to investigate the business dealings of the Bidens, which is a "threat to national security."

National security equals no questioning of the Bidens. Democracy equals removing an elected president.

All this rhetoric ignores the notion that the House impeachment itself proves he's not "unchecked." A Democratic-majority House has been aggressively "checking" Trump with oversight investigations, in effect trying to do what the Mueller report failed to do: establish that Trump is some sort of autocrat who's emptying American democracy of all meaning. House impeachment manager Adam Schiff will insert the word "cheat" into every paragraph going forward.

Desperation Overtook Reason

But that isn't half as shocking as the really unglued portions of Schiff's closing argument before the Senate. Desperation overtook reason. If Trump isn't removed, the congressman from Hollywood feverishly imagined, Trump "could offer Alaska to the Russians in exchange for support in the next election or decide to move to Mar-a-Lago permanently and let Jared Kushner run the country, delegating to him the decision whether to go to war."

This of course is a TDS false narrative as CNN did not convene a large panel discussion on whether Schiff is mentally unstable. The "nonpartisan fact-checkers" didn't look into Schiff's paranoid screenplay.

This "unchecked" president has been subjected to almost 1,100 hyper negative minutes—just about impeachment—on the evening news from late September 2019 through January 2020, while in the same time frame, the gangbusters economy drew a mere 14 minutes. This doesn't count more than 200 hours of soap opera-canceling live impeachment coverage on ABC, CBS and NBC. It doesn't count PBS' broadcasting the impeachment process live and then rerunning it in prime time. It doesn't hold a candle to cable news' 24/7 obsession with impeachment.

The left somehow feels Trump is unaccountable because this tsunami of scandal coverage isn't damaging his public standing. In fact, Gallup just found that "Trump's job approval rating has risen to 49%, his highest in Gallup polling since he took office in 2017." Since the start of the year, Trump's approval is up 6 points among Republicans and 5 points among independents.

This leaves the overall impression that Trump has a very good chance of becoming the first president to be impeached and then reelected. That's because this impeachment exercise was so transparently one-sided and partisan. And so was the press.

The Articles of Impeachment Against President Trump

From the A&E History Special "President Donald Trump impeached" in December 2019: The only way for Congress to remove a sitting president is to find him or her guilty during the Senate trial. In that trial, which comes after the House votes to approve articles of impeachment, the Chief Justice of the United States presides, and the 100 members of the Senate serve as the jury. A full two-thirds of the Senate jurors present needs to vote "guilty" for a president to be convicted.

Article I, Section 3 of the Constitution gives the Senate "sole power to try all impeachments" and sets forth three requirements that underscore the seriousness of an impeachment trial: 1) senators are put under oath; 2) the Chief Justice presides, not the vice president; and 3) a two-thirds "supermajority" is required to convict.

After weeks of discussions among legislators, the House of Representatives voted to impeach the 45th President, Donald Trump, for abuse of power and obstruction of Congress on December 18, 2019. The vote fell largely along party lines: 230 in favor, 197 against and 1 present. Trump became only the third president ever to be impeached, joining Andrew Johnson and Bill Clinton, after Democrats raised concerns about his alleged attempts to seek foreign interference in the 2020 election and to hamper their investigation.

Some Democrats had advocated impeaching Trump, a historically unpopular president to the left, liberals and Democrats who was elected by the Electoral College despite losing the popular vote, since the moment the moment he took office. After they regained control of the House of Representatives, Democrats launched multiple investigations into his business dealings and his campaign's ties to Russian hackers who targeted his 2016 opponent, Hillary Clinton. After an exhaustive effort failed to convince Speaker Nancy Pelosi and others that they had reason to impeach, a new scandal emerged that succeeded in doing so.

In September 2019, the public learned of a whistleblower complaint regarding a July phone call between Trump and Ukrainian President Volodymyr Zelensky. The complaint, which was corroborated by the acting Ambassador to Ukraine, stated that Trump had threatened to withhold U.S. foreign aid money until Zelensky promised to investigate Hunter Biden, son of leading Democratic 2020 candidate Joe Biden, for suspicious dealings in Ukraine.

The White House denied any "quid pro quo," but the administration's response was muddled. Rudy Giuliani, who was accused of helping Trump put pressure on Ukrainian officials to investigate Biden, made several media appearances in his capacity as Trump's personal attorney that only created more confusion and suspicion. By late November, it was clear that the Democrats felt confident enough in their case for wrongdoing and obstruction of Congress that they would go through with impeachment.

After both articles were approved in the House, the case then moved to a Senate trial, which began on January 16, 2020. U.S. Supreme Court chief justice John Roberts presided over the trial. On February 5, 2020, in a vote that again fell largely along party lines, the Senate voted to acquit President Trump on both charges.

Impeachment Gets 77x More TV Time than Trump's Economic Successes

According to a new February 2020 Media Research Center (MRC) study, reported by Rich Noyes, for *each minute* the broadcast evening newscasts spent talking about the President's successful economic programs, viewers heard 77 minutes about the Democrats' impeachment push, a massive disparity. Overall, coverage of the President was 93% negative during the last four months, reaching 95% negative in January 2020

Details: MRC analysts examined all 1,776 minutes of Trump administration coverage produced on the ABC, CBS and NBC evening newscasts since the formal launch of the impeachment investigation on September 24, 2019, through the Senate vote against additional witnesses on January 31, 2020.

The vast majority of this airtime (1,082 minutes, or 61%) was spent on the Democrats' ultimately futile impeachment probe, which culminated in an acquittal vote. Only twice during these four months did the networks permit policy to dominate the newscasts—and both times, reporters and anchors cast it in heavily negative terms for the administration.

The top policy topic during these months was the U.S. showdown with Iran following the killing of their Quds Force commander, General Qasem Soleimani, which drew 197 minutes of evening news airtime in January 2020, nearly all of which (96%) was critical of the administration.

The President's decision to pull troops out of northern Syria in October 2019 was the second-most covered topic (126 minutes) and was even more one-sided—evening news viewers were treated to 99 percent negative coverage of his Syria pull-out.

On the other hand, the administration's economic policies were collectively given mostly (82%) positive coverage on the evening broadcasts. But the network coverage of these topics was so minuscule, viewers might have barely noticed the good news.

The administration's trade talks with China, culminating in the signing of a Phase One deal on January 15, 2020, were granted just 10 minutes of coverage during these 130 days, while the achievement of getting the USMCA trade deal through the House received a mere 90 seconds of airtime. Adding in the positive numbers on job creation and economic growth, total evening news coverage of the administration's economic program totaled just 14 minutes, or 0.7% of the total coverage of the administration.

That dearth of coverage of good news topics, plus heavy negative coverage of other policy topics as well as impeachment, makes it easy to see why overall coverage of President Trump has averaged 93% negative during these past four months (95% negative in January 2020).

According to Gallup (prior to the pandemic), Americans right now are more satisfied with the way things are going in the U.S. than at any point in the past 15 years, while confidence in the economy is at its highest since 2000. Imagine how those numbers would look if the networks gave the President's economic achievements the attention they deserve.

And, in case you were wondering—the evening newscasts didn't spare any seconds for those important Gallup results, either.

Inside the Media's Relentless Crusade to Destroy President Trump

From the October 13, 2019 article "Inside the media's relentless crusade to destroy President Trump" in the *New York Post* by Kimberley Strassel, she provides a critical insight from her 2019 book titled *Resistance at All Costs: How Trump Haters are Breaking America* of how far the press will go in its relentless crusade to destroy President Trump.

Since Donald Trump's election in 2016, the mainstream media has shed its once-noble mission—the pursuit of the truth—and instead, adopted a new purpose: to take down the president. The president regularly blasts the media for reporting "fake news" but when you see the evidence, it's hard to argue against him.

As an example, the *Washington Post* revealed the alarming news that House Democrats were considering having their anonymous "whistleblower" (of the Trump-Zelensky phone call) testify from a remote location, and in disguise. Just as shocking as the details of this plan was the justification the *Post* ladled on this Democratic effort to hide impeachment information from the public.

It explained, high up in the story, that the cloak-and-dagger approach was merely Democrats expressing "distrust of their GOP colleagues, whom they see as fully invested in defending a president who has attacked the whistleblower's credibility and demanded absolute loyalty from Republicans."

This, from a newspaper with a tagline of "Democracy Dies in Darkness." Maybe the better journalistic epitaph is: Democracy dies in bias. How did journalism get here?

Strassel has never engaged much in media criticism because it's almost too obvious. Yes, the mainstream media is liberal and biased. But at least in the past, that bias was largely a function of insularity. Most reporters weren't even fully aware they were prejudiced politically; everyone they worked and socialized with held the same left-of-center views.

That's changed in the age of Trump. The press has embraced its bias, joined the Resistance, and declared its allegiance to one side of a partisan war. It now openly declares those who offer any fair defense of this administration as Trump "enablers."

It writes off those who mention SpyGate or question the FBI or Department of Justice actions in 2016 as "conspiracy" theorists. It acts as willing scribes for Democrats and former Obama officials; peddles evidence-free accusations; sources stories from people with clear political axes to grind; and closes its eyes to clear evidence of government abuse.

This Media War is Extraordinary, Overt and Damaging to the Country

Here's one of many reasons why:

The latest installment of this Democratic-media tie-up is the Ukraine story that House Intelligence Committee Chairman Adam Schiff explained that the intelligence community inspector general wanted to transmit an anonymous "whistleblower" complaint to him but had been stopped by the Trump administration. Schiff has for 10 months been obsessing over how to impeach Trump, so his claim merited great skepticism.

Instead, the media ran with it.

Even as it acknowledged that it did not know the subject of the complaint, or the background of the accuser, it began running stories postulating that the Trump administration had engaged in a cover-up. It later accepted whole-cloth the whistleblower's hearsay accusation that Trump had demanded a Ukrainian investigation into former Vice President Joe Biden as a condition of military aid—before even seeing a transcript of the Trump call.

The New York Times was so eager to push the impeachment narrative forward (and give it credibility) that it divulged the sensitive detail that the whistleblower was a CIA officer detailed to the White House.

Sadly, this press behavior is nothing new since the election of Donald Trump that has led to the greatest disintegration of press standards in modern history. For those wondering if they are getting the "real story" in the Ukraine impeachment drama, it's worth taking a walk back through the past few years of what we now know was the Russia-collusion hoax.

One particularly bad decision helped drive all the rest of that false narrative: The press became willing advocates for government actors (at least the ones they liked). This is the reverse of the role the press is supposed to play. The media exists to be a government watchdog as was the case of Richard Nixon's Watergate.

Sure, when it comes to the Trump administration, the press rides herd on most every issue. But when it has come to former Obama officials (James Comey, Andrew McCabe, John Brennan), the media has swallowed everything it is told. It's hard to explain just how big a dereliction of duty this is.

The FBI's Trump-Russia investigation fell clearly into a government-abuse-of-power story, of the kind the press used to salivate for an in-depth expose. It came laden with red flags—opposition research from the rival campaign, backdoor channels to the IRS, surveillance of American citizens. And yet anything the former people of power told the press to write, the press wrote.

Ignoring Facts in Favor of Theory is What Feeds Collusion Conspiracy Theories

The best example is that infamous *New York Times* story about the "origin" of the FBI probe. In late 2017, when former House Intelligence Chairman Devin Nunes finally came close to winning his battle with the DOJ to see documents about the infamous Steele dossier, FBI protectors panicked. They knew how terrible it would look that they had used opposition research from a rival campaign to get surveillance warrants on at least one Trump campaign official. So, someone called the *New York Times* for help in getting ahead of the story. On Dec. 30, 2017, it published: "How the Russia Inquiry Began: A Campaign Aide, Drinks and Talk of Political Dirt."

The story was, of course, all about how George Papadopoulos had inspired the FBI's probe, and it flat-out narrated what would become the FBI line about its origins. It also flatly dismissed the dossier. The Papadopoulos take "answers one of the lingering mysteries of the past year: What so alarmed American officials to provoke the FBI to open a counterintelligence investigation into the Trump campaign months before the presidential election? It was not, as Trump and other politicians have alleged, a dossier compiled by a former British spy hired by a rival campaign," opined the *Times*. The story cited nobody in its story other than anonymous "American and foreign officials."

In May 2018, the paper ran another "blockbuster" story about the FBI's Trump investigation, which was code-named Crossfire Hurricane. The *Times* reported that "Only in mid-September, congressional investigators say, did the dossier reach the Crossfire Hurricane team." This is false. Justice Department official Bruce Ohr has testified under oath that he briefed a lot of people about the dossier—and its political provenance—not long after it was handed to him in late July. As of the writing of this book, the *Times* has never updated or corrected that piece.

The Willingness to be Spoon-Fed is What Drove so Many Big Press Bloopers

Were there a Collusion Press-Error Hall of Fame, CNN would be the first inductee. There was CNN's decision in 2017 to run a story, based on one unnamed source, claiming a presidential adviser, Anthony Scaramucci, was under investigation for his ties to a Russian investment fund. CNN had to retract the story, and three of its journalists resigned.

In December 2017, CNN announced a scoop for the ages. It claimed it had evidence that Donald Trump Jr. had been offered by advance access to hacked Democratic emails. MSNBC and CBS also claimed to have "confirmed" this evidence that the Trump campaign and WikiLeaks had been colluding. It later came out that the outlets had gotten the date on their evidence wrong. Donald Trump Jr. had been sent an email directing him to look at the WikiLeaks dump—after WikiLeaks had made it public the year before. Ouch!

Also don't forget BuzzFeed's epic "news" in January 2019 that President Trump personally directed his longtime attorney Michael Cohen to lie to Congress about the Trump Tower project in Moscow. Politicians seized on the news, and Adam Schiff promised to do what was "necessary" to find out if the president had committed "perjury." Democratic Rep. Joaquin Castro said that if the allegations were true, Trump "must resign." The problem? They weren't. This one was such an invention that special counsel Bob Mueller's team made a rare statement, denying the BuzzFeed report.

There are plenty more. *The Washington Post* claimed Russians had accessed the US electrical grid through a Vermont utility. Not true. Slate claimed a Trump server had been communicating with Russia. Not true. *The Guardian* claimed that Paul Manafort had visited Julian Assange in his hideout at the Ecuadorian Embassy in London—three times. If so, Mueller missed it. The press gets furious when Trump talks about "fake news." But what else would you call this?

Another low of the past few years—which we are seeing again now—has been the media's willingness to run fact-free accusations. Case in point claims from the Steele dossier. The specific charges in that document have never been proven. Opposition-research firm Fusion GPS was incredibly clever in its decision to feed that document to the FBI to give it more credibility. But the fact that the FBI had it or, that Schiff was irresponsible to quote from it during a hearing, didn't release the press from a basic obligation: to either verify the truth or treat the document for what it was—slander. Instead, the media repeated the dossier's claims ad nauseum, rarely bothering to note the partisan motivations behind its creation.

Hypothetics is When the Press Indulge in Endless "Connect the Dots" Exercises

By embracing hypothetics (rather than tracking down facts), the press indulged in endless "connect the dots" exercises.

In April 2018, two reporters from *McClatchy* cited "sources" who said, "Mueller has evidence Michael Cohen was in Prague in 2016, confirming part of the dossier." The story claimed Cohen had secretly snuck into the Czech Republic, through Germany, presumably for a clandestine meeting with Kremlin officials. It again quoted only "sources familiar with the matter." Yet Cohen had vehemently insisted that he'd never been there. And the Mueller report would later flatly say he had not.

McClatchy, as of the writing Kimberley Strassel's book *Resistance at All Costs: How Trump Haters are Breaking America* in 2019, still hasn't retracted the story. Why? It claims that what it was reporting was that Mueller had "received evidence," and it noted that Mueller never said he didn't receive evidence. See?

Liberal opinion writers were even worse. One of the standout headlines from 2018 came from Jonathan Chait, writing in *New York Magazine*. It read: "Trump-Putin: Will Trump Be Meeting with His Counterpart—Or His Handler?" Chait asked: "What if Trump has been a Russian asset from 1987?" Then followed thousands of words that purported to tie together Trump, obscure Russians, Stormy Daniels, Assange and so much more. The story, suffice it to say, did not age well.

All reporters sometimes bend a rule or go out on a limb or get something wrong. But the important thing is that they usually do this in aid of getting truth to the public. What has defined the media breakdown that started in 2016 was the press' abandonment of standards in aid of peddling a narrative—rather than reality. This abandonment has had terrible consequences for the industry and for the country.

A Monmouth University poll in early 2018 found that a whopping 77 percent of Americans believe traditional TV and newspaper outlets report "fake news." And 42 percent of respondents said they believed outlets did this specifically to promote a political agenda. These kinds of numbers are alarming for civil society. The more Americans are turned off from traditional news, the more they turn to dubious sources and read and listen only to things with which they agree. For those worried about our increasingly polarized society, the media is feeding that divide.

11 – WOWW's Journalism Code of Ethics, Practical Logic & Sapience

Credit: GOP. *"Newsweek FALSELY reported that Polish First Lady Kornhauser-Duda did not shake President Trump's hand."*

Once asked what it takes to be a successful writer, Ernest Hemingway replied, "A good crap-detector." Crude? Perhaps. What he meant was an ability to separate the authentic from the phony, the real from the illusory, the significant from the trivial, the artistic from the artful, the truth from the BS.

It's not only the writer and reader who needs that capacity. Everyone does, and more so these days with hip boots. Lacking it, we can do little more than slip and slide from the brainwashing effect of MSM. Or we can fight back and help eliminate it? One effective way to do that is to master practical logic and the correct rules of argument.

The SAPIENT Being utilizes the Society of Professional Journalists: Code of Ethics (Straubhaar, LaRose & Davenport, pages 478-79) in regard to its journalistic research and reporting standards. The Society of Professional Journalists created a code of ethics that are in effect today and outlined below.

These standards provide the foundation of journalistic ethics and they are supplemented with key practical logic fallacies, confirmation bias, constructive disagreement, replication crisis, along with the mission statement of the SAPIENT Being that promotes the return of free speech, open dialogue and civil discourse and the vision statement of creating a society advancing personal Intelligence and enlightenment now together (S.A.P.I.E.N.T.).

Society of Professional Journalists: Code of Ethics

The Code of Ethics from the Society of Professional Journalists used for the first half of this chapter is powerful list because it reminds oneself how mainstream fake news media flagrantly and continuously violate every item on the list. The Code can be used to critique fake news journalism, unsound research, fact checking, agendas, sources, stereotyping, and so on. In one item there is added term (ideology) that is shown in parenthesis.

Best Practices:

The main mantra of the code is "Seek truth and Report it!" The code also states that: "Journalists should be honest, fair, and courageous in gathering, reporting, and interpreting information. Journalists should:

- Test the accuracy of information from all sources and exercise care to avoid inadvertent error. Deliberate distortion is never permissible.

- Diligently seek out subjects of news stories to give them the opportunity to respond to allegations of wrongdoing.

- Identify sources whenever feasible. The public is entitled to as much information as possible on sources' reliability.

- Always question sources' motives before promising anonymity. Clarify conditions attached to any promise made in exchange for information. Keep promises.

- Make certain that headlines, news teases, and promotional material, photos, video, audio, graphics, sound bites, and quotations do not misrepresent. They should not oversimplify or highlight incidents out of context.

- Never distort the content of news photos or video. Image enhancement for technical clarity is always permissible. Label montages and photo illustrations.

- Avoid misleading reenactments or staged news events. If reenactment is necessary to tell a story, label it as so.

- Avoid undercover or other surreptitious methods of gathering information except when traditional open methods will not yield information vital to the public. Use of such methods should be explained as part of the story.

- Never plagiarize.

- Tell the story of the diversity and magnitude of the human experience boldly, even, when it is unpopular to do so.

- Examine their own cultural values and avoid imposing on those values on others.

- Avoid stereotyping by (ideology), race, gender, age, religion, ethnicity, geography, sexual orientation, disability, physical appearance, or social status.

- Support the open exchange of views, even views they find repugnant.

- Give voice to the voiceless; official and unofficial sources of information can be equally valid.

- Distinguish between advocacy and news reporting. Analysis and commentary should be labeled and not misrepresent fact or content.

- Distinguish news from advertising and shun hybrids that blur the lines between the two.

- Recognize the special obligation to ensure that the public's business is conducted in the open and that government records are open to inspection.

Minimize Harm:

Ethical journalists treat sources, subjects, and colleagues as human beings deserving of respect. Journalists should:

- Show compassion for those who may be affected adversely by news coverage. Use special sensitivity when dealing with children and inexperienced sources or subjects.

- Be sensitive when seeking or using interviews or photographs of those affected by tragedy or guilt.

- Recognize that gathering and reporting information may cause harm or discomfort. Pursuit of the news is not a license for arrogance.

- Recognize that private people have a greater right to control information about themselves that do public officials and others who seek power, influence, or attention. Only an overriding public need can justify intrusion into anyone's privacy.

- Show good taste. Avoid pandering to lurid curiosity.

- Be cautious of identifying juvenile suspects or victims of sex crimes.

- Be judicious about naming criminal suspects before the formal filing of charges.

- Balance a criminal suspect's fair trial rights with the public's right to be informed.

Act Independently:

Journalists should be free of obligation to any interest other than the public's right to know. Journalists should:

- Avoid conflict of interest, real or perceived.

- Remain free of associations and activities that may compromise integrity or damage credibility.

- Refuse gifts, favors, fees, free travel, and special treatment, and shun secondary employment, political involvement, public office, and service in community organizations if they compromise journalistic integrity.

- Disclose unavoidable conflicts.

- Be vigilant and courageous about holding those with power accountable.

- Deny favored treatment to advertisers and special interests and resist their pressure to influence news coverage.

- Be wary of sources offering information for favors or money; avoid bidding for news."

Be Accountable:

Journalists are accountable to their readers, listeners, viewers, and each other. Journalists should:

- Clarify and explain news coverage and invite dialogue with the public over journalistic conduct.

- Encourage the public to voice grievances against the news media."

- Admit mistakes and correct them promptly.

- Expose unethical practices of journalists and the news media.

- Abide by the same high standards to which they hold others.

All of these guidelines are for the betterment of society and the regulation of fake news and biased media. If you have any questions or require additional info regarding our code of ethics in journalism, please don't hesitate to contact SAPIENT Being HQ at (951) 638-5562 or at sapientbeing@att.net.

Practical Logic to the Rescue and Intervention

Per Vincent E. Barry, author of the 1980 timeless classic *Practical Logic*, listed in alphabetical order is a quick and short definition of the essential practical logic terms for your use as needed. There's no better written way of calling out fake news than quoting these:

Argument from analogy is an inductive argument in which a known similarity that two things share is used as evidence for concluding that the two things are similar in other respects.

Argument from ignorance fallacy is the argument that uses an opponent's inability to disprove a conclusion as proof of the conclusion's correctness.

Argument is any group of propositions true or false statements one of which is said to follow from the others.

Common practice fallacy is an argument that attempts to justify wrongdoing on the basis of some practice that has become commonly accepted.

Compatibility refers to whether or not a hypothesis fits in with a body of knowledge that is already accepted as true.

Deductive argument is one whose conclusion is claimed to follow from its premises with logical certainty in logic a deductive argument whose premises necessarily lead to its conclusion is termed a valid argument.

Fallacies of ambiguity are those fallacies arising from careless language usage.

Fallacies of relevance are those arguments whose premises are logically a relevant to their conclusions.

Fallacy is a type of argument that may seem to be correct but is not.

Fallacy of accent is an argument whose justification depends on a shift in emphasis on a word or phrase.

Fallacy of accident is an argument that applies a general rule to a particular case Whose special circumstances make the rule inapplicable.

Fallacy of ad hominem is an argument that attacks the person who makes an assertion rather than the person's argument.

Fallacy of begging the question is an argument that assumes as a premise the very conclusion it intends to prove.

Fallacy of biased question is an argument based upon the answer to a question that is worded to draw a predetermined reply.

Fallacy of biased sample is an argument that contains a sample that is not representative of the population being studied.

Fallacy of complex question is an argument that in asking a question assumes the conclusion at issue.

Fallacy of composition is an argument that attributes characteristics of the parts to a whole.

Fallacy of concealed evidence is an argument that presents only facts that are favorable to its conclusion while suppressing relevant but non-supportive facts.

Fallacy of division is an argument that attributes to the parts of a whole the characteristics of the whole itself.

Fallacy of equivocation is an argument that uses the word or phrase in such a way that it carries more than a single meaning.

Fallacy of false analogy is an argument that makes an erroneous comparison.

Fallacy of false authority is an argument that violates any of the criteria for a justifiable appeal to authority.

Fallacy of false dilemma is an argument that erroneously reduces the number of possible positions for alternatives on an issue.

Fallacy of fear or force is an argument that uses the threat of harm for the acceptance of a conclusion.

Fallacy of hasty conclusion is an argument that draws a conclusion based on insufficient evidence.

Fallacy of invincible ignorance is an argument that insists on the legitimacy of an idea or principle despite contradictory fact.

Fallacy of mob appeal is an argument that attempts to persuade by arousing a group's deepest emotions.

Fallacy of pity is an argument uses pity to advance a conclusion.

Fallacy of popularity is an argument the tries to justify something strictly by appeal to numbers.

Fallacy of positioning is an argument that tries to capitalize on the earned reputation of a leader in a field to sell something.

Fallacy of provincialism is an argument that views things exclusively in terms of group loyalty.

Fallacy of questionable causation is an argument that asserts that a particular circumstance produces that it causes a particular phenomenon when there is in fact little or no evidence to support set contention.

Fallacy of questionable classification is an argument that classifies somebody or something on the basis of insufficient evidence.

Fallacy of slippery slope is an argument that object to a position on the erroneous belief that the position if taken will set off a chain of events that ultimately will lead to undesirable action.

Fallacy of two wrongs make a right is an argument that attempts to justify what is considered wrong by appealing to other instances of the same action.

Fallacy of unknown fact is an argument that contains premises that are unknowable either in principle or in this particular case.

Generalization is a statement that covers many specifics.

Guilt by association fallacy is an argument in which people are judged guilty solely on the basis of the company they keep or the places they frequent.

Hypothesis must be relevant that is it should explain the problem directly.

Inductive argument is one whose conclusion is a generalization.

Inductive generalization is an inductive argument whose conclusion is a generalization.

Informal fallacies are commonplace errors in reasoning that we fall into because of careless language usage or inattention to the subject matter.

Intuition is the direct apprehension of knowledge that is not the result of conscious reasoning or of immediate sense perception.

Irreverent reason fallacy is the argument whose premises are totally irrelevant to the conclusion.

Justification refers to the reasonableness of the evidence to support a conclusion.

Method of agreement states that if two or more instances of a phenomenon have only one circumstance in common than that circumstance is probably the cause for the effect of the phenomena.

Method of concomitant variation states that whenever a phenomenon varies in a particular way as another phenomenon varies in a particular way then a causal relationship probably exists between them.

Method of difference states that if an instance where the phenomenon occurs in an instance where it doesn't occur have every circumstance in common except one in that circumstance occurs only in the former than the circumstances probably the cause or the effect of the phenomenon.

Necessary and sufficient cause any condition that must be present for the effect to occur in one that will bring about the effect to one and of itself.

Necessary cause is a condition that must be present if the effect is to occur.

Occam's razor is the problem-solving principle that "entities should not be multiplied without necessity", or more simply, the simplest explanation is usually the right one.

Objectivity refers to the quality of viewing ourselves in the world without distortion.

Persuasive definition is one that departs from conventional word meaning in order to influence attitudes.

Post-hoc fallacy is an argument that asserts that one event is the cause of another from the mere fact that the first occurred earlier than the second.

Predictability refers to the explanatory power that a hypothesis has.

Premises of arguments are those statements that are claimed to until the conclusion. The conclusion is the statement that supposedly is entailed by the premises.

Proposition is true means the proposition describes a state of affairs.

Public verification means that almost anyone wanting could verify the claim.

Reason is the capacity to draw conclusions from evidence.

Sampling technique is the method of procedure used to generate a sample.

Scientific method is a way of investigating a phenomenon that's based on the collective analysis and into interpretation of evidence to determine the most probable explanation. The five basic steps in scientific method: 1) statement of the problem, 2) collection of facts, 3) formulating a hypothesis, 4) making further inferences, and 5) verifying the inferences.

Simplicity refers to a hypothesis capacity to account for the facts and data in the most economical way of all the alternatives.

Statistical generalization is a statement that asserts that something is true of a percentage of a class.

Stipulative definition is one that attaches unique or at least unconventional meaning to a term.

Stratified sample is a sampling technique in which relevant strata within the group are identified and a random sample from each stratum is selected in proportion to the number of members in each stratum.

Straw man fallacy is an argument that alters a position that the result is easier to attack than the original.

Sufficient cause is any condition that by itself will bring about the effect.

Supporting testimony refers to the observations of other observers that tend to support the evidence presented.

Testability refers to whether or not a hypothesis offers observations that will confirm or disconfirm it.

True premises do not of themselves justify and inductive conclusion an argument is sound when in the case of induction, it is Justified; or win in the case of deduction it is both valid and true.

Universal generalization is a statement that asserts that something is true of all members of a class.

Recommendations for Tech Companies

The Media Research Center has undertaken an extensive study of the problem at major tech companies' effort to censor the conservative worldview from the public conversation and formulated a guidebook in 2018, titled *CENSORED! How Online Media Companies Are Suppressing Conservative Speech*.

Like it or not, social media is the communication form of the future—not just in the U.S., but worldwide. Facebook and Twitter combined reach 1.8 billion people. More than two-thirds of all Americans (68 percent) use Facebook. YouTube is pushing out TV as the most popular place to watch video. Google is the No. 1 search engine in both the U.S. and the world.

As previously covered, war is being declared on the conservative movement in this space and conservatives are losing—badly. If the right is silenced, billions of people will be cut off from conservative ideas and conservative media. It's the new battleground of media bias. But it's worse. That bias is not a war of ideas. It's a war against ideas. Below is a list of suggestions from MRC to deal with this problem:

People are Policy:

Tech companies like Google and Facebook are making a nominal effort to hire conservatives, but that doesn't address the core problems within those organizations. Companies need to eliminate policies and biases that discriminate against conservatives. They also need to protect employees' ability to disagree with the pervasive liberal groupthink that dominates the industry.

Tech Companies Must Provide Transparency:

People and organizations have their posts and videos either restricted or deleted on all major platforms. If those companies expect their users to trust them, they must make this system transparent. They must show at least when posts of organizations and public figures are deleted and when they aren't. That would give users a baseline of what speech is allowed on a platform, not just whatever the companies choose to delete.

Expect Regulation at This Pace:

Tech companies are facing calls for regulation from left and right. The firms should address this by setting rules about how they will treat both conservative and liberal organizations and information fairly. This means clear, published guidelines must be established that support free speech online. Algorithms, content guidelines and ad policies must be designed that don't target political speech. Firms must stop pretending disagreement is equivalent to hate speech. Fairness and transparency are equally essential.

Avoid Partnering With Bad Actors:

Twitter, YouTube and others had tried to establish policies that prevent so-called hate speech on their platforms. But those policies are being enforced by organizations that spew hate against the conservative movement and can't pretend to be neutral players. Groups like the SPLC and ADL label core conservative values as "hate" or "bigotry." Tech companies can't expect conservatives to trust a system that is so blatantly one-sided.

Modify Flagging Systems:

One of the worst problems tech companies grapple with is the abuse of their flagging and reporting systems. YouTube, Twitter and Facebook, in particular, succumb to liberal activists who game their systems and constantly report conservative content. These services must determine a better way to handle alerts that do not allow coordinated campaigns against the right.

Use Neutral Fact-Checkers:

If social media sites are going to attempt to be the arbiters of what is real news, they must rely on fact-checking sources that are neutral and fair toward stories on both sides of the aisle. Relying on sites like Snopes, which has a clear liberal bias, raises concerns over whether the tech giants are trying to promote a liberal political narrative.

Avoiding Personal Bias and Faulty Research Methods

The sections above provide a solid foundation for spotting and fighting fake news in all its forms and uses in an ethical and journalistic manner. The ones below from a sociological and psychological perspective, can also assist in our crusade to improve journalistic, media, and research standards and make them more sapient in the process.

Constructive Disagreement is Good

Constructive disagreement occurs when people who don't see eye-to-eye are committed to exploring an issue together, alive to their own fallibility and the limits of their knowledge—and open to learning something from others who see things differently than they do.

When people lack the skill or the will to disagree constructively, disputes about theories, methods, data, analysis, or solutions can take on the character of zero-sum power struggles rather than opportunities for mutual growth and discovery. People become more polarized and closed-minded. They grow less likely to share and cooperate, and more likely to withhold key information, or engage in bad faith for competitive advantage.

Mistakes and failures are more likely to be weaponized against scholars rather than being understood as an unavoidable part of the iterative process of exploration, trial, error, discovery, and revision that lies at the core of the scientific method. People grow less likely to take risks or tolerate uncertainty. Under these circumstances, increased diversity can become a liability—a source of additional paranoia and strife—rather than an asset.

Confirmation Bias is Bad and Everywhere

As an example, a *Reason* study by Ronald Bailey in 2011 titled "Climate Change and Confirmation Bias" suggests that your values, not science, determine your views about climate change.

The Pew Research Center conducted a 2009 survey comparing the political ideologies of scientists and the general public. Only 9 percent of scientists identified as conservative, 35 percent as moderate, and 52 percent as liberal, with 14 percent claiming to be very liberal. In contrast, the general public identifies as 37 percent conservative, 38 percent moderate, and 20 percent liberal, and 5 percent very liberal.

Slicing the data another way, the survey finds that 81 percent of scientists lean Democrat whereas 52 percent of the general public does. Another telling division between the beliefs of the general public versus scientists is their responses to this statement: "When something is run by the government, it is usually inefficient and wasteful." Fifty-eight percent of scientists disagreed, whereas 57 percent of the public agreed with it.

The quest for publication has led some scientists to manipulate data, analysis, and even their original hypotheses. In 2014, John Ioannidis, a Stanford professor conducting researching on research (or 'meta-research'), found that across the scientific field, "many new proposed associations and/or effects are false or grossly exaggerated." Ioannidis, who estimates that 85 percent of research resources are wasted, claims that the frequency of positive results well exceeds how often one should expect to find them. He pleads with the academic world to put less emphasis on "positive" findings.

Ironically, the scientific method is meant to combat confirmation bias: scientists are encouraged to search primarily for falsifying evidence, then confirmation of their hypothesis. The rigors of science, however, are often outweighed by the realities of getting and keeping a job. With their academic careers and tenure contingent on getting published, scientists have moved from testing "How am I wrong?" to simply asking "How am I right?"

"At present, we mix up exploratory and confirmatory research," Brian Nosek, a psychologist with the University of Virginia, told Philip Ball. "You can't generate hypotheses and test them with the same data."

The Replication Crisis in Science is Real

Because the reproducibility of experimental results is an essential part of the scientific method, the inability to replicate the studies of others has potentially grave consequences for many fields of science in which significant theories are grounded on unreproducible experimental work. The replication crisis has been particularly widely discussed in the field of psychology and in medicine, where a number of efforts have been made to re-investigate classic results, to determine both the reliability of the results and, if found to be unreliable, the reasons for the failure of replication.

A 2016 poll of 1,500 scientists reported that 70% of them had failed to reproduce at least one other scientist's experiment (50% had failed to reproduce one of their own experiments). In 2009, 2% of scientists admitted to falsifying studies at least once and 14% admitted to personally knowing someone who did. Misconducts were reported more frequently by medical researchers than others.

The replication crisis in the sciences has just begun. It will be big when it's over. After a decade of slow growth beneath public view, the replication crisis in science begins breaking into public view. First psychology and biomedical studies, now spreading to many other fields—overturning what we were told is settled science, the foundations of our personal behavior and public policy.

This crisis emerged a decade ago as problems in a few fields—especially health care and psychology. Slowly similar problems emerged in other fields, usually failures to replicate widely accepted research. Economics, with its high standards for transparency—has been hit and even physics has been affected.

Is climate change next?

12 – 25 Other MSM Worst Fake News Examples

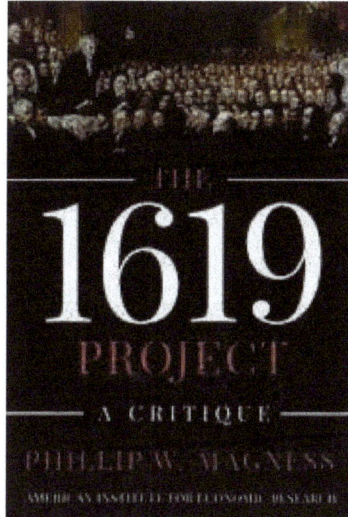

Credit: Amazon.com

Libertarian Wes Messamore published a November 2016 article titled "25 Fake News Stories From The Mainstream Media" at the Independent Voter News with an extensive example list presented below. At the top of this list is the "1619 Project" update added by the S.A.P.I.E.N.T. Being. The content for the other 24 examples is from Messamore's list.

When you look at mainstream media (MSM), more than 90% of the fake news and false stories come from liberal media. On this representative list below there is only one conservative news network, Fox on Item 13 below, and they are included in the "All" category of Item 25, that made the list. Yes, conservative MSM networks succumb to fake news, but on an exponentially smaller scale compared to liberal media.

So, it's important now for the independent, critically minded reader and sharer of news to note and reflect on the amount of fake news stories propagated by mainstream media sources, sometimes unknowingly through unacceptable carelessness and lack of proper journalistic rigor, other times knowingly and deliberately to influence elections or support a policy agenda.

Remember that after the 2016 election, even the *New York Times*, America's "newspaper of record," has had to apologize and "rededicate" itself to honesty, fairness, and scrutiny. The following list of 10 fake news stories from the mainstream media shows just how difficult it is to tackle the problem of fake news.

Using the "1619 Project" from project's creator Nikole Hannah-Jones, she and her 100-page August 2019 article in the *New York Times* provides the World Of Writing Warriors (WOWW) Program a prime example of the abuse and violation of the code of ethics in journalism (on an epic scale) using the Society of Professional Journalists: Code of Ethics as a litmus test.

Hannah-Jones once wrote in a 1995 letter to the editor of Notre Dame's student newspaper, "The white race is the biggest murderer, rapist, pillager, and thief of the modern world." Let that sink in if your school is considering and/or adding the "1619 Project" to their curriculum.

Below is a copy of the entire article from *The Wall Street Journal* titled "The '1619 Project' Gets Schooled" by Elliot Kaufman, Dec. 16, 2019. The subheading reads: "The *New York Times* tries to rewrite U.S. history, but its falsehoods are exposed by surprising sources."

All WOWW members are encouraged, but not required, to use the 100 page "1619 Project" article to critique the number and location of the extensive violations and abuses to the journalistic code of ethics and demonstrate this is the kind of fake news journalism that the WOWW Program is fighting.

25 Examples of Fake News Stories: The "1619 Project" is the Worst

1. (*The New York Times*) Article: The "1619 Project"

Per Elliot Kaufman: 'So wrong in so many ways" is how Gordon Wood, the Pulitzer Prize-winning historian of the American Revolution, characterized the *New York Times's* "1619 Project." James McPherson, dean of Civil War historians and another Pulitzer winner, said the *Times* presented an "unbalanced, one-sided account" that "left most of the history out."

Even more surprising than the criticism from these generally liberal historians was where the interviews appeared: on the World Socialist Web Site, run by the Trotskyist Socialist Equality Party.

The "1619 Project" was launched in August 2019 with a 100-page spread in the *Times's* Sunday magazine. It intends to "reframe the country's history" by crossing out 1776 as America's founding date and substituting 1619, the year 20 or so African slaves were brought to Jamestown, Virginia. The project has been celebrated up and down the liberal establishment, praised by Kamala Harris and Pete Buttigieg, and won a Pulitzer.

A September 2019 essay for the World Socialist Web Site called the project a "racialist falsification" of history. That didn't get much attention, but in November the interviews with the historians went viral. "I wish my books would have this kind of reaction," Wood says in an email. "It still strikes me as amazing why the *NY Times* would put its authority behind a project that has such weak scholarly support."

He adds that fellow historians have privately expressed their agreement. McPherson coolly describes the project's "implicit position that there have never been any good white people, thereby ignoring white radicals and even liberals who have supported racial equality."

The project's creator, Nikole Hannah-Jones, is proud that it "decenters whiteness" and disdains its critics as "old, white male historians." She tweeted of McPherson: "Who considers him preeminent? I don't."

Her own qualifications are an undergraduate degree in history and African American studies and a master's in journalism. She says the project goes beyond McPherson's expertise, the Civil War. "For the most part," she writes in its lead essay, "black Americans fought back alone" against racism. No wonder she'd rather not talk about the Civil War.

To the Trotskyists, Hannah-Jones writes: "You all have truly revealed yourselves for the anti-black folks you really are." She calls them "white men claiming to be socialists."

Perhaps they're guilty of being white men, but they're definitely socialists. Their faction, called the Workers League until 1995, was "one of the most strident and rigid Marxist groups in America" during the Cold War, says Harvey Klehr, a leading historian of American communism.

"Ours is not a patriotic, flag-waving kind of perspective," says Thomas Mackaman, the World Socialist Web Site's interviewer and a history professor at King's College in Wilkes-Barre, PA. He simply recognizes that the arrival of 20 slaves in 1619 wasn't a "world-altering event." Slavery had existed across the world for millennia, and there were already slaves elsewhere in what would become the U.S. before 1619.

But "even if you want to make slavery the central story of American history," he says, the *Times* gets it backward. The American Revolution didn't found a "slavocracy," as Hannah-Jones puts it. Instead, in Mackaman's telling, it "brought slavery in for questioning in a way that had never been done before" by "raising universal human equality as a fundamental principle." Nor was protecting slavery "one of the primary reasons" the colonists declared independence, as Hannah-Jones claims. It's no coincidence the abolitionists rapidly won votes to end slavery in five of the original 13 states, along with Vermont and the new states of the Midwest.

Hannah-Jones insists "anti-black racism runs in the very DNA of this country." Mackaman calls that claim "anti-historical." Proving it requires her to belittle the most progressive declaration of modern history: "that all men are created equal." Hannah-Jones calls this a "lie" and claims its drafters didn't even believe it. The abolitionists disagreed. So did the reverend Martin Luther King Jr: He saw it as a "promissory note."

Mackaman also protests Hannah-Jones's "cherry-picking" of quotes to present Abraham Lincoln as a "garden-variety racist." He attributes the misleading picture to her "totally racialist interpretation." If whites and blacks are supposed to be "diametrically opposed to each other," he says, "then you have to disregard all the history that runs contrary to that—and there's an awful lot."

2. (CBS 60 Minutes) Dan Rather Publicizes Fake Memos About George W. Bush's National Guard Duty

Less than two months before the 2004 Presidential election, Dan Rathers, one of the most trusted names in news went way out on a limb in publishing unauthenticated National Guard memos that turned out to be forged.

The memos falsely attributed to Bush's commander Lt. Col. Jerry Killian suggested that Bush disobeyed direct orders and that the Bush family had exaggerated Bush's service in the National Guard.

When independent bloggers began to question the documents because they were in a computer word processor font that didn't exist at the time, CBS defended its reports until Killian's assistant told them she and Killian did not type the memos. Rather apologized and resigned from CBS.

3. (Huffington Post, *New York Times*, FiveThirtyEight, et al.) Hillary Has a 98% Chance of Winning The Election

Speaking of fake news to influence a campaign, as everyone knows now, the entire mainstream press painted a very false picture of the electoral odds in the 2016 presidential race. Days before the election, Huffington Post had Hillary Clinton at 98% likely to win the election.

With an electoral college gap of 232 to Donald Trump's 306, she was soundly defeated and the overwhelming media confidence in the inevitability of her victory turned out to be fake news. It was a blow of historical proportions to the credibility of the mainstream media and its polling methods.

4. (Salon, CNN, NBC News, MSNBC, CBS News, et al.) Donald Trump Requests Security Clearance for His Children

A widely reported story on mainstream news outlets this week was that President-designate Donald Trump requested secret security clearance for his kids in an act of nepotistic impropriety.

The story was reported, among others by CNN, NBC News, Rachel Maddow on MSNBC, CBS News, and Salon, which snarkily headlined, "Donald Trump's trying to give his kids top secret security clearance, making sure his conflicts of interest are extra bold."

But as *USA Today* reported, "Despite reports suggesting the contrary, a transition team official says Donald Trump did not request or begin paperwork to have his children gain top-level security clearance, according to a pool report."

5. (ABC News) In 2009, ABC News Blatantly Lied About The 1 Million Protesters in Attendance, Reports 60,000

This is a bad one because it was so brazenly false. Glenn Beck's 9-12 March on Washington DC brought in over a million Tea Party protesters to call for lower taxes and less federal spending.

Clear pictures of the crowds from the tops of Washington DC buildings can be cross-referenced with the *USA Today*/National Park Service schematic for estimating the turnout at President Obama's inauguration in January earlier that year. The turnout was undeniably one million plus.

But ABC News not only grossly distorted the turnout to a paltry 60,000, but they also actually went out of their way to correct a misattribution of the more accurate figure to them, wanting to be sure everyone was completely clear that their number was 60,000.

6. (CBS News) 1 Million Disenfranchised Black Voters in the 2000 Election

Less than a month before the 2000 presidential election, echoing an unsourced, unproven claim repeated *ad nausea* on the campaign trail by presidential candidate John Kerry, CBS News uncritically passed along the (mis)information from the mouth of Rev. Jesse Jackson:

"'Black votes have been targeted.' Jackson asserts. In 2000, 2.1 million votes were disenfranchised, 1 million were black.'"

The following January, with the election tallied and over, it was oddly enough CBS News that challenged the authenticity of its own reporting in an article entitled, "The Florida Myth Spreads": Last Thursday's challenge by certain congressional Democrats to the certification of the 2004 presidential election was but the latest chapter in the urban legend that began four years ago in Florida.

Back then, activists claimed that dogs and horses were used to keep black voters from the polls. Claims that thousands of blacks were disenfranchised, harassed, and intimidated from voting ran rampant. The U.S. Commission on Civil Rights conducted a six-month investigation of the charges and found absolutely no evidence of systematic disenfranchisement of black voters. The civil-rights division of the Department of Justice also found no credible evidence that any Floridians were intentionally denied the right to vote.

These findings did little to dispel the myth of "massive disenfranchisement." Maybe because CBS News itself helped spread the myth three months earlier.

7. (CNN, CBS News, NBC, et al.) TV Networks Call Critical Toss-Up Race in Florida for Al Gore Too Early

In a historically very tight toss-up race in a state with critical electoral votes, the mainstream media's television networks called Florida too soon for Al Gore in an "embarrassment of major proportions." Dan Rather was so bold as to make it a guarantee, "If we say somebody's carried the state, you can take that to the bank. Book it!"

The networks made the call just before 8pm Eastern and were forced to retract their call. By 1:30am the Sunshine State was still too close to call. The earlier pronouncement may have had the effect of chilling votes on either or both sides. The state was eventually carried by George W. Bush.

8. (ABC, CBS, CNN, Fox News, NBC, and MSNBC) TV Networks Falsely Claim the Polls In Florida Are Closed

Remember the election in Florida was extremely close. The number of electoral votes made the state pivotal in the 2000 electoral map. Both campaigns had spent no small fortune to secure those votes.

Anchors on every networked emphasized repeatedly that the polls in Florida would be closed at 7pm Eastern Time. Five anchors made sure to say it more than once: Cokie Roberts on ABC, Brian Williams on MSNBC, Judy Woodruff on CNN, Tom Brokaw on NBC, and Dan Rather on CBS.

Brokaw said, "We want to point out to our viewers that in half an hour, at 7 o'clock Eastern Time, we have a group of critical states that will be closing their polls, including the state of Florida," following up on that a few minutes later with, "The polls will close in Florida, as we said just a few moments ago, at 7 Eastern Time tonight."

But the problem with that, and it would be very hard to believe these professional election commentators didn't know it, was that Florida has two time zones, and the polls in the very reliably Republican panhandle did not close at 7pm Eastern. They closed at 8 pm Eastern.

It can't be interpreted any other way than a deliberate ruse to disenfranchise Republican voters in the Florida panhandle to steal the election for Al Gore, or an industry-wide amateur hour of severe journalistic malpractice.

9. (*Washington Post*, *Miami Herald*, et al.) Sources Falsely Claim Orlando Shooter Used an AR-15 Rifle

In a truly repugnant case of politicizing a tragedy to serve a policy agenda, multiple sources falsely reported that the Orlando nightclub shooter used an AR-15 rifle, a gun heavily targeted by the media and activists for more strict regulation or an outright ban.

An uncorrected article on the *Miami Herald* still conveys the misinformation: "Orlando shooter's AR-15: Accurate, lightweight and there are millions." Another uncorrected article on Mic.com still claims incorrectly that the Orlando shooter used the hated AR-15.

After running a piece incorrectly claiming the shooter used an AR-15, the *Washington Post* had the journalistic sense to go back and correct the piece, "The gun the Orlando shooter used was a Sig Sauer MCX, not an AR-15," glibly huffing, "That doesn't change much."

10. (Network Television Affiliates) Swing State Television Networks Aired Swift Boat Veterans for Truth's Blatant Lies About John Kerry's Service

Facebook and social media aren't the only places where fake news hoaxers buy ads to swing election results. In one of the most famous political hoaxes in US history, a 527 group was formed by Vietnam Veterans who didn't even serve with John Kerry in Vietnam to air four television ads claiming that John Kerry's actions in Vietnam were dishonorable, unreliable, and not befitting someone seeking the office of the US presidency. Their claims and credibility have since been widely debunked.

11. (*Daily Mail*) UK Newspaper Falsely Claims Donald Trump's wife, Melania, Worked as an Escort

The Daily Mail, prompted by some heavy litigation led by the same lawyer who represented Hulk Hogan in his successful lawsuit against Gawker, retracted a story in which it printed allegations that Melania Trump worked as an escort in the 1990s. The title of the article, which has now been taken down, was, "Naked photoshoots, and troubling questions about visas that won't go away: The VERY racy past of Donald Trump's Slovenian wife."

12. (*New York Times*) A National Desk Columnist for *The New York Times* Made A Career There Out of Faking News

Jayson Blair had a bright career at the *New York Times* that ended abruptly in 2003 when he was investigated for fabricating numerous stories. Keep that in mind when you consider the *New York Times'* recent rededication to honesty and fairness.

The last time the newspaper of record had to publish a mea culpa, calling the revelations, "a low point in the 152-year history of the newspaper," wasn't enough to keep the paper on track through this election.

The newspaper's internal investigation found problems with 36 out of the 73 columns Blair had written since transferring to the national desk.

13. (Fox News) Top Fox News Employee Confesses to "Selling" Americans on The Iraq War

Over at Fox News, Laurie Luhn, a top aide to former Chairman and CEO Roger Ailes revealed a lot about the network's inner workings when she went public with bombshell accusations of sexual abuse by Ailes, who has since resigned in disgrace after multiple other female employees at the news network shared their own similar stories of harassment.

In one expose, it was revealed that Fox News doesn't live up to its branding as "Fair and Balanced" or other tropes like, "We report, you decide." Instead, the network had a vested interested in making sure its viewers decided in favor of the 2003 Invasion of Iraq.

Listen to what Luhn said: "I was very proud of the product. I was very proud of how we handled 9/11. Very proud of how we handled the run-up to the Iraq War. My job was to sell the war. I needed to get people on the air that were attractive and articulate and could convey the importance of this campaign. It was a drumbeat."

Propaganda is just another way to say: fake news.

14. (*Washington Post, New York Times, Newsweek*, CBS) The CIA Recruited Leading American Journalists to Pass Off Propaganda As News

Sometime read the Wikipedia entry about Operation Mockingbird and marvel that you are on a non-profit encyclopedia's well-sourced article, not some seedy conspiracy blog.

The details read like something you would expect out of Soviet-era Russia, campaign by the Central Intelligence Agency from the 1950s - 1970s recruiting major journalists from respected news sources to present the agency's propaganda as news.

It wouldn't be complete without bribes for journalists and publishers.

15. (*Rolling Stone*) A Completely Fabricated Story of Campus Rape is Published In a Catastrophic Failure of Editorial Process

In November 2014, *Rolling Stone* magazine published an article entitled, "A Rape on Campus," by Sabrina Erdely about a UVA student who was raped by a group of fraternity members at a party, sending the school and community into shock.

As other journalists and bloggers began to note inconsistencies in the story and improprieties in how it was investigated by Erdely before publication, the entire story unraveled until it was soundly discredited.

Rolling Stone issued a retraction and called on Steve Coll, the Pulitzer Prize-winning dean of America's most prestigious journalism school to investigate what went wrong. His conclusion was a thorough indictment of the magazine's practices, issuing a report detailing, "how traditional safeguards broke down at pretty much every level of the editorial process."

16. (Reuters) Photographer Doctors a Photo of Smoke at the Site of an Israeli Airstrike

In 2006, Reuters published photos of an Israeli airstrike in a suburban neighborhood of Beirut. A skeptical American blogger criticized the photo: "This Reuters photograph shows blatant evidence of manipulation. Notice the repeating patterns in the smoke; this is almost certainly caused by using the Photoshop 'clone' tool to add more smoke to the image."

When interviewed by *Ynet News*, he said, "This has to cast doubt not only on the photographer who did the alterations, but on Reuters' entire review process. If they could let such an obvious fake get through to publication, how many more faked or 'enhanced' photos have not been caught?" Reuters investigated and fired the photographer.

17. (The Huffington Post, *The Independent*, International Business Times et al.) Media Falsely Reports Hit and Run in Brussels as Right-Wing Hate Crime

When a Muslim women was struck and knocked down by a hit and run driver in the Brussels district of Molenbeek, mainstream news sources rushed to call it a hate crime perpetrated by a far-right wing activist.

The Huffington Post's headline was later amended, but the URL still contains the original report of a "far right activist" at work. *The Independent* also corrected the narrative-driven, knee jerk reporting still evident in their article's URL. So too, the International Business Times.

As the *Independent* reports in a correction at the bottom of their article, the hit and run driver was a young Muslim local named Mohamed.

18. (*The Guardian*) UK Newspaper Publishes Chain Email Hoax Claiming President Bush Has The Lowest IQ of Any President

In 2001 after the election of President George W. Bush, a hoax email began circulating claiming that a study of presidential IQs by the Lovenstein Institute of Scranton, Pennsylvania found that George W. Bush had an IQ of 91, the lowest of any US president, while outgoing President Bill Clinton had the highest at 182.

The study was a fabrication, and the Lovenstein Institute doesn't even exist. Neither do the sociologists quoted in the email. But in a stunning display of the journalistic standards at *The Guardian*, the fairly obvious chain email hoax was published as news! The paper retracted the story when the Associated Press pointed out their error.

19. (CBS 60 Minutes) Lara Logan Reports Fake News Story About Benghazi, Leading to Her Suspension

In 2013, CBS 60 Minutes aired an "eyewitness" report from a security contractor who turned out not to have been present for the events he claims to have witnessed. The story unraveled when it became evident that his reports didn't match with what he told the FBI.

The boondoggle was a result of poor standards of journalism. No calls were made to the FBI or State Department to verify the contractor's statements. The misstep left the *Washington Post* in shock: "That '60 Minutes' suddenly and inexplicably got out of the business of fact-checking boggles the mind."

Perhaps more damaging, the 60 Minutes report "was flawed in other ways, including Lara Logan making unsourced assertions that Al Qaeda was behind the attack that killed four Americans and controlled a local hospital. It's still not clear where Logan got this information." Apparently, Senator Lindsey Graham had told Logan it was a "fair thing to say" in his opinion, because there had been a "build-up of Al Qaeda types" in the area.

20. (*Washington Post*) Pulitzer Prize Awarded to Journalist for Fake Story About an 8-Year-Old Heroin Addict

In 1980, as the War on Drugs started by President Richard Nixon raged on, a *Washington Post* journalist named Janet Cooke published a story entitled, "Jimmy's World," about an 8-year-old heroin addict.

The piece profiled Jimmy's travails in tragic detail, noting the "needle marks freckling the baby-smooth skin of his thin brown arms," and chronicling his aspirations to become a drug dealer. The piece resonated so strongly it led to an all-out police search to find the boy and Cooke was awarded a Pulitzer Prize.

That's when Cooke admitted the story was a hoax and returned the Pulitzer, the only person to do so in the award's history.

21. (The Huffington Post) A Photoshopped Receipt With a One Percent Tip From a "One Percent" Banker Makes Headlines

In 2012, with the Occupy Wall Street movement in full force and rage against "the One Percent" angrily fomenting, The Huffington Post could not pass up on publishing what turned out to be a hoax.

A wealthy banker's underling and dinner companion was so outraged by a nasty tip the boss left a server on a $133.54 ticket, that the disgruntled employee snapped a picture, showing a tip amount of $1.33 with the word "Tip" circled and an arrow pointing to some harsh words: "Get a real job."

But the image was Photoshopped and the actual credit receipt on file with the restaurant showed a bill of $33.54, not $133.54. The tip was $7.00, slightly more than the customary 20% for good service.

22. (NBC) Nightly News Anchor Brian Williams Lied About an Iraq War Helicopter Incident

In 2003 Dateline NBC headlined a story, "Target Iraq: Helicopter NBC's Brian Williams Was Riding In Comes Under Fire." In a 2007 retelling of the story, Williams said, "I looked down the tube of an RPG that had been fired at us, and it hit the chopper in front of us." By 2013, Williams said, the helicopter he was in had been "hit ... and landed very quickly."

In February of 2015, Williams had to recant the story after criticism from the Chinook crew who said the helicopter Williams was riding in was not hit by an RPG and that he could not have seen the one that was hit ahead of the one he was riding in because it was a half hour ahead of his flight.

Further scrutiny prompted by this revelation found that Williams had told inconsistent stories about a man committing suicide in the New Orleans Super Dome during Katrina, falsely claimed he was at the Brandenburg Gate the night the Berlin Wall came down and lied about flying into Baghdad with SEAL Team Six.

23. (The Associated Press, *Boston Globe*, CNN, Fox News) FBI Criticizes Media for False Reports Regarding The Boston Marathon Bombers

In the aftermath of the Boston Marathon Bombings in 2013, with the perpetrators still at large, several news sources falsely reported that an arrest had been made.

The FBI released a statement scolding the media for its inaccurate and premature reporting on a sensitive terrorism investigation still in progress:

"Over the past day and a half, there have been a number of press reports based on information from unofficial sources that has been inaccurate. Since these stories often have unintended consequences, we ask the media, particularly at this early stage of the investigation, to exercise caution and attempt to verify information through appropriate official channels before reporting."

Judy Muller, who teaches journalism at the University of Southern California, wrote the *New York Times* to say: "I fear we have permanently entered the Age of the Retraction. All the lessons of the past—from Richard Jewell to NPR's announcement of the death of Gabby Giffords to CNN's erroneous report on the Supreme Court Ruling on Obamacare—fail to inform the present. The rush to be first has so thoroughly swallowed up the principle of being right and first that it seems a little egg on the face is now deemed worth the risk."

24. (The *Washington Post*, MSNBC, ABC, NBC, CBS, et al.) Media Spreads Inflammatory Fake News Story About a Police Shooting in Ferguson, MO

In 2014, when a Ferguson, Missouri Police Officer confronted a suspect who matched the description of an assault and robbery that had just taken place at a convenient store, the young man, 18-year-old Michael Brown, fought with the Police Officer, Darren Wilson, struggling to wrest his gun away. When Wilson pursued him on foot, Brown turned and charged at him, and Wilson fired several shots into the front of Brown's body, killing him.

This was a very delicate tragedy with strong racial overtones, and in a rush to support a racially-charged, inflammatory media narrative, journalists enthusiastically spread a fake news story: that Michael Brown had his hands up and yelled "Don't shoot!" at the time Wilson fatally discharged his firearm. It turned out to be false. Upon investigation by the Federal Justice Department, eyewitnesses changed their stories or admitted they didn't see the shooting take place.

The eager embrace of this narrative by the media had real world consequences, stoking tensions and anger in Ferguson, and leading to looting of local businesses and protests that turned violent. The shooting happened in August 2014. By March 2015, MSNBC anchor and *Washington*

Post columnist Jonathan Capehart finally offered a mea culpa with a column entitled, "'Hands Up, Don't Shoot' Was Based on a Lie."

25. (*The Daily Mirror*) Piers Morgan Fired From UK Newspaper for Hoaxing Photos of Iraqi Prisoner Abuse

Before he got his cable television show on CNN, Piers Morgan was the editor of *The Daily Mirror*, one of the UK's biggest newspapers, which in 2004, published photos of Iraqi prisoners of war being abused by British Army soldiers from the Queen's Lancashire Regiment.

Then the picture editor at *The Guardian* published a point-by-point analysis of the photos arguing that they looked to be a hoax. When they turned out to be fake news, Piers Morgan was sacked from the publication, not for his editorial slip, but for refusing to apologize for it.

13 – Spotting Fake News Media Like a Media Watchdog

Credit: MRC

Over the years, the Media Research Center (MRC) has catalogued the views of journalists on the subject of bias and most of the content for this chapter is from their extensive reports.

A number of journalists have admitted that the majority of their brethren approach the news from a liberal angle. But many journalists continue to deny the liberal bias that taints their profession. Following Obama's election in November 2008, Reuters ran a headline baldly declaring: "Media bias largely unseen in U.S. presidential race." Fake news madness and clearly false!

During the height of CBS's forged memo scandal during the 2004 campaign, Dan Rather ridiculously insisted that the problem wasn't his bias, it was his critics: "People who are so passionately partisan politically or ideologically committed basically say, 'Because he won't report it our way, we're going to hang something bad around his neck and choke him with it, check him out of existence if we can, if not make him feel great pain.'" This is an example of denial of his forgery and criminal fake news.

In the words of Steve Forbes, "Before the emergence of talk-radio, before Fox News, before online center-right alternative media, there was Brent Bozell. He pioneered an entire cottage industry that effectively holds the national media accountable before the public. The exponential growth of alternative media owes a lot to Brent Bozell, as his relentlessness in exposing and documenting media bias is the foundation upon which they have succeeded."

The Media Research Center (MRC) is America's premier media watchdog, and since its founding in 1987 by Brent Bozell , the MRC has worked to expose and neutralize the propaganda arm of the Left: the national news media. The MRC's commitment to neutralizing leftist bias in the news media and popular culture has had a critical impact on the way Americans view the liberal media.

The MRC is able to effectively educate the public about left-wing media bias by integrating cutting-edge news monitoring capabilities with a sophisticated marketing operation. MRC generated an average of 376.8 million impressions each week in 2019. This includes radio, television, social media, email, and websites. Their mission is to, "Create a Media Culture in America Where Truth and Liberty Flourish."

MRC's guidebook, *CENSORED! How Online Media Companies Are Suppressing Conservative Speech* by the Media Research Center has undertaken an extensive study of the problem at major tech companies effort to censor the conservative worldview from the public conversation and formulated this informative guidebook.

Be Skeptical of Other 'Media Watchdog' Impersonators

There are many liberal and leftist imposters claiming to "objective" media watchdogs that are the darlings of social and mainstream media—but none of them have advanced the science of exposing media bias like Media Research Center (MRC) has for more than thirty years and during those years they have grown to include seven departments as follows:

- **CNSNews** reports the stories the liberal media refuse to cover. Under the skillful editorial stewardship of long-time conservative writer and Pulitzer Prize nominee Terry Jeffrey, CNSNews has emerged as the conservative media's lynchpin for original reporting and breaking news.

- **NewsBusters**, the News Analysis Division's fast paced and popular blog, is the leader in documenting, exposing, and neutralizing liberal media bias. Its team of expert news analysts monitor all the major media outlets 24 hours a day and produce comprehensive bias analysis as well as posts showcasing the most ridiculous examples of leftist bias in the media.

- **MRC Business** is dedicated to advancing the culture of free enterprise in America. MRC Business is the only organization dedicated to correcting the media's anti-free enterprise biased reports, reporting the truth about the American economy, and promoting a fair portrayal of the business community in the news and entertainment media.

- **MRC Culture** fights to preserve and restore America's culture, character, traditional values, and morals against the assault of the liberal media elite, and to promote fair portrayal of social conservatives and religious believers in the media. MRC Culture is dedicated to correcting misconceptions in the media about social conservatism and religious faith.

- **MRC Latino** advocates for comprehensive, fair, and accurate news coverage in U.S. Spanish-language media by exposing and countering bias against conservatives in this significant segment of American media. MRC Latino's ongoing content analysis and special reports are featured in both English and Spanish. MRC Latino educates all audiences of the problem of liberal bias in Spanish-language media.

- **MRCTV** is the multimedia division of MRC featuring original content and aggregated videos of the news, people, and events conservatives care about. The site features all of the MRC's television appearances and serves as an online platform for conservatives to share and view videos on topics ranging from breaking news to political analysis and humor.

- **MRC Action** is the grassroots arm of the Media Research Center. The team directly contacts hundreds of thousands of Americans each week, urging citizens with its MRC Action e-newsletter to take action in neutralizing the left-wing press. MRC Action mobilizes its members to counter left-wing media bias with petitions, email campaigns, and phone banks all demanding fair and accurate reporting in the media.

The Fact Checkers' Fact Checker: Real Clear Politics

News media fact checkers were once a rarity, but according to a report titled "Who Is Fact Checking The Fact Checkers?" by *Investor's Business Daily* in August 2018, they're now in a position to determine what people can read online, despite their own checkered past. So, who keeps the fact checkers honest? Thankfully, Real Clear Politics has stepped into the breach by creating what it calls Fact Check Review.

If a fact-checking outfit deems a story not entirely true, for example, Facebook can limit its reach on its News Feed. Google now includes a "fact check" box on its main search results page to help "people make more informed judgments."

The problem is that fact checkers themselves can be unreliable sources for what's true or not. Fact checkers make their own mistakes. They sometimes change ratings based on new information. Or they make determinations based on arbitrary standards that can change from one review to the next.

Per a report titled "Facebook Censors Pro-Trump Ad After Fact-Checker Admits Claim May Be True" by John Bickley in a September 2020 edition of the DailyWire.com, amid pressure from left-wing activists and media outlets to clamp down on "misinformation" from the right, Facebook has begun censoring political ads that receive negative fact-checks—fact-checks that are produced by mostly left-leaning fact-checkers and that mostly target right-leaning ads.

In at least two new cases, these fact-checks do not actually check facts—they instead merely state that factually true claims are "missing context," then downgrade the ads.

The danger of this political speech-silencing policy by the social media giant—which nearly 70% of Americans use and where more than 40% read their news—is on full display in the case of the censoring of the pro-Trump 30-second political ad "Too Risky."

The ad launched on August 4, 2020 before getting slapped with a "mostly false" rating by PolitiFact and subsequently blocked by Facebook the next month. The ad directly quotes Biden declaring, "If you elect me, your taxes are going to be raised, not cut," and warns that his plan will raise taxes "on all income groups."

Fact Checkers Often "Check" Opinions

Fact checkers also often "check" opinions, rather than factual claims, even though two people can form diametrically opposed opinions based on the same facts.

Worse, many media "fact checks" use other media sources to check facts, apparently forgetting that journalists get their facts wrong almost as often as politicians. (Take a look at the list of corrections on any given day in *The New York Times*.)

On top of this are legitimate complaints of political bias among fact checkers, who often seem to spend most of their time trying to debunk claims made by conservatives rather than liberals.

Thankfully, Real Clear Politics has stepped into the breach by creating what it calls Fact Check Review.

Not only does the site regularly review problematic "fact checks," it constantly updates a database on fact checks published by Snopes, FactCheck.org, PolitiFact, *New York Times*, *Washington Post* and the *Weekly Standard*.

It then rates them based on how often each site checks opinions rather than facts. In July 2020, for example, a quarter of the *Post's* "fact" checks were of opinions, as were 18% of PolitiFact's. It also looks at how often fact checkers rely on other news outlets to verify claims. In July, 90% of Snopes fact checks used other media sources.

There's a bigger problem with this fact-checking trend, however. As the *Weekly Standard's* Mark Hemingway explained: "It's basically a way for a bunch of reporters with no particular expertise to render pseudoscientific judgments on statements from public figures that are obviously argumentative or otherwise unverifiable. Then there's the matter of them weighing in with thundering certitude—pants on fire!—on complex policy debates they frequently misunderstand."

Become Better Informed About the Issues

In the end, the best way to judge the veracity of claims being tossed around is to become better informed about the issues, not contract out that job to people who aren't necessarily qualified to do for you.

The goal of the RCP Fact Check Review project is to understand how the flagship fact-checking organizations operate in practice, from their claim and verification sourcing to their topical focus to just what even constitutes a "fact." To answer these questions, RCP created a centralized searchable database, updated weekly, that codifies key characteristics of all fact checks bearing on issues of civic and public concern published by six major fact-checking organizations:

- FactCheck
- *New York Times*
- PolitiFact
- Snopes
- *Weekly Standard*
- *Washington Post*

These fact checkers were selected due to their outsize influence in the fact-checking landscape and the reliance of major internet platforms such as Facebook on their decisions. Each relevant fact check is recorded using a dual coder reconciliation workflow that codifies several key attributes.

We rely on a human review workflow due to the nuanced nature of some of the attributes we compile about each fact check. While some of the basic attributes could be extracted using automated tools, many of the fields are more resistant to high-quality, automated extraction.

For example, RCP breaks each fact check into the discrete claims it evaluates; summarize each claim using the fact checker's own words; separate the list of sources to associate each source with the specific claim(s) it was used to confirm or refute; assess a claim as "fact" or "opinion"; and record whether the fact checker specifically notes that their determination was based on a lack of evidence or belief that the claim is misleading and classify each source into a type taxonomy.

MSNBC Producer's Scathing Exit Letter: Ratings Model 'Blocks Diversity of Thought and Content'

Joe Concha's August 2020 article in *The Hill* titled "MSNBC Producer's Scathing Exit Letter: Ratings Model 'Blocks Diversity of Thought and Content'" is one of many and his is highlighted below:

Producer Ariana Pekary recently resigned from MSNBC with an open letter accusing the news network of predicating its editorial process on ratings and alleging that its model "blocks diversity of thought and content because the networks have incentive to amplify fringe voices and events."

"I don't know what I'm going to do next exactly, but I simply couldn't stay there anymore," Ariana Pekary, a producer for MSNBC's second-most-watched program, "The Last Word with Lawrence O'Donnell," wrote on her website. "My colleagues are very smart people with good intentions. The problem is the job itself. It forces skilled journalists to make bad decisions on a daily basis."

"It's possible that I'm more sensitive to the editorial process due to my background in public radio, where no decision I ever witnessed was predicated on how a topic or guest would 'rate.'

The longer I was at MSNBC, the more I saw such choices—it's practically baked into the editorial process—and those decisions affect news content every day," she continued. "Likewise, it's taboo to discuss how the ratings scheme distorts content, or it's simply taken for granted, because everyone in the commercial broadcast news industry is doing the exact same thing."

"But behind closed doors, industry leaders will admit the damage that's being done," she continued. Pekary, who worked on O'Donnell's show until July 24, added that she believes the news media is making the same mistake it did in 2016 by focusing almost exclusively on President Trump in 2020 and not so much on presumptive Democratic presidential nominee Joe Biden

"This cancer risks our democracy, even in the middle of a presidential election," she writes. "Any discussion about the election usually focuses on Donald Trump, not Joe Biden, a repeat offense from 2016 (Trump smothers out all other coverage). Also important is to ensure citizens can vote by mail this year, but I've watched that topic get ignored or 'killed' numerous times."

"The model blocks diversity of thought and content because the networks have incentive to amplify fringe voices and events, at the expense of others," Pekary also wrote. "All because it pumps up the ratings."

Pekary joined MSNBC seven years ago as part of the launch of actor Alec Baldwin's weekly program, which lasted just five weeks.

The resignation echoes that of former *New York Times* columnist Bari Weiss, who penned a scathing resignation letter to *Times* published A.G. Sulzberger on her website claiming a "hostile work environment" by fellow staffers because of her centrist views.

Weiss also alleged that editors were reluctant to go "against the grain" with pieces that could spur a backlash on social media. "Showing up for work as a centrist at an American newspaper should not require bravery," she wrote in the letter, which quickly went viral.

MSNBC is having its best year from a ratings perspective in its 24-year history and is currently the second-most-watched channel on cable behind Fox News.

List of Popular Liberal Journalists Denying Liberal Bias

The liberal bias and fake new madness are eating away at the heart and soul of ethical journalism and is a cancer to MSM that must be cured. The Media Research Center (MRC) provides extensive documentation of every bias incident and below is just a tiny fraction of examples of how prevalent it is:

- "My work has been so cleansed, as I see it, and as I've tried, of political opinions over 27 years.... No one gives a rat's patootie about my opinion, so it's nice that I don't have to share it." *NBC Nightly News anchor* **Brian Williams** *on Alec Baldwin's Here's the Thing New York City radio show, March 4, 2013.*

- "Most of us, do not—you don't know whether we're Republicans or Democrats or exhibitionists." *Co-host **Barbara Walters** on ABC's The View, April 9, 2012.*

- "I think the thing that is underappreciated about MSNBC is that we don't really do anything as a company, that we all sort of get to do our own thing. There may be liberals on TV at MSNBC, but the network is not operating with a political objective." *MSNBC 9pm ET host **Rachel Maddow** in a December 21, 2011 interview posted at Slate.com.*

- "I do not have a liberal bias. I don't have a conservative bias, either. I don't have any bias. I am bias-free. Bias is what people who hear or read the news bring to the story, not what the journalist brings to the reporting. My newscast is a flavor of neutrality." *PBS's **Jim Lehrer** appearing on Comedy Central's The Colbert Report, November 27, 2006.*

- "Brent Bozell has, you know, an entire organization devoted to doing as much damage, and I choose that word carefully, as he can to the credibility of the news divisions. And now, on the Left, there are the young bloggers out there. These three aging white men are stuck somewhere in the middle trying, on a nightly basis, to give a fair and balanced picture of what's going on in the world." *NBC Nightly News anchor **Tom Brokaw**, sitting alongside **Dan Rather** and **Peter Jennings**, at an October 2, 2004 New Yorker Festival forum shown on C-SPAN the next day.*

- "Anybody who knows me knows that I am not politically motivated, not politically active for Democrats or Republicans, and that I'm independent. People who are so passionately partisan politically or ideologically committed basically say, 'Because he won't report it our way, we're going to hang something bad around his neck and choke him with it, check him out of existence if we can, if not make him feel great pain.' They know that I'm fiercely independent and that's what drives them up a wall." *CBS's **Dan Rather** as quoted by USA Today, September 16, 2004.*

- CBS's Lesley Stahl: "Today you have broadcast journalists who are avowedly conservative… The voices that are being heard in broadcast media today, are far more likely to be on the right and avowedly so, and therefore, more—almost stridently so, than what you're talking about." Host Cal Thomas: "Can you name a conservative journalist at CBS News?" Stahl: "I don't know of anybody's political bias at CBS News. We try very hard to get any opinion that we have out of our stories, and most of our stories are balanced." *Exchange on the Fox News Channel's After Hours with CBS's **Lesley Stahl** and Fox's **Cal Thomas**, January 18, 2003.*

- "I think there is a mainstream media. CNN is mainstream media, and the main, ABC, CBS, NBC are mainstream media. And I think it's just essentially to make the point that we are largely in the center without particular axes to grind, without ideologies which are represented in our daily coverage, at least certainly not on purpose." *ABC's **Peter Jennings**, CNN's **Larry King** Live, May 15, 2001.*

List of Journalists Admitting Liberal Bias

Again, and again, relentlessly since 1987, the Media Research Center (MRC) provides extensive documentation of every bias incident and as well as the ones where journalists admitted to it as the examples below show.

"Are reporters biased? There is no doubt that—I've worked at the *Wall Street Journal*, the *Washington Post* and worked here at Politico. If I had to guess, if you put all of the reporters that I've ever worked with on truth serum, most of them vote Democratic." *Politico's **Jim VandeHei** during C-SPAN's coverage of the GOP primaries, March 13, 2012.*

"No person with eyes in his head in 2008 could have failed to see the way that soft coverage helped to propel Obama first to the Democratic nomination and then into the White House." *New York Magazine political reporter **John Heilemann**, January 27, 2012.*

"The mainstream press is liberal. Since the civil rights and women's movements, the culture wars and Watergate, the press corps at such institutions as the *Washington Post*, ABC-NBC-CBS News, the *NYT*, the *Wall Street Journal*, *Time*, *Newsweek*, the *Los Angeles Times*, the *Boston Globe*, etc. is composed in large part of 'new' or 'creative' class members of the liberal elite— well-educated men and women who tend to favor abortion rights, women's rights, civil rights, and gay rights. In the main, they find such figures as Bill O'Reilly, Glenn Beck, Sean Hannity, Pat Robertson, or Jerry Falwell beneath contempt. If reporters were the only ones allowed to vote, Walter Mondale, Michael Dukakis, Al Gore, and John Kerry would have won the White House by landslide margins." *Longtime Washington Post political reporter **Thomas Edsall** in an October 8, 2009 essay for the Columbia Journalism Review, 'Journalism Should Own Its Liberalism.'*

"The elephant in the newsroom is our narrowness. Too often, we wear liberalism on our sleeve and are intolerant of other lifestyles and opinions. We're not very subtle about it at this paper: If you work here, you must be one of us. You must be liberal, progressive, a Democrat. I've been in communal gatherings in *The Post*, watching election returns, and have been flabbergasted to see my colleagues cheer unabashedly for the Democrats." *Washington Post "Book World" editor **Marie Arana** in a contribution to the Post's "daily in-house electronic critiques," as quoted by Post media reporter Howard Kurtz in an October 3, 2005 article.*

"I worked for the *New York Times* for 25 years. I could probably count on one hand, in the Washington bureau of the *New York Times*, people who would describe themselves as people of faith.... I think one of the real built-in biases in the media is towards secularism. .... You want diversity in the newsroom, not because of some quota, but because you have to have diversity to cover the story well and cover all aspects of a society. And you don't have religious people making the decisions about where coverage is focused. And I think that's one of the faults." *Former New York Times reporter **Steve Roberts**, now a journalism professor at George Washington University, on CNN's Reliable Sources, March 27, 2005.*

"Does anybody really think there wouldn't have been more scrutiny if this [CBS's bogus *60 Minutes* National Guard story fabricated by Dan Rather] had been about John Kerry?" *Former 60 Minutes Executive Producer* **Don Hewitt** *at a January 10, 2005 meeting at CBS, as quoted by Chris Matthews later that day on MSNBC's Hardball.*

Jack Cafferty: "The liberal talk radio station Air America debuts today. .... Does America need additional 'liberal' media outlet?" Bill Hemmer: "Why hasn't a liberal radio station or TV network never taken off before?" Cafferty: "We have them. Are you—did you just get off a vegetable truck from the South Bronx? They're everywhere. What do they call this joint? The Clinton News Network." *CNN's American Morning, March 31, 2004*

"At ABC, people say 'conservative' the way people say, 'child molester.'" *ABC 20/20 co-anchor* **John Stossel** *as quoted in a January 28, 2004 story on CNSNews.com.*

"There is just no question that I, among others, have a liberal bias. I mean, I'm consistently liberal in my opinions. And I think some of the, I think Dan [Rather] is transparently liberal. Now, he may not like to hear me say that. I always agree with him, too, but I think he should be more careful." *CBS's* **Andy Rooney** *discussing his ex-colleague Bernard Goldberg's book, Bias, CNN's Larry King Live, June 5, 2002.*

"Everybody knows that there's a liberal, that there's a heavy liberal persuasion among correspondents. Anybody who has to live with the people, who covers police stations, covers county courts, brought up that way, has to have a degree of humanity that people who do not have that exposure don't have, and some people interpret that to be liberal. It's not a liberal, it's humanitarian and that's a vastly different thing." *Former CBS Evening News anchor* **Walter Cronkite** *at the March 21, 1996 Radio & TV Correspondents Dinner.*

"The old argument that the networks and other 'media elites' have a liberal bias is so blatantly true that it's hardly worth discussing anymore. No, we don't sit around in dark corners and plan strategies on how we're going to slant the news. We don't have to. It comes naturally to most reporters." *Then-CBS reporter* **Bernard Goldberg** *in a February 13, 1996 Wall Street Journal op-ed.*

"As much as we try to think otherwise, when you're covering someone like yourself, and your position in life is insecure, she's your mascot. Something in you roots for her. You're rooting for your team. I try to get that bias out, but for many of us it's there." *Time Senior Writer* **Margaret Carlson** *talking about covering First Lady Hillary Clinton, as quoted in The Washington Post, March 7, 1994.*

"Coverage of the [1992] campaign vindicated exactly what conservatives have been saying for years about liberal bias in the media. In their defense, journalists say that though they may have their personal opinions, as professionals they are able to correct for them when they write. Sounds nice, but I'm not buying any." *Former Newsweek reporter* **Jacob Weisberg** *in The New Republic, November 23, 1992.*

"As the science editor at *Time* I would freely admit that on this issue we have crossed the boundary from news reporting to advocacy." *Time Science Editor **Charles Alexander** at a September 16, 1989 global warming conference, as quoted by David Brooks in an October 5, 1989 Wall Street Journal column.*

The Media Research Center (MRC) is Blacklisted

Per MRC'S NewsBusters (NB): The media are hard at work weaving a web of confusion, misinformation, and conspiracy surrounding every major issue or topic of the Trump administration. At MRC's NewsBusters, we cut through the hypocrisy and expose the media's bias, bringing the truth to the American people—but without you, our efforts can only go so far.

The media is using whatever crisis it can to swing the upcoming election—they have an agenda, and the truth is not part of it. When a sapient organization like MRC excels at calling out liberal and leftist bias in social media—they too have experienced their wrath.

This is why NewsBusters, a program of the MRC, exists. To take on the liberal media, expose their toxic bias, and stop them in their tracks. We are part of the only organization purely dedicated to this critical mission and we need your help to fuel this fight.

Media Research Center Founder and President Brent Bozell and the MRC's Free Speech Alliance released an open letter in July 2020 to Alphabet CEO Sundar Pichai ahead of the House Judiciary Committee and the Antitrust Subcommittee in the July 2020 hearing featuring Pichai, Amazon CEO Jeff Bezos, Apple CEO Tim Cook, and Facebook CEO Mark Zuckerberg.

The letter comes less than a week after major MRC's major sites (including NewsBusters) and other conservative platforms were blacklisted from Google's search results. The full text of the letter can be found below:

Dear Mr. Pichai,

This past Wednesday July 21 (2020), several conservative media platforms, including four of Media Research Center's (MRC) major sites, were removed from Google's search results. Google's official response was that this was the result of a technical glitch.

We don't believe you.

We believe Google is lying yet again. It's the same old game. Censor conservatives wait for someone else to call you out on it, then blame the algorithms or another technical problem for the censorship. Somehow you never manage to discover your own glitch. It's always your victims who do. Your approach to this scandal is one of an utter lack of transparency and has become second nature to you and your organization. It's not merely shameful, it's a clear and present danger to our civil society. You need to answer for this.

Who at Google was responsible for this latest instance of deliberate censorship against conservatives?

Why did they do it?

What are you doing about your employees who did this and who are trying to undermine our democratic process?

What information are you going to provide to both Congress and those impacted to show what actually happened?

How many more times will Google censor conservatives, and then lie about it before Congress has to take action against your company? The time has passed for lame excuses. If you won't be honest and fix the problem, then Congress must act decisively to counter the threat to freedom of speech from you and other Big Tech companies. It's time for the federal government to consider antitrust solutions for companies like Google and the rest of the Big Tech industry that have grown too powerful and too irresponsible.

Your claims that Google is neutral, while your company continues to censor conservatives deliberately and deceptively, are simply not credible.

On Wednesday, July 29, you are appearing before the House Judiciary Subcommittee on Antitrust. Google deliberately censors conservatives. We dare you to deny that under oath.

Sincerely,

L. Brent Bozell III
Founder and President
Media Research Center

14 – Ten Prevalent Liberal/Leftist Fake News Stories and Agendas

TECH COMPANIES CENSOR
TRUMP MORE THAN BIDEN
*5/31/18 to 11/30/20

TIMES BIDEN HAS
BEEN CENSORED

TIMES TRUMP HAS
BEEN CENSORED

0　VS　325

mrc

Credit: MRC

Unfortunately, we live in a world these days gone mad and turned up-side down it seems. Much like a witch-hunt, or where you're guilty first until proven innocent later, or simply a lack of free speech, many people cannot seem to separate their opinions from facts. Have you had enough of the idiocracy of illiberalism and fake news madness?

As the time-tested saying goes, "Everyone is entitled to their own opinions, but they're not entitled to their own facts." Facts are facts, the truth is the truth, but they can be skewed and manipulated for disingenuous methods and false narratives. We don't do that at the SAPIENT Being or Fratire Publishing. In fact, we'll go out of our way to point out and correct such fallacies. This is part of the higher calling of being a journalist and a sapient being.

Here are 10 powerful and relevant examples of fake news stories and false agendas that fail the criteria set in the WOWW's Journalism Code of Ethics, Practical Logic & Sapience and they also comprise the bulk of fake news stories and journalism seen and read today. Many of the WOWW Program 's *MADNESS* titles tackle head on these subject areas and by having a clear, truthful, and sapient understanding of these issues, one can make sense of them and make smarter choices and decisions at the ballot box and public policy.

FYI: There are many more than these ten examples. Looks for others and report about them.

1. Refusing to Accept There is 'No' Gender Pay Gap

In a 2019interview with Christina Hoff Sommers of the American Enterprise Institute (AEI) with Prager U, she explains the fallacious 77-cents-on-the-dollar statistic is calculated by dividing the median earnings of all women working full-time by the median earnings of all men working full-time. In other words, if the average income of all men is, say, 40,000 dollars a year, and the average annual income of all women is, say, 30,800 dollars, which would mean that women earn 77 cents for every dollar a man earns. 30,800 divided by 40,000 equals 77.

But these calculations don't reveal a gender wage injustice because it doesn't take into account occupation, position, education, or hours worked per week. A sapient analysis *must* include these critical variables.

Even a study by the American Association of University Women, a feminist organization, shows that the actual wage gap shrinks to only 6.6 cents when you factor in different choices men and women make. And the key word here is "choice." The small wage gap that does exist has nothing to do with paying women less, let alone with sexism; it has to do with differences in individual career choices that men and women make.

In 2009, the U.S. Department of Labor released a paper that examined more than 50 peer-reviewed studies and concluded that the oft-cited 23 percent wage gap "may be almost entirely the result of individual choices being made by both male and female workers." If true, let's look at some of those choices.

Georgetown University compiled a list of the five best-paying college majors, and the percentage of men or women majoring in those fields: Number 1 best-paying major: Petroleum Engineering: 87% male Number 2: Pharmaceutical Sciences: 48% male 3: Mathematics and Computer Science: 67% male 4: Aerospace Engineering: 88% male 5: Chemical Engineering: 72% male

Notice that women out-represent men in only one of the five top-paying majors—by only a few percentage points.

Now consider the same study's list of the five worst paying college majors: Number 1: Counseling and Psychology: 74% female Number 2: Early Childhood Education: 97% female 3: Theology and Religious Vocations: 66% male 4: Human Services and Community Organization: 81% female 5: Social Work: 88% female.

Notice that women out-represent men in all but one of the five low-paying majors. So, it seems that business leaders aren't bad at math simply because they don't only hire women. Those who claim that for the same work women earn 77 cents on the dollar compared to men, on the other hand, are not merely bad at math—but at telling the truth.

2. Promoting the Myth of Democratic Socialism Over American Capitalism

From a July 2018 article in *Forbes* titled "Sorry Bernie Bros: But Nordic Countries Are Not Socialist" by Jeffrey Dorfman, a professor of economics at the University of Georgia, he explains:

The myth of Nordic socialism is partially created by a confusion between socialism, meaning government exerting control or ownership of businesses, and the welfare state in the form of government-provided social safety net programs. However, the left's embrace of socialism is not merely a case of redefining a word. Simply look at the long-running affinity of leftists with socialist dictators in Cuba, Nicaragua, and Venezuela for proof many on the left long for real socialism.

To the extent that the left wants to point to an example of successful socialism, not just generous welfare states, the Nordic countries are actually a poor case to cite. Regardless of the perception, in reality the Nordic countries practice mostly free market economics paired with high taxes exchanged for generous government entitlement programs.

First, it is worth noting that the Nordic counties were economic successes *before* they built their welfare states. Those productive economies, generating good incomes for their workers, allowed the governments to raise the tax revenue needed to pay for the social benefits. It was not the government benefits that created wealth, but wealth that allowed the luxury of such generous government programs.

Second, as evidence of the lack of government interference in business affairs, there is the fact that none of these countries have minimum wage laws. Unions are reasonably powerful in many industries and negotiate contracts, but the government does nothing to ensure any particular outcome from those negotiations. Workers are paid what they are worth, not based on government's perception of what is fair.

A third example of Nordic commitment to free markets can be found in Sweden which has complete school choice. The government provides families with vouchers for each child. These vouchers can be used to attend regular public schools, government-run charter schools, or private, for-profit schools. Clearly, the use of government funds to pay for private, for-profit schools is the opposite of socialism.

Socialism can take the form of government controlling or interfering with free markets, nationalizing industries, and subsidizing favored ones (green energy, anyone?). The Nordic countries don't actually do much of those things. Yes, they offer government-paid healthcare, in some cases tuition-free university educations, and rather generous social safety nets, all financed with high taxes.

However, it is possible to do these things without interfering in the private sector more than required. It is allowing businesses to be productive that produces the high corporate and personal incomes that support the tax collections making the government benefits feasible. The Nordic countries are smart enough not to kill the goose that lays the golden egg.

If the left insists on naming a system of generous government benefits combined with a free market democratic socialism, we cannot stop them. That seems unnecessarily confusing since the government is actually running no industries other than education (and meddling somewhat in healthcare). It certainly isn't socialism. In fact, the only reason most such countries can afford those benefits is that their market economies are so productive they can cover the expense of the government's generosity. Perhaps a better name for what the Nordic countries practice would be compassionate capitalism.

3. Unverifiable and Incorrectly Painting Trump as a Racist

From an interview of Nikki Haley and article by Kristine Marsh in August 2020 titled "Nikki Haley Destroys ABC for Ignoring What Trump's Done for Black, Hispanic Americans":

Former U.N. Ambassador Nikki Haley embarrassed ABC and CBS journalists by responding to their leading questions with reason and facts. During her two interviews, she was repeatedly badgered to attack President Trump, but wouldn't take the bait. Instead, she made a powerful case skewering ABC for ignoring what the president has done for minorities as well as schooling CBS on how he's handled the coronavirus pandemic.

On ABC's Good Morning America, anchor George Stephanopoulos immediately tried to "fact-check" Haley for saying that Democrats think America is a "racist" country, during last night's Republican National Convention. He also wanted "specifics" on what President Trump has done to fight the left-wing construct of "systemic racism:"

You spoke last night about our racial divide and criticized Democrats who you say call this a racist country. Joe Biden has not said America is racist, but he and other Democrats have decried patterns of what they say is systemic racism in housing, education employment, law enforcement, the latest possible example, that shooting of Jacob Blake in Kenosha, Wisconsin last night. Do those barriers exist and what specifically has President Trump done to address them?

Funny how Joe Biden was in office for how many decades and he doesn't get this question from journalists?

Haley responded by pointing out examples of America's accomplishments in disavowing and combating racism before Stephanopoulos asked the question again. He tried to trap her by bringing up her criticism of President Trump's Charlottesville comments in 2017. But Haley was ready to educate Stephanopoulos and ABC viewers on all the things Trump has done for black Americans which Obama and Biden didn't do.

Stephanopoulos: Right but I asked you what President Trump has done to heal that racial divide and, you know, you wrote that you were deeply disturbed by President Trump's comments after Charlottesville. Since then, he's tweeted out a video of his supporters chanting white power, praised the Confederate flag which you call divisive in your speech last night, so I'll ask the question again, what specifically has President Trump done to address this systemic racism and the racial divide?

Haley: I will tell you first of all President Trump has passed criminal justice reform which Obama and Biden didn't do. We saw the lowest unemployment of African Americans and Hispanics which wasn't under President Obama or Biden. We have seen more funding go to the historically black colleges. That never happened under Obama and Biden, so this is more about opinions of you thinking that the President hasn't done enough. I'm looking at results at what the President has done.

"He cared about making sure that he left his mark on improving America for when he was done, and I think that we have to look at that. To just think and to have, you know, media outlets say he is just a bad person is not fair," she argued.

4. Denying Black Lives Matter is a Marxist Organization

Black Lives Matter is run by Marxist organizers and their agenda is far different from the slogan. From the July 2020 interview on Prager U between Professor Carol M. Swain, PhD and Will Witt, she explains why:

Many see the slogan Black Lives Matter as a plea to secure the right to life, liberty, and the pursuit of happiness for all Americans, especially historically wronged African Americans. They add the BLM hashtag to their social-media profiles, carry BLM signs at protests, and make financial donations.

Tragically, when they do donate, they are likely to bankroll a number of radical organizations, founded by committed Marxists whose goals aren't to make the American Dream a reality for everyone—but to transform America completely.

Just ask BLM leaders Alicia Garza, Patrisse Cullors and Opal Tometiln from a revealing 2015 interview, Cullors said, "Myself and Alicia in particular are trained organizers. We are trained Marxists." BLM not "fringe?" Two of BLM's leaders are self-described Marxists. Furthermore, the group's New York leader stated: "If this country doesn't give us what we want, then we will burn down this system and replace it."

Visit the Black Lives Matter website, and the first frame you get is a large crowd with fists raised and the slogan "Now We Transform." Read the list of demands, and you get a sense of how deep a transformation they seek.

One proclaims: "We disrupt the Western-prescribed nuclear-family-structure requirement by supporting each other as extended families and 'villages' that collectively care for one another." There are more manifestos just as extreme—if not hateful and racist.

The goals of the Black Lives Matter organization go far beyond what most people think. But they are hiding in plain sight, there for the world to see, if only we read beyond the slogans and the innocuous-sounding media accounts and sound bites of the movement.

Mike Gonzalez at the Senior Fellow, Center for Foreign Policy notes the BLM and their activists have not been silent about their agenda to dismantle the nuclear family, transform gender/sexual identity, and force radical change. So why are so many eagerly following along? For more answers look for SAPIENT Being's future book *Crime Rate Madness* to learn why their model for a fundamental change of American values is a blueprint for Marxism, not justice, and why sapient beings reject it.

Just as extreme, a partner organization, the Movement for Black Lives, or M4BL, calls for abolishing all police and all prisons.

5. Censoring Antifa and Leftist Violence & Destruction

As Mark Dice points out in *The True Story of Fake News: How Mainstream Media Manipulates Millions*:

During the 2016 presidential campaign when peaceful Trump supporters kept being assaulted as they were leaving Trump rallies or targeted on the street for wearing their red "Make America Great Again" (MAGA) hats, most incidents were only briefly covered in local papers or by online conservative outlets. These politically motivated attacks weren't just rare or isolated incidences, they were part of a disturbing pattern that was ignored by the liberal media, despite videos and photos of the attacks going viral online.

The mainstream media is also always reluctant to call politically motivated riots what they are when leftists instigate them, and instead usually just call them 'protests' when they're perpetrated by Black Lives Matter supporters and instigated by Antifa, college students trying to prevent conservative speakers from holding their events, and even in the case of leftist anarchists rioting after Trump's inauguration.

In Ferguson, Missouri, the birthplace of Black Lives Matter, Michael Brown's stepfather urged an angry crowd to "burn this bitch down" after a grand jury decided not to indict officer Darren Wilson for shooting and killing Brown, the 6-foot-4, three-hundred-pound thug who attacked him after being confronted shortly after robbing a convenience store. CNN host Jason Carroll admitted that the network chose to censor footage of people rioting in Ferguson, because it didn't fit with how they were trying to frame their coverage.

Anti-police hatred boiled over in July 2016 when a black supremacist opened fire on police officers in Dallas, Texas during a Black Lives Matter march, killing five officers and wounding nine others. The perpetrator was a 25-year-old black man who was incited to violence from the mainstream media continuing to paint police as racists who regularly kill African Americans and get away with it. This horrible tragedy was in the news for just a few days, and then it was quickly forgotten.

When we began seeing the rise of Antifa in 2016, which are leftist anarchists who wear all black (including ski masks) and see themselves as "freedom fighters" who embrace violence and assault Trump supporters and anyone who supports Conservatism (or as they call them "Nazis"), the liberal media compared them to American patriots who stormed the beaches of Normandy on D-Day. Many in the liberal media framed conservative ideas as 'violent' and claimed that Antifa's violence was 'ethical' because they aimed to stop 'hate speech.'

6. Denying Anti-White Racism & Victimization

Mark Dice is also brave enough to point out in *The True Story of Fake News: How Mainstream Media Manipulates Millions* how for decades MSM has denied anti-white hatred, racism and victimization throughout America.

Dice notes that while giving nonstop coverage to incidents of alleged racism committed by random white people, police officers, or businesses, the major news networks do their best to never report on racist black people who commit hate crimes against whites. They want people to believe that racism is a one-way street and that only white people can be racist, when in fact many in the black community harbor hatred for whites and frequently commit hate crimes against them.

There are too many incidences to be listed here (see *Crime Rate Madness* for more), but one reporter in particular Shepard Smith's comments, to suppress this conversation, stands out:

Shepard Smith, a then liberal host at Fox News, cut off a reporter mid-sentence when he was reporting on this crime after he mentioned the fact that many were concerned that the Black Lives Matter movement were fanning the flames of anti-white racism and might have helped create an environment which incited the perpetrators. "Wait, wait, wait, Matt, Matt, Matt, Matt, Matt, Matt, Matt, Matt, Matt, Matt, Matt, Matt. The police chief made clear what this was...let's leave the politics of this alone," Smith interjected.

Shepard Smith also cut off Louisiana governor Bobby Jindal while he was live on the air commenting on a black perpetrator who ambushed three police officers in Baton Rouge, Louisiana, killing them for Black Lives Matter. Jindal was saying, "It is time for folks across party lines, across ideological lines, to condemn this violence, to condemn this insanity, we've got to come together, we've got to say that all lives matter. It doesn't matter what color you are, black, white, brown, red, it doesn't matter, all lives matter. We've got to protect and value our police."

Smith interrupts him, saying, "Governor you know that that phrase you just used is one that's seen by many as derogatory, right? (referring to 'All Lives Matter') I'm just wonder why it is that you used that phrase when there's a certain segment of the population that believes it's a real dig on them?"

Jindal responded, "Well, Shepard, it's not meant to be. The point is we've got to move beyond race. Look, these police officers, these are the men and women that run towards danger, not away from it, so that we can be safe. It is time for us to be unified as, as a country. We've got to look beyond race. I think that's one of the dumbest ways for us to divide people. It's one of the dumbest ways to for us to classify people or categorize people. We shouldn't be divided; we do need to be united. These are police officers—they don't care whether you' re black or white, they will turn towards danger to protect you. That's what they swear, that's their duty, that's what they do first. These are heroes!"

7. The SpyGate 'Soft' Coup Against Trump That MSM Fails to Cover

From the August 2020 Brian Cates article in the *Epoch Times* titled "The Russiagate Hoax Is Dead—But the Fake News Media Can't Admit It" and Kristine Phillips and Kevin Johnson's comments in *USA Today* the same month, their latest update on SpyGate is as follows:

John Durham was tapped by Attorney General William Barr in May 2019 to investigate alleged misconduct on behalf of intelligence officials, law enforcement, and other actors in relation to the FBI's investigation into alleged links between Russia and President Donald Trump's 2016 campaign. Durham is looking into the origins of the FBI's investigation into Russian election interference.

Trump has long asserted that the FBI and Obama administration-era officials spied on his campaign and later attempted to spread disinformation tying him to the Kremlin. British intelligence played a part in helping the Democrats to nail down Trump. Ukrainians played a part in promoting the view that the Russians and Trump colluded. The Clinton Foundation has connections with foreigners who spread the news about the Trump-Russia collusion.

Former FBI lawyer Kevin Clinesmith pleaded guilty in August 2020 to falsifying an email used to support the surveillance of President Donald Trump's former campaign aide Carter Page. This very first indictment shows the FBI Crossfire Hurricane team, and the Mueller special counsel team were well aware by June 2017 of the compelling necessity of hiding Carter Page's longstanding relationship with the CIA from the FISA Court.

Why did they need to hide that relationship? Because their "evidence" for the warrant alleging Page was a Russian agent came from a political propagandist named Christopher Steele, who was being paid by the Clinton campaign, and misrepresenting the key source providing the Page allegations (who turned out to be a low-level research assistant at the Brookings Institute named Igor Danchenko).

What if the FBI admits to the FISA Court the relevant facts that Steele was a paid employee of the Clinton campaign, who is using a Brookings research assistant disguised as a top Russian intelligence official as his source, but that the CIA itself says Page isn't a Russian agent and is, instead, a CIA intelligence asset reporting all his Russian contacts to their agency?

The moment the FISA Court was alerted to the fact the CIA claimed Page as one of their own, the judge would have had to take a closer look at the Steele information. If that happened, the entire carefully managed fraud would begin unraveling.

How could Page be a Russian agent if he's been keeping the CIA up to date about his contacts with top Russian officials, the same contacts the FBI is attempting to use in the warrant to claim he is working for the Russians?

If that happened, Steele's hearsay allegations against Page would be exposed and the FBI was very likely not going to have the warrant approved. So not only did the FBI hide at least three key relevant facts from the FISA Court to get the original warrant, they kept the fraud going through the three subsequent renewals.

Guess what that's going to allow Durham to prove? I will prove that most involved knew the truth behind the deceptions. It will allow Durham to prove with documentary evidence that, just like Clinesmith, other FBI/Mueller team members knew the truth about Page, and they still hid that from the court as they continued to obtain warrants through what can only be described as acts of deliberate fraud.

It's all there in Department of Justice Inspector General Michael Horowitz's FISA abuse report from December 2019 that FBI Special Supervisory Agent (SSA) Stephen Somma deliberately hid several things from the FISA Court to obtain the Page warrant—including Page's relationship with the CIA.

For more information on this topic, look for the SAPIENT Being's future *Justice Madness* book and read all about it.

8. MSM Pushes Fake News About Trump's Pandemic Management

At the Media Research Center (MRC) NewsBusters division, Rich Noyes provides numerous statistics in April 2020 as to how the media are hard at work weaving a web of confusion, misinformation, and conspiracy surrounding the COVID-19 pandemic with 25-to-1 negative headlines for Trump's handling of the Chinese Communist Party (CCP) COVID-19 pandemic. The media is using whatever crisis it can to swing the upcoming election—they have an agenda, and the truth is not part of it.

As the leading newspaper in the nation's capital, the editors of *The Washington Post* are a great example of abusing their influence to set an agenda for the many powerful political and media people who read it on a daily basis. And the first thing those powerful readers see every morning are the big headlines on the *Post's* front page, framing the news the way *The Post's* editors want them to see it.

In the 100 days since the coronavirus epidemic began to receive significant news coverage, *The Post* has used its front page to undermine the administration's response to the unprecedented crisis, with dozens of headlines flagrantly editorializing against the President and nearly everyone on his team.

The MRC reviewed the headlines of all 136 *Washington Post* front-page news stories about the U.S. government's response to the coronavirus from January 17 through April 25, 2020. None of these articles was labeled as an editorial or an opinion piece, but many of the headlines employed heavy-handed rhetoric to slam the administration, from the President and the White House down to departments and agencies such as the Department of Health and Human Services (HHS) and the Centers for Disease Control (CDC).

Their analysts tallied 53 obviously negative headlines during this 100-day period, compared with just two that were clearly positive, a greater than 25-to-1 disparity. (The remaining 81 headlines were neutral, although that does not mean that the articles did not convey an obvious slant.)

Most of the *Post's* venom was directed at President Trump himself, with highly-opinionated language such as: "A confused effort to show calm control" (March 1); "Trump's error-filled speech rattled rather than reassured" (March 13); "White House's chaotic response evokes Trump's early days" (March 15); "70 days of denial, delays and dysfunction" (April 5); and "Hostility to criticism, hunger for praise are central to his response" (April 9).

The Trump team's many accomplishments—assistance deployed to hard-hit areas, millions of tests administered, deals struck to build ventilators, testing kits, quarantining China, and the dramatic lowering of fatality estimates as Americans implemented the administration's strategy to "flatten the curve"—were either ignored, buried inside the newspaper, or relayed with neutral headlines that refused to celebrate good news.

Strung together, the *Post's* headlines read like a dismal daily diary of dysfunction, all aimed at conveying that agenda to its elite readership who would multiply their negative take throughout the political establishment.

9. MSM Trashes Trump 2020 Election and the Republican Party

Another Media Research Center (MRC) analysis by Rich Noyes in August 2020, shows of all evening news coverage of President Donald Trump and former Vice President Joe Biden in June and July, the networks chose to aim most of their attention and nearly all of their negative coverage on Trump, so Biden escaped any scrutiny of his left-wing policy positions, past job performance or character, etc.

From June 1 through July 31, 2020, the ABC, CBS and NBC evening newscasts focused 512 minutes of airtime on the President, or nine times more than the 58 minutes allotted to Biden. (This excludes coverage of the Trump administration in general when not associated with the President himself.) This is an even wider gap than the spring when Trump received seven times more coverage than Biden (523 minutes vs. 75 minutes).

The extra airtime devoted to Trump consisted almost entirely of anchors and reporters criticizing the President. During these two months, their analysts documented 668 evaluative statements about the President, 95 percent of which (634) were negative, vs. a mere five percent (34) that were positive. Using the same methodology, MRC found very few evaluative statements about Joe Biden—just a dozen, two-thirds of which (67%) were positive.

Do the math, and viewers heard *150 times* more negative comments about Trump than Biden. That's not news reporting—that's a negative advertising campaign in action.

If you consider the evening newscasts a reliable gauge of the liberal media at large (cable news, big newspapers, etc.), it means Biden has enjoyed an army of so-called journalists conducting a massive negative information campaign against his opponent, while he is sheltered from any scrutiny. Controversies from the spring, such as allegations from former staffer Tara Reade that he sexually assaulted her in the 1990s, completely disappeared from his evening news coverage in June and July.

Biden's various policy proposals—which by his own admission would take his administration farther to the Left than the very liberal Obama administration—received a meager 5 minutes, 22 seconds of airtime, not one second of which included any critical analysis from any journalist.

There were no labels of Biden as "progressive," "left-wing," or even "liberal" on any of these newscasts, either; reporters also neglected to tell viewers how much the Democrat would raise taxes if he were elected (spoiler: more than $4 trillion).

Biden's plan for $700 billion more federal spending (what he called "investments"), announced July 9, 2020, received a scant 40 seconds of evening news airtime (25 seconds on ABC, 15 seconds on CBS, nothing on NBC). When he outlined his massively expensive ($2 trillion) plan to combat climate change on July 14, it received six seconds, all of it on CBS.

No presidential candidate (i.e., Biden)—not even Barack Obama in 2008—has ever been on the receiving end of such a wide array of media favors. (While Obama received highly positive coverage, there was no massive media effort to destroy his GOP opponent, Senator John McCain.) While the former Vice President sat snugly in his basement before his nomination, the entire liberal "news" media complex has spent the summer on the attack against his opponent, even as they refuse to report anything negative about Biden himself.

10. Media Lockdown on the Hunter Biden Scandal

Media Research Center (MRC) Founder and President Brent Bozell laid out on the Mark Levin Show on Tuesday, November 10, 2020 survey data indicating that the media's bias by omission of the Hunter Biden scandal, resulted in the defeat of President Donald Trump. Enough of Joe Biden's voters would have switched their selection had they known about his son Hunter's money scandal, enough to give President Trump a clear victory.

Bozell explained that it is well-known how the mainstream media dedicates over 90% of its Trump airtime to negative coverage of the president, but the MRC president argues that their omission of Trump's successes and Joe Biden's failures is much more dangerous.

"We took a survey after the elections, on the night of the elections, and asked Democrats if they knew about the Hunter Biden story. A full 36% of Democrats knew nothing about the Hunter Biden story," Bozell said. "Further, 4.6% of Democrats said they would not have voted for Joe

Biden had they known this story. We then took that 4.6% and we spread it across the electoral landscape."

"Guess what? Had they known this story, Joe Biden would not have carried Arizona, Georgia, Pennsylvania, Wisconsin, and the Trump lead would have been definitive in North Carolina. Meaning what? Meaning that Donald Trump would have won 289 electoral votes and would be the re-elect president of the United States."

A November 2020 poll by Paul Bedard, Washington Examiner reporter led to this conclusion per his article titled "Media's hiding of Hunter Biden scandal robbed Trump of clear win: Poll."

The story was not covered much in non-conservative media, and Twitter and other social media platforms that banned many of the reports on their sites. On the contrary, *Newsmax* and the *Epoch Times* covered it closely as they did SpyGate where other fake-news media feared to tread and held off declaring a winner until the courts and Congress had fully investigated the numerous claims of voter fraud.

"Now we know the impact of that cover-up," said MRC President Brent Bozell, adding, "4.6% of Biden voters say they would not have voted for him had they been aware of evidence of this scandal. This story would have potentially changed the outcome of this election. The media and Silicon Valley were fully aware of this, so they actively tried to prevent it from reaching the American public. The American people deserved to know the truth; now it's too late."

15 – Which Media Sources Can We Trust and Not Trust?

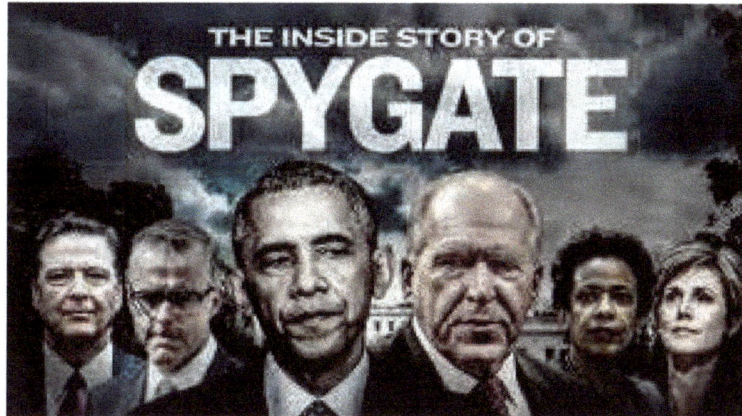

Credit: The Epoch Times

In July 2016, the Pew Research Center's Pathway to News report by Amy Mitchell, Jeffrey Gottfried, Michael Barthel and Elisa Shearer, observed that Americans express a clear preference for getting their news on a screen—though which screen that is varies. TV remains the dominant screen, followed by digital. Still, TV news use is dramatically lower among younger adults, suggesting further shake-ups to come.

About four-in-ten Americans often get news online and as of early 2016, just two-in-ten U.S. adults often get news from print newspapers. This has fallen from 27% in 2013. This decrease occurred across all age groups, though the age differences are still stark: Only 5% of 18- to 29-year-olds often get news from a print newspaper, whereas about half (48%) of those 65 and older do.

TV continues to be the most widely used news platform; 57% of U.S. adults often get TV-based news, either from local TV (46%), cable (31%), network (30%) or some combination of the three. This same pattern emerges when people are asked which platform they prefer—TV sits at the top, followed by the web, with radio and print trailing behind.

TV's staying power over print is buttressed by the fact that Americans who prefer to watch news still choose TV, while most of those who prefer to read the news have migrated online. News watchers overwhelmingly prefer television, while readers prefer the web and the greatest portion of U.S. adults, 46%, prefer to watch news rather than read it (35%) or listen to it (17%).

When paired with the platforms people prefer, the data reveal that as of now, the web has largely pulled in "readers" rather than "watchers." While those who prefer watching news predominantly opt for TV and listeners turn to radio, most of those who prefer reading news now opt to get news online rather than in print (59%, compared with 26% of news readers who opt for print).

Beware of Fake News Organizations Trying to Discredit Their Non-Fake News Rivals

When primarily fake news *The New York Times* parrots Chinese propaganda in a failed takedown of a rising star and non-fake news organization the *Epoch Times*, readers beware. The Libby Emmons article in The Post Millennial in October 2020 titled *"The New York Times* parrots Chinese propaganda in failed takedown of *Epoch Times"* shows us why.

As Emmons explains: *The New York Times'* hit piece on *The Epoch Times* focused on Epoch's critique of China, and their founding as an outlet that called out the Chinese Communist Party (CCP) treatment of the Falun Gong religious movement. They use *The Epoch Times* opposition to human rights abuses and extensive inquiries into the origin of the coronavirus as a reason to bash them.

The *Epoch Times* was founded, in large part, to call out the atrocities committed by the CCP against the Falun Gong religious minority, but for *The New York Times*, this religious group is the subject of scorn, and so is the paper that documents the crimes committed against them.

The *New York Times* wrote: "*The Epoch Times*] is a remarkable success story for Falun Gong, which has long struggled to establish its bona fides against Beijing's efforts to demonize it as an 'evil cult,' partly because its strident accounts of persecution in China can sometimes be difficult to substantiate or veer into exaggeration." For this statement, *The New York Times* provides no substantiation.

As regards *The New York Times* portrayal of Falun Gong, and their use of the movement as a means to discredit *The Epoch Times*, Senior Editor Jan Jekielek said that, "Any of such pieces that come out painting Falun Gong in a negative light, they're used by the CCP, they get translated into Chinese, and then they get used by the CCP to target Falun Gong, to justify the persecution of Falun Gong practitioners, as they do the Uighurs and Tibetans."

The *New York Times*, however, which has recently published in support of China's intentions toward annexation of Hong Kong, does not appear concerned with China's human rights violations against Falun Gong, and portrays the movement as suspect. Regardless of one's feelings on a religion, there can be no condoning of the persecution of its members for their beliefs.

It doesn't appear that the *New York Times* dug into these claims at all, despite the fact that, as Jekielek said, "The *New York Times* has such massive resources at their disposal, and there are so many highly newsworthy things they don't cover."

So, what of the *New York Times*' claims? Jekielek said of *Epoch Times'* founding that "*The Epoch Times* was founded to counter Chinese influence operations, with the knowledge that what journalists were doing in the west, with few exceptions, was repeating Chinese Communist Party-approved narratives." That sounds like what the *New York Times* is doing to a "T."

Of *The Epoch Times*' reporting on the coronavirus, *The New York Times* said that it has "promoted the unfounded theory that the coronavirus—which the publication calls the 'CCP Virus,' in an attempt to link it to the Chinese Communist Party—was created as a bioweapon in a Chinese military lab." The truth and investigative reporting will tell.

The New York Times, as well as other mainstream media outlets, have consistently refused to dig into the origins of the virus. Earlier in the pandemic it was somehow believed to be racist to blame the Chinese government for the virus that they perhaps unwittingly let spread around the world. It is as though editorial outlets just couldn't believe that the CCP would either do this intentionally, intentionally cover it up, or alter a virus for research purposes, as virology labs so often do.

It is this "oh, that couldn't be true," approach that has led mainstream media outlets to ignore and pass over stories that do not conform with their world view. So, too, it appears that is the case with *The New York Times* reporting on *The Epoch Times*.

Jekielek said that "*The New York Times* published a piece that is low on facts and high on bias. It rehashes a whole bunch of inaccurate stuff from an NBC story, that we've responded to repeatedly."

But as with the origins of the coronavirus, or the Steele dossier, or the recent allegations with regard to the Biden family, *The New York Times* is content to spread their own version of the truth, not because it is researched and well-reasoned, but because it just feels right to them and their editorial board.

The Epoch Times' Stephen Gregory responded to more false claims and narratives by NBC and MSNBC with their August 27, 2019 response titled "*The Epoch Times*' Stephen Gregory Responds to NBC & MSNBC's Gross Misrepresentations of Our Media" and like the *NYT* hit piece, both reports from NBC and MSNBC were discredited. Per Gregory, "*The Epoch Times* seeks to restore traditional journalism, seeks to restore honest journalism. Our motto is 'truth and tradition.' We want to provide readers with honest, truthful reporting about the important events of the day."

Three Prime Examples of the Good, Bad & Ugly of Media Organizations

Here we highlight three prominent examples of media organizations that the SAPIENT Being chose because they are outstanding, significant, and noteworthy examples of non-fake news, illiberal resources, and an unholy Trinity of fake news journalism. The good, the bad, and the ugly!

These examples, amongst the ones covered in *Fake News Madness*, can be the inspiration for the world of writing warriors to fight back and reverse the prevalent fake news bias in mainstream journalism, social media, and illiberal establishments that in principle and practice are antithetical to an intellectually vibrant and viewpoint diverse sapient being mindset.

Good: *Newsmax* Cable News Beats Out Fox News For Election 2020 Coverage

A new August 2020 poll by Public Policy Polling confirms Fox News is now the most trusted television news network in America.

However, four months later in December 2020, a Reuters' article titled "*Newsmax* plans expansion to capitalize on Trump support, anger at Fox News" by Lisa Richwine and Helen Coster, notes how *Newsmax*, a conservative cable news channel aided by shout-outs from Trump on Twitter, saw their weekly primetime viewership jump 68% since the U.S. presidential election as the channel refused to declare Joe Biden the winner and aired controversial theories about voter fraud.

The network plans to hire more staff in the United States and London, debut a new primetime host and add more weekend programming to capitalize on post-election gains and some viewers' discontent with Rupert Murdoch's longtime ratings king Fox News.

During the 2020 presidential election, *Newsmax* early evening host Greg Kelly averaged 229,000 viewers ages 25 to 54, the group most coveted by cable news advertisers, for the first-time beating Fox's Martha MacCallum, who brought in 203,000 viewers in that age range at that hour. The network had its highest-rated November in history, drawing 3.9 million primetime viewers, beating all cable networks, not just cable news.

Newsmax sees the 40 million viewers not on cable as the next battleground for growth. In addition to cable news, the network streams for free on platforms including YouTube and a *Newsmax* app, which roughly doubles their nighttime audience. "People are really tired of Fox News," Chief Executive Chris Ruddy told Reuters in a recent interview. "There is a perception that they really tried to torpedo the president."

Trump has complained many times about Fox's coverage of his presidency. The network further irked the president and some viewers on election night with a projection that Biden had won Arizona — nine days before most major news organizations confirmed that win.

"Newsmax, I think, has been gaining ground against Fox News because it's been able to convince some fraction of Fox's audience that it is more loyal to the president than Fox is," said Matt Gertz, a senior fellow at liberal media watchdog Media Matters for America.

Fox's more recent challengers on the right remain independent networks like *Newsmax*, *The Epoch Times*, and One America News Network (OAN), rather than major media conglomerates, because large players view the conservative media business as too risky, said Christopher Balfe, partner at media firm Red Seat Ventures, which advises on new media startups.

"None of (the independents) have deep enough pockets from a resource perspective to be truly competitive," Balfe said. Fox spent $1 billion before Fox News became profitable, per Fox Corp Chief Financial Officer Steve Tomsic. "It's not a small undertaking to try to compete at that level," Tomsic said at a UBS conference. "When people think about competition, their knee-jerk reaction is to think 'Well, all we need is two or three talking heads to go head-to-head with ours.' The business is much bigger than that."

Overall, using a more recent confirmation of this analysis, in August 2020, Media Research Center (MRC) President Brent Bozell responded to the new nationwide survey confirming that Americans overwhelmingly trust the Fox News Channel more than any other network per his report as follows:

"The proof is in the pudding. Americans want balanced news, not liberal advocacy." Fox offered them 'fair and balanced' journalism, and America has embraced them. "In terms of quantity, Fox has been pulling the highest numbers for quite some time."

"Now comes the quality meter, the new polling data showing that Fox News is also the most trusted name in news," states Bozell. "In fact, no one comes close. Fox is trusted a staggering 10 percentage points above any other network. And it is the only network to earn more trust (49%) than distrust (37%) among those polled.

"Liberal politicians and liberal journalists who regularly bash Fox News need to realize it is *they* who are completely out of touch with the American people. The bottom line is that Americans now trust Fox far more than any other network. Liberal bias has come back to bite the networks where it hurts.

The poll was conducted by the Public Policy Polling between January 18—19, 2020, and found that among the 1,151 registered voters they surveyed, Fox crushed the other networks in trust as follows:

- 49% trusted the Fox News Channel, 10 percentage points more than any other network.
- 39% said they trusted CNN.
- 35% said they trusted NBC and sister cable network MSNBC.
- 32% said they trusted CBS.
- 31% said they trusted ABC.

Fox News is also the only network to be trusted more than distrusted:

- Both ABC and CBS were not trusted by 46% of those surveyed.
- And NBC/MSNBC was not trusted by 44%.
- Only 37% did not trust Fox, the lowest level of distrust among all the networks recorded.

In an August 2020, Fox News report by Brian Flood with contribution by Paul Steinhauser, "A whopping 9.2 million people tuned in to Fox News from 10 p.m. to 11:45 p.m. to watch

President Trump accept his party's renomination for president to close the Republican National Convention."

By contrast, no other network garnered more than 2.6 million viewers. More people tuned into Fox News Thursday night than did CNN, MSNBC, ABC, NBC and CBS combined. The viewing figures more than double the combined viewership of the two liberal cable news networks, with CNN averaging 2.2 million viewers and MSNBC pulling in 1.9 million viewers.

Bret Baier and Martha MacCallum co-anchored Fox News' record-breaking coverage, helping the network finish with an average primetime viewership of 7.8 million during the fourth night of the Republican National Convention (RNC). That figure is the highest primetime total viewership average for any political party convention in cable news history.

In addition, "Hannity" averaged 7.8 million viewers and "Tucker Carlson Tonight" averaged 6.3 million viewers on Thursday, as both programs garnered the highest ratings in network history for their respective timeslots. Fox News averaged 7.9 million total viewers during the four-day RNC, keeping its title of cable's most-watched television network.

Fox News also thrived among the key demographic of adults age 25-54, averaging 2.2 million demo viewers during Trump's speech compared to only 757,000 for CNN and 391,000 for MSNBC. Fox News also topped CNN, MSNBC, ABC, CBS and NBC combined among the key demographic. Fox News had 2.6 million interactions across Facebook, Twitter and Instagram on the final day of the RNC, according to Socialbakers.

Bad: Wikipedia is Riddled With Liberal Bias

Wikipedia was launched in 2001 as an online encyclopedia that "crowdsourced " its articles by allowing anyone to write and edit them, which has surprisingly led to them becoming the fifth most popular website in the world.

Unlike traditional encyclopedias written and edited by experts in their field, pretty much anyone can add almost anything to Wikipedia articles, making it the most popular online "encyclopedia" and one of the most visited websites online. Therefore, we must take a serious look at articles published on the site and how they are fact checked, edited, and censored.

Per Mark Dice, and in his own words: Editors at most newspapers and traditional encyclopedia companies have names and titles, not to mention bosses and company policies they must abide by, but much of what happens on Wikipedia is a mystery, and most of the editors and writers are anonymous or only referred to by their online handles which rarely reveal any information about who they actually are or what credentials they have.

Wikipedia has been involved in several lawsuits over defamation, and a substantial amount of their money has been spent defending them. Comedian Stephen Colbert once sarcastically praised Wikipedia for their 'quality' by pointing out that the article on Lightsabers (the handheld weapon from Star Wars) was longer than the article about the printing press. Since its editorial policies and oversight are so flawed, the site has been called "the abomination that causes misinformation."

Pages of popular conservatives often have large "Controversies" sections which contain long lists of every little thing they've said that liberals find objectionable or want to amplify. Pages for Ann Coulter, Sean Hannity, Rush Limbaugh, and Michael Savage all have the "Controversy" section or equivalent which nitpick things they've said or done.

Conversely, there are relatively few liberal journalists or talk show hosts who have a 'Controversy' section in their articles or have much negative information about them even mentioned at all. For example:

Liberal political figures also appear to get special treatment on Wikipedia by editors who carefully guard their pages, trying to keep them portrayed in a positive light. One investigation revealed that a single Wikipedia editor made 2,269 changes to Hillary Clinton's page over a ten-year period from 2006 up until the time she announced she was running for president in 2016 in order to keep as much criticism off it as possible.

Sometimes Wikipedia editors will even create an entire article about a topic or an issue hoping to shine a spotlight on it to further promote their political leanings. For example, there was a lengthy article titled "Criticism of George W. Bush," but the "Criticism of Barack Obama" page had been deleted four different times by Wikipedia editors who kept claiming the article "has no meaningful, substantive content," and called it an, "Attack page" that was "unsourced" (which it wasn't)

After the edit wars continued, the site finally allowed the "Criticism of Barack Obama" page to stay but renamed it to "The Public Image of..." and of course Obama's main page is mostly praise. The edit summary for the decision to rename and redirect the 'Criticism' section of Obama's page reads, "so the conservatards [conservative retards] won't get their knickers in a twist."

Dice compared the pages of several prominent conservative political commentators like Ann Coulter to popular liberals like Michael Moore and found that the negative bias was overwhelming. At the time of his search, the "Controversies and Criticism" section of Ann Coulter's page was over 35% of the article, where Michael Moore's was under 5% in terms of the word count.

Editors also guard the Southern Poverty Law Center (SPLC) which is the organization dedicated to painting conservatives as racists, homophobic, xenophobic, and anti-government extremists.

Ugly: Columbia University's Trinity of Fake News Journalism, Leftist Pulitzer Prize Choices & Soros Foundation Funding Connections

Why the extreme ugly categorization? The ratings below are from the Media Research Center (MRC) and show the enormous, and "enormous" is no exaggeration, influence this Ivy League university has on the mainstream, social, and journalistic mediums in the United States.

In America there is NO other concentration of power, influence, and bias—from one over-arching organization as Columbia University. In the past century, the Columbia University School of Journalism was considered America's most respected liberal journalism programs along with their *Columbia Journalism Review (CJR)* and Pulitzer Prize choices. However, their ideology and focus has shifted ever more leftward over the course of the last two decades to a dangerous and unacceptable leftist bias with many negative consequences (covered below)—that qualifies them with the worst fake news madness rating.

Combine their past liberal and now leftist influence from the Columbia University School of Journalism and its *CJR,* their past liberal and now leftist Pulitzer Prize winner choices, and their immense financial backing from the leftist and anarchist George Soros Foundation—they're a fake news leftist behemoth without equal!

Exhibit A: Columbia University School of Journalism

Columbia University helps define the news business. Its School of Journalism is perhaps the foremost institution of its kind in the United States, and its alumni fill the ranks of fake news organizations. It is also home to the Pulitzer Prize—the top award in the industry. Each May, it graduates a new class and sends a fresh crop of young editors, writers, and producers into the field.

The "About" page of the Columbia University School of Journalism website says that the school provides its students with the opportunity "not only to succeed, but to shape the future of journalism." By merit of their job placement alone, they definitely are shaping that future, but not in a positive way.

Unfortunately, Columbia's journalism program is not committed to honest journalism. Instead, it delivers a one-sided education that celebrates left-wing policies and is overwhelmingly run by liberal journalists, most of whom work for liberal news outlets in addition to their jobs at the school. Sixty-eight percent of the full-time faculty at Columbia University School of Journalism write for explicitly left-wing news outlets. Many of the adjunct faculty and guest lecturers also work for these operations.

With its substantial influence, Columbia has become a force to shape the future of journalism. Alumni have gone on too many prominent news organizations but have often retained a bias that mirrors that of the faculty and donors of the school.

The faculty list of the Columbia University School of Journalism reads like a Who's Who of left-wing organizations. Of the 40 full-time members of the faculty, 27 work at explicitly left-wing outlets including The Huffington Post, Slate, *The American Prospect*, *Mother Jones*, Salon, *The Nation* and Greenpeace.

Many of these professors not only write for these liberal outlets, but actually work full-time for them as well. A few (Thomas B. Edsall with the Huffington Post, Todd Gitlin with Greenpeace and Victor Navasky with *The Nation*) have actually sat on the boards of these outlets.

Alumni have secured jobs at such prominent media outlets as *The New York Times*, Bloomberg, ABC News, NBC News, CBS News, CNN, *The Los Angeles Times*, *The Washington Post* and *USA Today*. Alumni have also worked at a number of left-wing outlets including *Mother Jones*, The Huffington Post, NPR and *The Nation*—the same operations their former professors staff.

The Media Research Center's Business and Media Institute (BMI) has extensively researched Columbia University School of Journalism, including its faculty, alumni, student publications, funding, guest lecturers, endorsements and awards. BMI found that there was a significant left-wing bias prevalent at the school—a bias that then migrates with its graduates to permeate the daily operations of news organizations across the United States.

Columbia has received $9.7 million from left-wing billionaire George Soros, more support than he has given to all but three other schools. Soros is also connected to the newly appointed dean of Columbia University Graduate School of Journalism, Steve Coll, is currently the head of the New America Foundation, a progressive public policy organization that has received $4.2 million from Soros since 2000.

The Media Consortium, to which many of these outlets belong, is a Soros liberal echo chamber where blogs and news operations like The Nation, *The American Prospect* and *Mother Jones* can share ideas. The Media Consortium ($675,000), *The Nation* ($77,000), *The American Prospect* ($1,280,000), *Mother Jones* ($485,000), and National Public Radio ($1,800,000) all receive funding from George Soros's Open Society Foundations.

At least seven Columbia professors have strong ties to Soros. Nina Berman, Howard French, Todd Gitlin, Victor Navasky, as well as full-time professors June Cross, Rhoda Lipton and James Stewart, have also directly received awards or funding from Soros's Open Society Foundations. Navasky is also the chairman of the Soros-funded *Columbia Journalism Review (CJR)*, a publication affiliated with Columbia University School of Journalism.

These professors have also been treated as experts by major news outlets, such as *The New York Times*, ABC, CBS, NBC, *The Washington Post* and *USA Today*, thanks to their status as Columbia faculty. Professor Edsall is a respected political commentator for *The New York Times*, using his position to publish attacks against the Republican Party's "ideological rigidity, its preference for the rich over workers, its alienation of minorities, its reactionary social policies and its institutionalized repression of dissent and innovation."

Nearly half (47 percent) of Columbia's journalism faculty work for liberal publications. These publications are not just liberal leaning like the *New York Times* and MSNBC, but outspokenly websites and magazines like Alternet, *Mother Jones* and the Huffington Post. Columbia even hired the former president of a violent radical group as a full-time professor. These professors are instilling a liberal worldview in their students, who then go on to have jobs at respected news organizations.

Forty Percent (51 out of 127) of the adjunct faculty also work at left-wing news outlets and organizations. The Business and Media Institute contacted the school to try to attain numbers of how many alumni went on to work at each of these organizations. CUSJ officials told BMI that no such records exist at this time. Columbia University's Graduate School of Journalism has graduated 12,642 students since its founding in 1912.

Exhibit B: *Columbia Journalism Review (CJR)* and Pulitzer Prize Choices

Once upon a time, it meant something for a reporter to be called a "Pulitzer Prize-winning journalist." The prestige of this designation is quickly eroding. The 2020 Pulitzer Prizes looked less like an excellence-in-media competition and more like an exercise in leftist self-affirmation and Trump Derangement Syndrome.

From the Washington Secrets Columnist April 2019 article, "Pulitzer judges: 'Not one anywhere close to a conservative'" by Paul Bedard:

The 19-member Pulitzer Prize Board convenes semi-annually in the Joseph Pulitzer World Room at Columbia University's Pulitzer Hall. It comprises major editors, columnists and media executives in addition to six members drawn from academia and the arts, including the president of Columbia University, the dean of the Columbia University Graduate School of Journalism and the administrator of the Prizes, who serves as the Board's secretary.

The judging process leans heavily liberal and the history of winners in the Trump era favors his critics, including those who got the collusion story wrong.

The number of Pulitzer Prize winners with heavy criticism of Trump over the last four years have led in many of the awards categories. Here are but a few examples:

- *The New York Times* won the explanatory prize for "an exhaustive 18-month investigation of President Donald Trump's finances that debunked his claims of self-made wealth and revealed a business empire riddled with tax dodges."

- The national reporting prize went to the *Wall Street Journal* "for uncovering President Trump's secret payoffs to two women during his campaign who claimed to have had affairs with him, and the web of supporters who facilitated the transactions, triggering criminal inquiries and calls for impeachment."

- The distinguished reporting award went to the *Washington Post* and *New York Times*, "For deeply sourced, relentlessly reported coverage in the public interest that dramatically furthered the nation's understanding of Russian interference in the 2016 presidential election and its connections to the Trump campaign, the president-elect's transition team and his eventual administration."

And of the 18 members on the board, sometimes dubbed "the deciders," there are no notable conservatives, but several famous liberals and many Trump critics abound. In an ideology review, the conservative media watchdog Media Research Center (MRC) found nobody from the center-right. "If this isn't the ultimate evidence of the left—and far left—dominance of the so-called 'news media,' what is?" asked L. Brent Bozell, president of MRC.

"Eighteen judges and not one—let this sink in—not one anywhere close to a conservative. The Pulitzer Prizes have always been liberal, but this is now not just leftist, it is a mockery of itself. And then they wonder why they're not trusted to tell the truth," he added.

Exhibit C: Soros Foundation Funding and Its Liberal Media Echo Chamber

George Soros is arguably the most influential liberal financier in the United States, donating more than $8 billion just to his Open Society Foundations. In 2004, he spent more than $27 million to defeat President George W. Bush and has given away millions more since to promote the left-wing agenda. But what goes almost without notice is Soros' extensive influence on and involvement with the media.

Since 2003, Soros has donated more than $52 million to all kinds of media outlets—liberal news organizations, investigative reporting, and even smaller blogs. He has also been involved in funding the infrastructure of supposedly "neutral" news, from education to even the industry ombudsman association. Many other operations Soros supports also have a media component to what they do.

His media funding has helped create a liberal "echo chamber," in the words of one group he backs, "in which a message pushes the larger public or the mainstream media to acknowledge, respond, and give airtime to progressive ideas because it is repeated many times." The goal is "Taking Down Fox News," as the Soros-supported "*Mother Jones*" described it.

Despite his denials, Soros has extensive reach into the media. The Media Research Center's Business & Media Institute conducted a detailed analysis of George Soros and his influence on the media. It found:

- Breach of Ethics: Prominent journalists like ABC's Christiane Amanpour, *New York Times* Executive Editor Jill Abramson and former *Post* editor and now Vice President Len Downie serve on boards of operations that take Soros cash. But according to the Society of Professional Journalists' ethical code, journalists should 'avoid all conflicts real or perceived.' Reporters and editors serving on boards of groups funded by Soros openly violate both aspects of this guideline.

- Reaching More Than U.S. Population: Every month, reporters, writers and bloggers at the many outlets Soros funds—from big players like NPR to the little-known Project Syndicate and Public News Service, both of which claim to reach millions of readers— easily reach more than 332 million people around the globe. FYI: For comparison of reach, the population of the entire United States was approximately 331 million in 2020.

- Fox News is Target No. 1: Nearly 30 groups funded by the liberal billionaire have attacked Fox News in the six months since the beginning of December 2010. Soros-funded media operations claim Fox News has a "history of inciting Islamophobia and racial and ethnic animosity" and that it tries to "race bait its viewers."

MRC's recommendations for addressing these issues are as follows and supported by the SAPIENT Being:

The Business & Media Institute has some recommendations for the media to better handle their obvious conflicts of interest when it comes to Soros:

- Just Say No to Soros Cash: No purportedly "objective" journalist should serve on a board or advise any outlet that is financed by Soros. If academics do so, they should be open about their affiliations. But working journalists like Downie, Amanpour and Abramson should divorce themselves from the conflict.

- Question Motivations of News Sources: Reporters and editors should be aware when a story is being deliberately hyped by a web of linked organizations. Such times should always have reporters questioning not just the motives, but the facts of the case— whether it's on the right or the left.

- Spend Time Investigating the Left: Journalists have no trouble finding incentive to do detailed analysis of conservatives, but spend little time questioning the motives or funding of liberal organizations. Reporters should do a more detailed investigation into the Open Society Foundations and their influence throughout the media.

Some Final Thoughts and Words to Live By

Don't trust anything you read, view, or hear—especially from academia, mainstream, and social media.

When in doubt about the viewpoint orthodoxy, confirmation bias, and hidden agenda from all media sources, refer back to Chapter 11 WOWW's Journalism Code of Ethics, Practical Logic & Sapience for advice and direction on the essentials of spotting, correcting, and fighting fake news, false agendas, and fallacies of logic.

Former London Mayor Ken Livingstone was suspended for a month after comparing a reporter to a concentration camp guard and once stated, "The world is run by monsters and you have to deal with them. Some of them run countries, some of them run banks, some of them run news corporations. And as you will see, those are often the real monsters we need to be concerned about."

English writer, philosopher, and lay theologian Gilbert Keith Chesterton noted a century ago, "Journalism possesses in itself the potentiality of becoming one of the most frightful monstrosities and delusions that have ever cursed mankind. This horrible transformation will occur at the exact instant at which journalists realize that they can become an aristocracy."

And my favorite from the young journalist Samuel Langhorne Clemons, better known by his pen name Mark Twain, an American humorist, essayist, novelist, and lecturer who found satire to his liking because of his early experience and success with it. He came to the conclusion that "a lie can travel halfway around the world—while the truth is putting on its shoes."

Hopefully, this book was a breath of fresh air and enlightening and your journey from chapter to chapter has made you more sapient and aware of the preponderance of fake news issues facing us. If it has, your journey towards becoming a sapient being is only beginning. If it hasn't, you're still our future and here's the onramp!

Appendix

1619 Project: Frederick Douglass vs. the 1619 Project: https://youtu.be/ajJIu3eoRlk

50 *MADNESS* Book Titles: https://www.fratirepublishing.com/madnessbooks

AllSides: "Form the Left" and "From the Center" and "From the Right" News Comparison: https://www.allsides.com/unbiased-balanced-news

Fact Check Review Methodology—RealClearPolitics: https://www.realclearpolitics.com/fact_check_review_methodology.html

MEDIA RESEARCH CENTER (MRC) NEWS BUREAUS & REPORTS:
<u>Bureaus:</u>
- **CNSNews:** https://www.cnsnews.com/
- **NewsBusters:** https://www.newsbusters.org/
- **MRC Business:** https://www.newsbusters.org/business
- **MRC Culture:** https://www.newsbusters.org/culture
- **MRC Latino:** https://www.newsbusters.org/latino
- **MRCTV:** https://www.mrctv.org/
- **MRC Action:** https://www.mrc.org/action

<u>Reports:</u>
- **Special Report: Columbia University:** https://www.mrc.org/special-reports/special-report-columbia-university
- **Journalists Denying Liberal Bias—Parts One, Two & Three:**
  https://www.mrc.org/media-bias-101/journalists-denying-liberal-bias-part-one
  https://www.mrc.org/media-bias-101/journalists-denying-liberal-bias-part-two
  https://www.mrc.org/media-bias-101/journalists-denying-liberal-bias-part-three
- **CENSORED! How Online Media Companies Are Suppressing Conservative Speech:**
  https://cdn.mrc.org/static/censored/mrc-censorship-report.pdf

PEW RESEARCH CENTER REPORTS LIST:
- **How Americans Get Their News:** https://www.journalism.org/2016/07/07/pathways-to-news/
- **How We Evaluated Americans' Trust in 30 News Sources:** https://www.pewresearch.org/fact-tank/2020/01/24/qa-how-pew-research-center-evaluated-americans-trust-in-30-news-sources/
- **The Modern News Consumer:** https://www.journalism.org/wp-content/uploads/sites/8/2016/07/PJ_2016.07.07_Modern-News-Consumer_FINAL.pdf

PRAGER U & VIDEOS:
- **Website:** https://www.prageru.com/
- **Prager U Five-Minute Videos Library:** https://www.prageru.com/series/5-minute-videos/
- **Prager U Takes Legal Action Against Google and YouTube for Discrimination:**
  https://www.prageru.com/press-release/prageru-takes-legal-action-against-google-and-youtube-for-discrimination/
- **What is Fake News?** https://www.youtube.com/watch?v=FOZ0irgLwxU&app=desktop

- **Watch the 21 Prager U Videos That YouTube Is Censoring:**
  https://www.dailysignal.com/2016/10/14/watch-the-21-prageru-videos-that-youtube-is-censoring/

SAPIENT BEING PROGRAMS:
- **Make Free Speech Again On Campus (MFSAOC) Program:**
  https://www.sapientbeing.org/programs
- **World Of Writing Warriors (WOWW) Program:** https://www.sapientbeing.org/programs
- **World Of Writing Warriors (WOWW) Journalism Code of Ethics, Practical Logic & Sapience Guidelines:** https://www.sapientbeing.org/resources

The S.A.P.I.E.N.T. Being: https://www.fratirepublishing.com/books

Glossary

Academy – Is an institution of secondary education, higher learning, research, or honorary membership. Academia is the worldwide group composed of professors and researchers at institutes of higher learning.

Confirmation Bias – Happens when a person gives more weight to evidence that confirms their beliefs and undervalues evidence that could disprove it.

Conspiracy Theory – The idea that many important political events or economic and social trends are the products of deceptive plots that are largely unknown to the general public:

Constructive Disagreement – Occurs when people who don't see eye-to-eye are committed to exploring an issue together, alive to their own fallibility and the limits of their knowledge—and open to learning something from others who see things differently than they do.

Critical Theory – Is a social theory oriented toward critiquing and changing society as a whole. It differs from traditional theory, which focuses only on understanding or explaining society. Critical theories aim to dig beneath the surface of social life and uncover the assumptions that keep human beings from a full and true understanding of how the world works.

Cultural Relativism – Cultural relativism is the idea that a person's beliefs, values, and practices should be understood based on that person's own culture, rather than be judged against the criteria of another.

Deplatforming – Also known as no-platforming, is a form of political activism or prior restraint by an individual, group, or organization with the goal of shutting down controversial speakers or speech or denying them access to a venue in which to express their opinion.

Emoluments Clause – Also called the foreign emoluments clause, is a provision of the U.S. Constitution (Article I, Section 9, Paragraph 8) that generally prohibits federal officeholders from receiving any gift, payment, or other thing of value from a foreign state or its rulers, officers, or representatives.

Fake News – A broad term that collectively includes media bias manifested in many different ways in mainstream journalism, social media, and illiberal establishments that in principle and practice are antithetical to an intellectually vibrant and viewpoint diverse sapient being mindset. Per Andrew Klavan's edited definition at: https://www.youtube.com/watch?v=FOZ0irgLwxU.

False Equivalency – A phenomenon that once a candidate 's rhetoric ventures beyond the accepted mainstream paradigm and proves offensive to the sensibilities of elite gatekeepers (i.e., the media), that balance, objectivity, and fairness become moot.

Frankfurt School – The Frankfurt School's biggest intellectual creation was Critical Theory, an approach to cultural analysis that focuses on criticizing existing social structures. It's founding members included Max Horkheimer, Theodor Adorno, Erich Fromm, Walter Benjamin, Jürgen Habermas, and Herbert Marcuse.

Groupthink – A phenomenon that occurs when a group of individuals reaches a consensus without critical reasoning or evaluation of the consequences or alternatives. Groupthink is based on a common desire not to upset the balance of a group of people.

Hypersensitivity – Symptoms of hypersensitivity include being highly sensitive to physical (via sound, sigh, touch, or smell) and or emotional stimuli and the tendency to be easily overwhelmed by too much information.

Hypothetics – A form of fake news where (rather than tracking down facts), the press indulged in endless "connect the dots" exercises.

Idiocracy – An idiocracy is a disparaging term for a society run by or made up of idiots (or people perceived as such). Idiocracy is also the title of 2006 satirical film that depicts a future in which humanity has become dumb.

Illiberalism – In popular usage, the word is used to describe an attitude that is close-minded, intolerant, and bigoted.

Intellectual Humility – A mindset that encompasses empathy, trust, and curiosity, viewpoint diversity gives rise to engaged and civil debate, constructive disagreement, and shared progress towards truth.

Intersectionality – A theoretical framework for understanding how aspects of one's social and political identities might combine to create unique modes of discrimination.

Liberating Tolerance – Herbert Marcuse propounded this Orwellian and illiberal oxymoron in the 1960s that would involve "the withdrawal of toleration of speech and assembly from groups and movements" on the Right, as opposed to the aggressive partisan promotion of speech, groups, and progressive movements on the Left.

Locke, John – An English philosopher and physician, widely regarded as one of the most influential of Enlightenment thinkers and commonly known as the "Father of Liberalism." Considered one of the first of the British empiricists, following the tradition of Sir Francis Bacon, Locke is equally important to social contract theory. His work greatly affected the development of epistemology and political philosophy. His writings influenced Voltaire and Jean-Jacques Rousseau, and many Scottish Enlightenment thinkers, as well as the American Revolutionaries. His contributions to classical republicanism and liberal theory are reflected in the United States Declaration of Independence.

Mainstream Media (MSM) – Traditional forms of mass media, as television, radio, magazines, and newspapers, as opposed to online means of mass communication.

Marcuse, Herbert – A German-American philosopher, sociologist, and political theorist, associated with the Frankfurt School of Critical Theory. Author of the *One-Dimensional Man: Studies in the Ideology of Advanced Industrial Society*, a 1964 best seller primarily known by the "power of negative thinking" became the standard for revolutionary speech in the movement he called the "Great Refusal." Marcuse distinguished between repressive tolerance, a form of tolerance that favors the already powerful and suppresses the less powerful, and a liberating tolerance, a form of tolerance that discriminates in favor of the weak and restrains the strong.

Marxism – The political, economic, and social principles and policies advocated by Marx and a theory and practice of socialism including the labor theory of value, dialectical materialism, the class struggle, and dictatorship of the proletariat until the establishment of a classless society.

Media Bubble – An environment in which one's exposure to news, entertainment, social media, etc., represents only one ideological or cultural perspective and excludes or misrepresents other points of view.

Mediacrats – A term to mean that the media and Democrats are closely aligned in their philosophical views and association with each other.

Multiculturalism – The view that cultures, races, and ethnicities, particularly those of minority groups, deserve special acknowledgement of their differences within a dominant political culture.

Occam's Razor – Is the problem-solving principle that "entities should not be multiplied without necessity", or more simply, the simplest explanation is usually the right one.

Open Inquiry – Is the ability to ask questions and share ideas without risk of censure.

Political Correctness – A term used to describe language, policies, or measures that are intended to avoid offense or disadvantage to members of particular groups in society.

Postmodernism – Is an intellectual stance or a mode of discourse that rejects the possibility of reliable knowledge, denies the existence of a universal, stable reality, and frames aesthetics and beauty as arbitrary and subjective.

Progressivism – A political philosophy in support of social reform based on the idea of progress in which advancements in science, technology, economic development, and social organization are vital to improve the human condition.

Replication Crisis – An ongoing methodological crisis in which it has been found that many scientific studies are difficult or impossible to replicate or reproduce.

Sapience – Also known as wisdom, is the ability to think and act using knowledge, experience, understanding, common sense and insight. Sapience is associated with attributes such as intelligence, enlightenment, and unbiased judgement and also recognizes the humanistic concepts of Western European culture, American exceptionalism, and conservative values.

Scientific Method – A way of investigating a phenomenon that's based on the collective analysis and into interpretation of evidence to determine the most probable explanation. The five basic steps in scientific method: 1) statement of the problem, 2) collection of facts, 3) formulating a hypothesis, 4) making further inferences, and 5) verifying the inferences.

Social Justice – A political and philosophical theory which asserts that there are dimensions to the concept of justice beyond those embodied in the principles of civil or criminal law, economic supply and demand, or traditional moral frameworks.

Social Media – Websites and other online means of communication that are used by large groups of people to share information and to develop social and professional contacts.

Tyranny of Public Opinion – Discourages students and others from dissenting from prevailing views on moral, political, and other types of questions.

Viewpoint Diversity – Viewpoint diversity occurs when members of a group or community approach problems or questions from a range of perspectives.

Woke – Having or marked by an active awareness of systemic injustices and prejudices, especially those related to civil and human rights.

Words Are Violence – An illiberal notion meant to stifle free speech and viewpoint diversity. Popularized by Millennial aged college students affected by the tyranny of feelings, it now guides the editorial pages of major newspapers.

References

33 Examples of Twitter's Anti-Conservative Bias, The Duran, https://theduran.com/33-examples-of-twitters-anti-conservative-bias/.

Adl-Tabatabai, Sean. "Nearly All Mainstream Media Leans Left, Study Shows." News Punch, January 29, 2019. https://newspunch.com/mainstream-media-leans-left-study/.

al-Gharbi, Musa. "The Media Bubble is Real—And Worse Than You Think." Heterodox Academy. April 27, 2017. https://musaalgharbi.com/2017/04/27/media-bubble-homogeneity/.

Attkisson, Sharyl. *Stonewalled: My Fight for Truth Against the Forces of Obstruction, Intimidation, and Harassment in Obama's Washington*. Harper Collins: New York, 2015.

Bailey, Ronald. "Climate Change and Confirmation Bias." Reason.com. Jul. 12, 2011. https://reason.com/2011/07/12/scientific-literacy-climate-ch/.

Barkoukis, Leah. "Report: 91 Percent of Media's Trump Coverage Has Been Negative." Townhall, Oct 26, 2016. https://townhall.com/tipsheet/leahbarkoukis/2016/10/26/report-91-percent-of-medias-trump-coverage-has-been-negative-n2237193.

Bedard, Paul. "Media's hiding of Hunter Biden scandal robbed Trump of clear win: Poll." Washington Examiner. Nov. 13, 2020. https://www.msn.com/en-us/news/politics/media-s-hiding-of-hunter-biden-scandal-robbed-trump-of-clear-win-poll/ar-BB1aZGcF.

Bedard, Paul. "Pulitzer judges: 'Not one anywhere close to a conservative.'" Washington Secrets Columnist. April 15, 2019. https://www.washingtonexaminer.com/washington-secrets/pulitzer-judges-not-one-anywhere-close-to-a-conservative.

Beyond Red vs. Blue: The Political Typology. Pew Research Center. May 4, 2011. https://www.pewresearch.org/politics/2011/05/04/beyond-red-vs-blue-the-political-typology/.

Bickley, John. "Facebook Censors Pro-Trump Ad After Fact-Checker Admits Claim May Be True." DailyWire.com. Sep 16, 2020. https://www.dailywire.com/news/facebook-censors-pro-trump-ad-on-biden-raising-taxes-after-fact-checker-admits-claim-may-be-true-rules-mostly-false-anyhow?itm_source=parsely-api.

Black Lives Matter Is a Marxist Movement. Prager U. Interview: Professor Carol M. Swain, PhD sits down with Will Witt to discuss. https://www.prageru.com/video/black-lives-matter-is-a-marxist-movement/.

Bloom, Allan. *Closing of the American Mind: How Higher Education Has Failed Democracy and Impoverished the Souls of Today's Students*. Simon & Schuster: New York. 2012.

Bozell III, L. Brent and Graham, Tim. "Impeachment Dies in Desperation." CNSNews: Media Research Center (MRC). Feb. 5, 2020. https://www.cnsnews.com/commentary/l-brent-bozell-iii/impeachment-dies-desperation.

Bozell III, L. Brent and Tim Graham. *Unmasked: Big Media's War Against Trump* Humanix Books: West Palm Beach. 2019.

Bozell to Levin: Survey Shows 4.6% of Democrats Would Not Have Voted for Joe Biden Had They Known Hunter Biden Story. The Spectator, November 12, 2020. https://thespectator.info/2020/11/11/bozell-to-levin-survey-shows-4-6-of-democrats-would-not-have-voted-for-joe-biden-had-they-known-hunter-biden-story/.

Bozell, Conservative Leaders Demand Answers From Google CEO After Blacklisting NB Staff. MRC NewsBusters, July 27, 2020. https://www.newsbusters.org/blogs/techwatch/nb-staff/2020/07/27/bozell-conservative-leaders-demand-answers-google-ceo-after.

Campbell, W. Joseph. *Getting It Wrong: Debunking the Greatest Myths in American Journalism.* University of California Press, Oakland. 2017.

Cates, Brian. "The Russiagate Hoax Is Dead—But the Fake News Media Can't Admit It." *Epoch Times.* August 24, 2020 Updated: August 26, 2020. https://www.theepochtimes.com/the-russiagate-hoax-is-dead-but-the-fake-news-media-cant-admit-it_3473422.html.

CENSORED! How Online Media Companies Are Suppressing Conservative Speech. Media Research Center (MRC). https://cdn.mrc.org/static/censored/mrc-censorship-report.pdf

Ciandella, Mike. "Special Report: Soros Funds Next Generation of Liberal Journalism." August 29, 2013. https://www.newsbusters.org/blogs/nb/mike-ciandella/2013/08/29/special-report-soros-funds-next-generation-liberal-journalism.

Code of Ethics of the Society of Professional Journalists. Society of Professional Journalists. https://journalistsresource.org/tip-sheets/foundations/code-of-ethics/.

Codevilla, Angelo M. "America's Ruling Class: And the perils of revolution." The American Spectator. July 16, 2010. https://spectator.org/americas-ruling-class/.

Columbia University: Special Report. Media Research Center (MRC). https://www.mrc.org/special-reports/special-report-columbia-university.

Concha, Joe. "Fox News tops broadcast networks for first time in 3rd quarter." *The Hill*, Sep. 29, 2020. https://thehill.com/homenews/media/518827-fox-news-tops-broadcast-networks-for-first-time-ever-in-3rd-quarter.

Concha, Joe. "MSNBC Producer's Scathing Exit Letter: Ratings Model 'Blocks Diversity of Thought and Content.'" *The Hill*, Aug. 8, 2020. https://www.msn.com/en-us/news/politics/msnbc-producer-pens-scathing-exit-letter-ratings-model-blocks-diversity-of-thought-and-content/ar-BB17yhp9.

Dice, Mark. *The True Story of Fake News: How Mainstream Media Manipulates Millions.* The Resistance Manifesto: San Diego. 2017.

Dorfman, Jeffrey. "Sorry Bernie Bros But Nordic Countries Are Not Socialist." *Forbes.* Jul 8, 2018. https://www.forbes.com/sites/jeffreydorfman/2018/07/08/sorry-bernie-bros-but-nordic-countries-are-not-socialist/.

Emmons, Libby. "*The New York Times* parrots Chinese propaganda in failed takedown of *Epoch Times*." The Post Millennial. Oct. 2020. https://thepostmillennial.com/the-new-york-times-parrots-chinese-propaganda-in-failed-takedown-of-epoch-times/.

Epstein, Joseph. "The New Pandemic: Trump Derangement Syndrome." *Wall Street Journal*. July 9, 2020. https://www.wsj.com/articles/the-next-pandemic-trump-derangement-syndrome-11594336574.

Fact Check Review Methodology—RealClearPolitics. https://www.realclearpolitics.com/fact_check_review_methodology.html.

Fair, Julia. "Nick Sandmann's settlement with CNN was almost public." *Cincinnati Enquirer*. Aug. 25, 2020. https://www.dispatch.com/story/news/local/2020/08/25/nick-sandmanns-settlement-with-cnn-was-almost-public/113489358/.

Flood, Brian. "Former *NYT* Journalist Resigns, Exposes Truth Behind Fake News Media." Life & Liberty. Jul. 15, 2020. https://lifeandlibertynews.com/2020/07/15/former-nyt-journalist-resigns-exposes-truth-behind-fake-news-media/.

Free Speech Is Under Attack On the Nation's Campuses With Too Few Willing to Defend It. Chronicles. Blog. November 30, 2015. https://www.chroniclesmagazine.org/article/free-speech-is-under-attack-on-the-nations-campuses-with-too-few-willing-to-defend-it/.

Goldberg, Bernard. "No rush to judgment on Trump—it's been ongoing since Election Day." TheHill.com. Jan. 23, 2020. https://www.realclearpolicy.com/2020/01/27/no_rush_to_judgment_on_trump_-_its_been_ongoing_308437.html.

Gonzalez, Mike, and Andrew Olivastro. "The agenda of Black Lives Matter is far different from the slogan." *New York Post*. July 1, 2020.

Gramlich, John. "How We Evaluated Americans' Trust in 30 News Sources." Pew Research Center. Jan. 24, 2020. https://www.pewresearch.org/fact-tank/2020/01/24/qa-how-pew-research-center-evaluated-americans-trust-in-30-news-sources/.

Hoff Sommers, Christina. "There Is No Gender Wage Gap!" Prager U. Video. Mar. 06, 2017. https://www.prageru.com/. https://www.prageru.com/video/there-is-no-gender-wage-gap/.

How 'Social Media' Became 'Anti-Social Media': Twitter's and Facebook's Reckoning. *Investor's Business Daily*. Jul. 27, 2018. https://www.investors.com/politics/editorials/social-media-bias/.

Journalists Denying Liberal Bias: Parts One, Two & Three. Media Research Center (MRC). https://www.mrc.org/media-bias-101/journalists-denying-liberal-bias-part-one and https://www.mrc.org/media-bias-101/journalists-denying-liberal-bias-part-two and https://www.mrc.org/media-bias-101/journalists-denying-liberal-bias-part-three.

Jurkowitz, Mark and Amy Mitchell, Elisa Shearer, Mason Walker. "U.S. Media Polarization and the 2020 Election: A Nation Divided." Pew Research Center. Jan. 24, 2020. https://www.journalism.org/2020/01/24/u-s-media-polarization-and-the-2020-election-a-nation-divided/.

Kiersz, Andy and Hunter Walker. "These Three Charts Confirm Conservatives' Worst Fears About American Culture." Yahoo Finance, Nov. 3, 2014. https://sg.finance.yahoo.com/news/three-charts-confirm-conservatives-worst-222121403.html.

Lawton, Dan. "Nearly all my professors are Democrats. Isn't that a problem?" *Christian Science Monitor.* July 13, 2009. https://www.csmonitor.com/Commentary/Opinion/2009/0713/p09s02-coop.html.

Marsh, Kristine. "Nikki Haley Destroys ABC for Ignoring What Trump's Done for Black, Hispanic Americans." Patriot Daily Press. August 25, 2020. https://patriotdailypress.org/2020/08/25/nikki-haley-destroys-abc-for-ignoring-what-trumps-done-for-black-hispanic-americans/.

Matthews, Stacey. "NYT's '1619 Project' Founder Once Wrote Whites Were 'Bloodsuckers' in Black Community, Equated Columbus to Hitler." Legal Insurrection. June 26, 2020. https://legalinsurrection.com/2020/06/nyts-1619-project-founder-once-wrote-whites-were-bloodsuckers-in-black-community-equated-columbus-to-hitler/.

McCann, Steve. "The Mainstream Media Is at the Point of No Return." American Thinker. August 11, 2020. https://www.americanthinker.com/articles/2020/08/the_mainstream_media_is_at_the_point_of_no_return.

Media Bias 101. Media Research Center. https://www.mrc.org/sites/default/files/uploads/documents/2014/MBB2014.pdf.

Media Bias: Pretty Much All Of Journalism Now Leans Left. Investor's Business Daily. Nov. 16, 2018. https://www.investors.com/politics/editorials/media-bias-left-study/.

Messamore, Wes. "25 Fake News Stories From the Mainstream Media." Independent Voter News. Nov. 21, 2016. https://ivn.us/2016/11/21/25-fake-news-stories-mainstream-media/.

Mettler, Zachary. "Another Poll Confirms the Media's Credibility is Cratering." The Daily Citizen. May 14, 2020. https://dailycitizen.focusonthefamily.com/another-poll-confirms-the-medias-credibility-is-cratering/.

Mitchell, Amy, and Jeffrey Gottfried, Michael Barthel, Elisa Shearer. "The Modern News Consumer." Pew Research Center. July 7, 2017. https://www.journalism.org/wp-content/uploads/sites/8/2016/07/PJ_2016.07.07_Modern-News-Consumer_FINAL.pdf.

Mitchell, Amy, and Jeffrey Gottfried, Michael Barthel, Elisa Shearer. "How Americans Get Their News." Pew Research Center. Jul. 7, 2016. https://www.journalism.org/2016/07/07/pathways-to-news/.

Noyes, Rich. "Impeachment Gets 77x More TV Time than Trump's Economic Successes." February 4, 2020. Media Research Center (MRC). https://www.newsbusters.org/blogs/nb/rich-noyes/2020/02/04/impeachment-gets-77x-more-tv-time-trumps-economic-successes.

Noyes, Rich. "MRC Study: Documenting TV's Twelve Weeks of Trump Bashing." MRC NewsBusters. October 25, 2016. https://www.newsbusters.org/blogs/nb/rich-noyes/2016/10/25/mrc-study-documenting-tvs-twelve-weeks-trump-bashing.

Noyes, Rich. "Study: 150 Times More Negative News on Trump than Biden." NewsBusters: Media Research Center (MRC). August 17, 2020. https://www.newsbusters.org/blogs/nb/rich-noyes/2020/08/17/study-150-times-more-negative-news-trump-biden.

Noyes, Rich. "The Eight Worst 'Fake News' Stories of the Trump Years: MRC Special Report." May 5, 2020. https://www.newsbusters.org/blogs/nb/rich-noyes/2020/05/05/special-report-eight-worst-fake-news-stories-trump-years.

Noyes, Rich. "*WaPo* Bashes Trump Virus Response." April 25, 2020. MRC NewsBusters. https://www.newsbusters.org/blogs/nb/rich-noyes/2020/04/25/study-washington-post-bashes-trump-virus-response-25-1-negative.

Perazzo, John. "In the Tank: A Statistical Analysis of Media Bias." FrontPageMagazine.com. October 31, 2008. https://www.worldviewweekend.com/news/article/tank-statistical-analysis-media-bias.

Phillips, Kristine, and Kevin Johnson. "Ex-FBI lawyer Clinesmith pleads guilty to falsifying email in Russia probe in Durham's first case." *USA Today*, Aug. 19, 2020.

Prager U Besieged By Big Tech And The Left—Expose. Video. https://www.prageru.com/. https://exposethemedia.com/prageru-besieged-by-big-tech-and-the-far-left/.

Prager U Takes Legal Action Against Google and YouTube for Discrimination. https://www.prageru.com/. https://www.prageru.com/press-release/prageru-takes-legal-action-against-google-and-youtube-for-discrimination/.

President Donald Trump impeached. LibertyVoter.Org. Dec. 18, 2019. www.libertyvoter.org. https://history.com/this-day-in-history/president-trump-impeached-house-of-representatives.

Prestigiacomo, Amanda. "WATCH: Shepard Smith Goes OFF on Bobby Jindal for Saying 'All Lives Matter.'" Jul 19, 2016. DailyWire.com. https://www.dailywire.com/news/watch-shepard-smith-goes-bobby-jindal-saying-all-amanda-prestigiacomo.

Pryor, J.J. "Who is the Least Biased News Source? Simplifying the News Bias Chart." Towards Data Science. Sep 9, 2020. https://towardsdatascience.com/how-statistically-biased-is-our-news-f28f0fab3cb3.

Research on Media Bias, Discover the Networks. David Horowitz Freedom Center. https://www.discoverthenetworks.org/organizations/research-on-media-bias/.

Richwine, Lisa and Helen Coster. "Newsmax plans expansion to capitalize on Trump support, anger at Fox News." Reuters. Dec. 10, 2020.

Shapiro, Ben. "Shapiro At 'National Review': Facebook, Google, YouTube, and Twitter Move Against Conservatives." Mar 7, 2018. DailyWire.com. https://www.dailywire.com/news/shapiro-national-review-facebook-google-youtube-ben-shapiro.

Shapiro, Ben. "Viewpoint Discrimination with Algorithms." March 7, 2018. National Review. https://www.nationalreview.com/2018/03/social-media-companies-discriminate-against-conservatives/.

Simon, Roger L. "Twitter as Prototype of the New High-Tech Totalitarianism." *The Epoch Times*, May 28, 2020. Updated: June 1, 2020. https://www.theepochtimes.com/twitter-as-prototype-of-the-new-high-tech-totalitarianism_3368875.html.

Smeaton, Paul. "LifeSite joins media leaders to demand Google answer for censoring conservatives." LifeSite. Jul. 28, 2020. https://www.lifesitenews.com/news/lifesite-joins-media-leaders-to-demand-google-answer-for-censoring-conservatives.

Smith, Kyle. "Ex-CBS Reporter's Book Reveals How Liberal Media Protects Obama." October 26, 2014. *New York Post*. https://www.weaselzippers.us/203630-ex-cbs-reporters-book-reveals-how-liberal-media-protects-obama/.

Stepman, Jarrett. "Social Justice Warriors Taking Over and Purging Newsrooms." June 10, 2020. The Daily Signal. https://www.cnsnews.com/index.php/commentary/jarrett-stepman/social-justice-warriors-taking-over-and-purging-newsrooms.

Strassel, Kimberley. "Inside the media's relentless crusade to destroy President Trump." October 13, 2019. *New York Post*. https://nypost.com/2019/10/13/inside-the-medias-relentless-crusade-to-destroy-president-trump/.

STUDY: Corrupt and Biased *Washington Post* Bashes Trump Virus Response with 25-to-1 Negative Headlines. Geller Report Staff. April 27, 2020. https://gellerreport.com/2020/04/study-corrupt-and-bias-washington-post-bashes-trump-virus-response-with-25-to-1-negative-headlines.html/.

Three CNN journalists resign after Trump aide article removed. BBC News. June 27, 2017. https://www.bbc.com/news/world-us-canada-40414886.

Tierney, John. "Journalists Against Free Speech." City Journal. Autumn 2019. https://www.city-journal.org/journalists-against-free-speech.

Turley, Jonathan. "The Dangerous Liberal Ideas For Censorship in the United States." May 2, 2020. *The Hill*. https://thehill.com/opinion/civil-rights/495788-the-dangerous-liberal-ideas-for-censorship-in-the-united-states.

Watch the 21 Prager U Videos That YouTube Is Censoring. Prager U. https://www.prageru.com/. https://www.dailysignal.com/2016/10/14/watch-the-21-prageru-videos-that-youtube-is-censoring/.

Weaver, Corinne. "Censorship Insanity: Twitter Goes After Trump and Campaign 194 Times." Nov. 16, 2020. MRC NewsBusters. https://www.newsbusters.org/blogs/techwatch/corinne-weaver/2020/11/16/censorship-insanity-twitter-goes-after-trump-and-campaign.

Weiss, Rusty. "Pew Study: Media Bias Against Trump is Real and Extreme." Liberty Unyielding, October 9, 2017. https://libertyunyielding.com/2017/10/09/pew-study-media-bias-trump-real-extreme/.

Who Is Fact Checking The Fact Checkers? *Investor's Business Daily*. Aug. 2, 2018. https://www.investors.com/politics/editorials/fact-checkers-big-media/.

Index

N

O

Author Bio

Corey Lee Wilson was raised an atheist by his liberal *Playboy* Bunny mother, has three Anglo-Hispanic siblings, a brother who died of AIDS, baptized a Protestant by his conservative grandparents, attended temple with his Jewish foster parents, baptized again as a Catholic for his first Filipina wife, attends Buddhist ceremonies with his second Thai wife, became an agnostic on his own free will for most of his life, and is a lifetime independent voter.

Corey felt the sting of intellectual humility by repeating the 4th grade and attended eighteen different schools before putting himself through college at Mt. San Antonio College and Cal Poly Pomona University while on triple secrete probation). Named Who's Who of American College Students in 1984, he received a BS in Economics and won his fraternity's most prestigious undergraduate honor, the Phi Kappa Tau Fraternity's Shideler Award, both in 1985. In 2020, he became a member of the Heterodox Academy.

As a satirist and fraternity man, Corey started Fratire Publishing in 2012 and transformed the fiction "fratire" genre to a respectable and viewpoint diverse non-fiction genre promoting practical knowledge and wisdom to help everyday people navigate safely through the many hazards of life. In 2018, he founded the SAPIENT Being to help promote freedom of speech, viewpoint diversity, intellectual humility and most importantly advance sapience in America's students and campuses.

The SAPIENT Being has two programs, the Make Free Speech Again On Campus (MFSAOC) and World of Writing Warriors (WOWW) to promote its mission and vision of sapience. The WOWW program plans to self-publish 50 *MADNESS* non-fiction textbooks in partnership with Fratire Publishing over the span of the 2020 decade in alliance with the MFSAOC program to start 50 chapters on America's high school and college campuses by 2030.

If you're interested in the MFSAOC Program and starting a S.A.P.I.E.N.T. Being club, chapter, or alliance please visit https://www.SapientBeing.org/start-a-chapter, e-mail SapientBeing@att.net, or call (951) 638-5562 for more information.

If you're interested in the WOWW Program and their 50 *MADNESS* series of textbooks from the S.A.P.I.E.N.T. Being, please check them out at https://www.FratirePublishing.com/madnessbooks, e-mail SapientBeing@att.net, or call (951) 638-5562 for more information.

Hopefully, this book was enlightening and your journey through it made you aware of the issues and challenges ahead of us. If it has, your journey towards becoming a sapient being has begun. If it hasn't, there's no better time to start than now. Come join us in creating a society advancing personal intelligence and enlightenment now together (S.A.P.I.E.N.T.) and become a sapient being.